LOVE
AND
SEXUALITY
Part 1

Translated from the French
Original title: «L'amour et la sexualité» *Part 1*

Prosveta S.A – B.P.12 – 83601 Fréjus CEDEX (France)
ISBN 2-85566-740-2
original edition: 1976 (France)

Omraam Mikhaël Aïvanhov

LOVE
AND
SEXUALITY
Part 1

Complete Works – Volume 14 AN

P R O S V E T A

Readers will better understand certain aspects of the lectures published in the present volume if they bear in mind that Master Omraam Mikhaël Aïvanhov's teaching was exclusively oral and that the editors have made every effort to respect the flavour and style of each lecture.

The Master's teaching is more than a body of doctrines; it is an organic whole, and his way of presenting it was to approach it from countless different points of view. By treating certain aspects in many different contexts he constantly reveals a new dimension of the whole, and at the same time throws new light on the individual aspects and their vital links with each other.

Omraam Mikhaël Aïvanhov

CONTENTS

I   The Masculine and Feminine Principles –
Love of God, Neighbour and Self 11

II   Taking the Bull by the Horns –
The Caduceus of Hermes, Part I and II 29

III   The Serpent – Isis Unveiled 47

IV   The Power of the Dragon 63

V   Spirit and Matter: the Sexual Organs, Part I and II ... 69

VI   The Manifestations
of the Masculine and Feminine Principles, Part I and II   81

VII Jealousy 95

VIII The Twelve Doors of Man and Woman 105

IX   From Yesod to Kether:
the Sublimation of Sexual Energy 117

X   A Spiritual Filter 121

XI   Learn to Love by Learning to Eat, Part I and II 129

XII Woman's Role in the New Culture 147

XIII Nudism and the Initiatic Significance of Nakedness,
Part I and II 157

XIV The Masculine and Feminine Principles:
A Relationship of Exchange, Part I and II 171

XV Emptiness and Fullness – Poros and Penia 187

XVI The Teaching of Love in the Mysteries 197

XVII Love is Everywhere 205

XVIII   A Broader Concept of Marriage, Part I 215

XIX   Sister Souls 221

XX   Everything Depends on How We See Things 229

XXI   A Broader Concept of Marriage, Part II and III 237

XXII   Analysis and Synthesis 247

XXIII   Love is Like the Sun:
         It Organizes Life, Part I and II 255

XXIV   A Mother's Love 265

XXV   Emptiness and Fullness:
         the Meaning of Renunciation 277

XXVI   The Bonds that Bind Us 287

XXVII   Youth and the Problem of Love: 297
         I   The Currents of a New Age 299
         II   Marriage 305
         III   The Argument for Self-control 314
         IV   The Need for a Guide 320
         V   Send your Love to Heaven
               before Sending it to Human Beings 326

Chapter One

THE MASCULINE
AND FEMININE PRINCIPLES

LOVE OF GOD,
NEIGHBOUR AND SELF

There are two essential principles in the universe and their reflection can be seen in every manifestation of life and nature. The whole of creation is the handiwork of these two principles which, for the sake of convenience, we call the masculine and feminine principles. These two principles are a reproduction, a reflection, of the heavenly Father and the divine Mother, the two divine principles that created all things and that must be understood as the polarization of the one, unique principle, the Absolute, the Unmanifest, that which Cabbalists call Ain Soph Aur. It is said that man was created in the image of God, that is to say, in the image of these two principles, and each human being possesses within himself a masculine and a feminine aspect. One aspect is visible and the other hidden: it cannot be seen but it is there. Every woman is outwardly a woman but, inwardly, she also possesses the masculine principle. And every man is outwardly a man, but he also possesses the feminine principle within himself. If you knew this law of polarity and how to use the two principles, masculine and feminine, emissive and receptive, positive and negative, you would be capable of solving so many problems.

Each human being has these two principles in them, therefore; their imprint can be seen everywhere: on the faces and bodies of human beings, on their hands, in nature, in flowers and animals and fruits, in the mountains, rivers and caves of the earth and in the stars. Wherever we look, we can see the manifestations of these two principles in countless different forms. On the earth and under the earth, in the depths of the oceans and high in the heavens, everything we see is the work of these two principles.

Consciously or unconsciously, all living creatures have the same reaction to this question of the two principles: they all recognize that it is of absolute importance; nothing matters but the two principles. When a man is looking for a wife he is ready to give up everything for her sake. A king is willing to abandon his kingdom with his army, his subjects and all his personal wealth for the sake of a woman. But what is it about a woman that makes her worth more than a nation of millions? In reality, it is not the individual woman, it is the feminine principle; nothing is of greater value than this. A man who abandons everything for the sake of a woman is simply being faithful; it is the principle he is interested in. And a woman does exactly the same; she is willing to defy her whole family, the whole world, for the sake of the man she loves. Why? Is she wrong to do so? No, she is not. The Lord himself and mother nature have engraved this law into the hearts of men and women: 'Therefore a man shall leave his father and mother and be joined to his wife (or a woman to her husband), and they shall become one flesh.' It is written in the depths of every creature that the first principle must seek the second, and the second must seek the first. Human beings are not always conscious of this, because their seeking takes so many different forms, depending on whether they are seeking in the sphere of science, philosophy, art or religion.

Mystics say that they are seeking God but, actually, what they call God is simply the part of themselves that is missing. This is the true object of all their seeking and yearning: fusion with that other part of themselves so as to be a whole, complete entity. They sense that until this union is achieved they will always be mutilated and incomplete. The desire of every living being is always the same: to be united to his complementary principle, that which initiatic science calls the sister or twin soul, so as to find total fulfilment and peace, knowledge and power, so as to resemble God himself. The only difference is in the different ways in which individuals seek this principle.

Think about this: everything is a question of love; apart from love there is only emptiness, nothingness. Religious people, puritans or hypocrites may not admit it but, in reality, even they seek only one thing: love. They don't show it because they try to conform to old traditions of purity and chastity, but nature does not recognize human inventions of that kind; she continues to work in every single being and the inner fires burn unabated. The only question, therefore, is to learn how to find true love as God sees it and, having found it, to manifest it according to the divine rules so as to achieve that union, that perfect blending into one.

Everything we see and do is an expression of the two principles. When you eat or drink, when you look at or listen to something, when you work and, even, when you sing together in the choir, you are manifesting the two principles. You don't realize what happens when you sing. Do you imagine that the high notes sung by the sisters and the deep bass notes of the brothers just drift away and lose themselves in space? Not at all; without your realizing it, they mingle in the atmosphere over your heads and give each other something marvellous, something divine. Each one of your voices is impregnated with your magnetism, your vitality, your fragrance. You are tied to your voice as though it were a kite on the end of a string. It soars into the air, where it meets and fuses into one with other voices, before coming back to you, amplified and enriched by all that it has received in that union. Singing is a means for the sisters and brothers to give each other certain divine, etheric elements that they cannot receive by other, cruder means. Your souls and spirits find nourishment in what they receive in this subtle give and take of voices, and they also pass on a few crumbs of that nourishment to your physical body so that it shall not be too hungry or thirsty.

When we sing together, therefore, the masculine and feminine principles join together in a creative work on a higher plane and we receive the fruits of that work and benefit from this chaste, divine intercourse. No one can accuse us of transgressing the laws of purity by an exchange of this nature which leaves us nourished and strengthened. This is why, since the world began, the custom of singing together has always existed but, today, the light has been lost; the underlying initiatic meaning of these things has been lost, only the external practice remains. Men and women continue to sing in duets, trios and choirs. Even peasants in rural communities are happy when they can sing and dance together, because, although they don't realize it, music and song are the means by which their souls and spirits enter into communion with each other, and for a brief moment they are satisfied and fulfilled by what they receive in this exchange.

Nature has invented hundreds and thousands of different ways for human beings to enjoy intercourse on a subtle level when they cannot do so physically: beaches and swimming pools, for example, dance-halls... even churches. Of course, you can't be sure that everything that is exchanged between them will be perfectly orthodox – even if they take place in an Orthodox church. A boy sees a dainty young miss, for instance, and starts to follow her down the street when, all of a sudden, she disappears into a church. 'Hmm,' he thinks, 'I'd feel more sure of myself if she'd gone into a disco!' but he follows her, all the same, and as she has seen this, she strikes a pose and puts on an expression of great piety. As for the boy, he moves gradually closer and, instead of paying attention to the priest and following the Mass, he has eyes only for her. You see? Some subtle forms of exchange can take place even in a church. Of course, the thoughts that may be going through their minds is quite another matter. There's no knowing whether they are orthodox or highly unorthodox.

But, let's get back to the question of singing. If you did not have a mouth – that is to say a tongue and two lips – you could neither speak nor sing. Speech and song, therefore, depend on the masculine and feminine principles in the form of the tongue and the lips. Don't think that I am suggesting anything indecent; I am simply stating a fact. It is nature that designed the mouth, not I. The tongue and lips have to work together to produce words; without that collaboration there can be no speech, no song. Song and speech are a result, a product. They are the children of a father and mother that are more highly evolved, more spiritual, since God has placed them in our head. The tongue and lips have the same function as the sexual organs. By working together they have the power to create, but their creativity is on the spiritual level. *'In the beginning was the Word...'* If we really want to find the two principles we must look for them on the higher, not on the lower level. The sexual organs of men and women are simply a repetition, a cruder reflection on the lower level, of the two higher principles which are also creative and which, like the two lower principles, can also transmit life.

There, what I have been saying should help you to see the importance of singing, and above all, of course, the importance of the spiritual, mystical songs that we sing here. Until now, singing has been simply a pastime, a form of recreation for you. From now on, you must understand that it is a form of nourishment, a necessity, a spiritual need. If you do not learn to nourish yourself with music and song, the less subtle forms of exchange will bring you nothing but bitterness and regrets.

But this question of exchange, of intercourse, is still not properly understood. Mystics, hermits and ascetics have sometimes been so ignorant and narrow-minded that they became completely unbalanced. Many of them destroyed their own health and happiness by refusing every form of exchange and ended up as lifeless, barren, dried-up corpses. In their own minds, of course, they were doing the Lord's will. But how could anyone imagine that dead, inanimate bodies were pleasing to God, who is only interested in life and creation, who does nothing but create? No, it is human beings who turn everything upside down and imagine that God is against love and marriage and the procreation of children. In their minds, this is what religion means – but what a strange religion!

You will say, 'But many great Masters and initiates never married; was it because they were like those fanatics?' No, initiates and great Masters have a very broad, clear vision of reality; they understand God's creation. If they live in purity and chastity it is because the exchanges that they enjoy on subtler levels are so rich and rewarding that they have no need to burden and limit themselves by seeking them on a lower, material level. They don't choose to live in celibacy and chastity because they are opposed to love; on the contrary, they nourish themselves and drink from sources and regions unknown to the masses, regions in which every exchange takes place in the utmost light and purity. They are visited by angels and archangels; the sun and the stars smile on them; even human beings give them their love and trust. Thus, all their wishes are gratified; what more do they need? Why should they give up such treasures and allow themselves to get bogged down in swampy regions that can give them nothing but disappointments? You don't understand what I am saying, yet, but you will understand.

We read in the Scriptures: *'You shall love the Lord your God with all your heart, with all your soul, with all your mind, and with all your strength; you shall love your neighbour as yourself.'* You see: we are told to love God and our neighbour; there is no mention of our having to love ourselves. And yet, what do human beings do? They love themselves first and foremost; if there is a little something left over they may give it to their neighbour, but the only thing they do for God is to light a candle in church, once a year. Why is this? Although the Bible never says that we must love ourselves, we do nothing else, whereas we never have time for the two commandments it actually gives us. The initiates have never taught that we should love ourselves, because they know that man's most natural, his deepest and most tenacious inclination is to love himself, to satisfy his own needs, to eat and drink – even to take for himself what belongs to his neighbour. Self-love is all we see around us, night and day. And yet, in fact, when initiates tell men to love God and their neighbour, what they are actually saying is, 'Love yourselves.' They have never said this in so many words, because they knew that they would not be understood, but that is what they meant.

Love of self, love of one's neighbour and love of God: these are three forms of love which correspond to three phases in the life of man. A child loves himself, he is only interested in himself; later on he begins to love his father and mother, his brothers and sisters and friends, and still later, his wife and children. Finally, when he has loved all kinds of people – people who have often betrayed him and let him down – he turns to the Lord and begins to love him and wants to be with him. Actually, I could show you that the higher degrees of love are contained in the love of self, for love of God and of our fellow men is still a form of self-love. It is a subtler, more luminous, more spiritual form, but it is still self-love. Why do you love one particular woman and not all the women in the world? Because that one woman reflects something of yourself, and that something is your other half, your missing part. Men and women are polarized beings and it is this polarization that drives them to look for their missing half in each other and even in the Lord. It is always himself that man is looking for, himself that he loves, not the self that he can see in a mirror but his other principle, his other pole. If you are a man, your other pole is a feminine principle; if you are a woman, it is a masculine principle.

A human being, such as initiates understand him, is a whole being. The two poles, positive and negative, are two halves of a unit which became divided in the course of evolution. In the beginning, each human being was androgynous, that is to say, both man and woman. When sexual separation was effected, male and female went their separate ways but each continues to bear the imprint, the image, of the other in the depths of his or her soul. This is why, when, amongst all the hundreds and thousands of women in the world, a man sees one face that has some resemblance to that inner image, he does everything he can to hold on to her. Unfortunately, as time passes, he often finds that the resemblance is not as close as he had thought and he abandons her and starts looking for someone else hoping, once again, to find his other half, his sister soul. This applies equally to both men and women; there are no exceptions. One day, the two principles will truly come together, for the love between them is more powerful than anything else.

In reality, our sister soul is our self, the other pole of our true self. We exist here below, but our other pole is in the world above; it dwells in the perfection and fulfilment of a constant communion with heaven and the angels, with God himself. This is why all initiations have taught their disciples how to become one with their other pole. In India, Jnana-yoga teaches methods by means of which a yogi may achieve union with his higher self, because when man becomes one with his higher self he becomes one with God. In Greece, the same idea was expressed in the inscription on the pediment of the temple at Delphi: 'Man, know thyself.' To know oneself, in this context, does not mean to know one's own character, one's strengths and weaknesses – that is too easy. The *Book of Genesis* says, *'Adam knew Eve,'* or *'Abraham knew Sarah;'* true knowledge is the fusion of two principles. 'Know thyself' means, 'Find your other pole within yourself and you will become a divinity.' If you are a man, your other pole is a woman and you will know her, just as a lover knows his beloved, although not in quite the same way, of course, for this fusion, this knowledge takes place in the regions of light. It is when you enter that light that you become one with yourself.

The Gospels give us the same precept, although they express it rather differently; they say: *'You shall love the Lord your God with all your heart, with all your soul, with all your mind, and with all your strength.'* And this implies that man can be united to God only through his higher soul. This is, also, what Christ meant when he said, *'No one comes to the father except through me.'* Christ symbolizes the Godhead, the Logos, the Son of God who lies buried in every soul like a hidden spark. By uniting himself with his higher soul, man forms a bond between himself and the Christ-principle, who is everywhere, in all souls, and, through the Christ-principle, between himself and God. You can only reach God through your higher self for it is this higher self that contains and represents all that is best and purest in you. This is why all the different methods of meditation teach us to put as much distance as possible between ourselves and the physical, material world, by means of thought, and to rise to the highest, most luminous world in order to reach the Godhead, the principle of our higher soul. And, as polarization is an ever-present reality, an affinity, a bond of sympathy is formed with our complementary principle, for the masculine is always attracted to the feminine and the feminine to the masculine.

Every being possesses this complementary principle within himself and can reach God only through that principle. This is why woman finds God through man. Man represents that other principle, and it is through that principle that she can be united with the heavenly Father. And man can only attain the Godhead through the feminine principle, whether it be in a woman, in nature (which is a feminine principle) or in the divine Mother. In the absence of the feminine principle, there can be no drive, no inspiration, no realization... nothing. And similarly, without the masculine principle, the feminine principle remains inert, formless and barren. Study the way nature does things and you will see that, by projecting its light and warmth, the sun – the masculine principle – vivifies all creatures. In our inner life we, too, have to be fertilized, animated and vivified by the divine principle of the sun. This is easier for women because they are more receptive, but men, who are predominantly positive and emissive, must learn to change their polarization and become receptive as well.

And now, let's get back to the three degrees of love I spoke of a moment ago. It does not take much reflection to realize that human beings don't know how to love themselves; in fact, they actually destroy themselves. Is it really a sign that you love yourself if you eat and drink without discrimination, if you smoke and indulge all kinds of unreasonable foibles? Are you really doing yourself any good when you give vent to anger or hatred, for example? On the contrary: you are poisoning yourself. You will say, 'But I want to poison So-and-so.' I know, but the poison has to travel through your own system before it can reach someone else. In other words, the poison will hurt you before it affects him. How little people know and understand what they are doing. They love themselves in all the wrong ways and they have got to learn to love themselves properly.

Suppose that you are determined not to let anything impure enter you... Ah, then I can say that you really love yourself, because, thanks to your purity, everything within you will become so shining and bright that the angels will want to come and stay with you. If you are careful never to do wrong by your thoughts, feelings or words, that is already a way of making things ready for the Lord to come and dwell within you. This kind of self-love is divine; this is the right way to love oneself. Those who don't know how to love themselves in this way, love neither God nor their neighbour. The love of God begins with love of self, for love has to pass through you before it can reach that other self, above. It is to please yourself, to please that higher part of your self that is constantly watching you, that you want to live in purity and light. This is how we should love ourselves: by keeping everything pure and whole within.

It is normal for human beings to love themselves; it was nature that gave her children this instinct. The only thing is that they have to learn to love themselves in a way that respects order and harmony and in an awareness of their true dignity, of their divine nature. Most people understand love as the gratification of their desires, the pursuit of pleasure, whereas it should be understood as sacrifice, intelligence, purity, detachment and selflessness. All happiness and fulfilment depend on a correct understanding of love but, unfortunately, the experience most people have of love leaves them with confused ideas on the subject. When a man falls in love with a woman, for example, instead of realizing that he has been given something divine and making the most of it to undertake some immense spiritual work, he ruins everything by wanting to gratify his desire immediately. Why couldn't he wait and benefit from that attraction, that love? If you fall in love with someone, don't show it, don't talk about it, be content to thank heaven for the gift of love, for it means that you are being given exceptionally favourable conditions that can help you to rise to a higher level, to have courage and drive and inspiration, to be victorious. Don't destroy these conditions by insisting on kissing or sleeping with the object of your affections at once; if you do that you will spoil everything: all joy, happiness and inspiration will disappear and you will be left with nothing but recriminations and arguments about who said this and who did that.

To love is a blessing. This is why you must protect your love for as long as you can, because, as soon as you begin to give expression to it, a new chapter begins, a chapter of upheavals and disasters. Love is God himself; love gives you everything: life, happiness, inspiration, wealth. Why are you in such a hurry to spoil everything by getting rid of it instead of living the eternal, divine life it offers? It is possible for you to live in love day and night, but on condition that you have intercourse only with the highest, most sublime regions and beings and that you do not waste it in cheap, crude exchanges that leave you with nothing but ashes. Love yourself, therefore, but love your divine self; do everything for that self. If you want to win that beloved being, to hold her in your embrace, to hear all nature sing, no sacrifice should seem too great.

All success and all happiness depend on this Centre, on this point that we call God. Look at this symbol I have had engraved on my pen: a circle with a point in the centre.[1] This symbol contains the whole of initiatic science. How do we interpret it? Well, you have all seen a classroom: when the teacher is not there, the pupils laugh and play and get into mischief. That is only to be expected – when the schoolmaster is absent it is time to let off steam – but as soon as he arrives, every child is back in his place, like a shot. Or take the example of an army: if the commanding officer is absent, the soldiers rush about without order or discipline and the battle is on the point of being lost. Then the general arrives; the soldiers obey his orders and the battle is won.

I could give you any number of examples to illustrate this, but the essential thing to understand is that identical laws exist within us. The Lord is the head, the general, the centre, and when he is not there... Well, you know the saying, 'When the cat's away, the mice will play...' Yes, and they devour all the cheese, too. So, when someone says, 'I don't need God; I can get along quite well without him,' my answer is that he may think he's getting along all right, but that rats and mice will be dancing within him because the head is absent. The head, that is to say, the Lord, brings order into our cells; when he is present, they all work together in harmony and peace and the flow of life is unimpeded. If the head is absent, a man can still get along in his everyday life, he can still go about his business, but his inner life is a shambles and soon shows signs of rot. Why is it essential to make the Lord the centre of your

---

[1] On the symbolism of the circle, see *The Symbolic Language of Geometrical Figures*, Izvor Collection, No. 218.

inner being? Human beings still don't know the answer, so that is why I am telling you, today: if you want order and harmony to reign within you, you must find the head, the centre of the circle, because it is this central point that organizes all the rest. There is no higher truth than this.

We have to love God, not for his sake but for ours; he is so rich that he does not need us. You may have seen the film 'Dieu a besoin des hommes' (God Needs Men)... Well, that may be so, but he can perfectly well do without us. What could we add to all that God already possesses? Our pride and vanity? Our viciousness or our mediocrity? What splendid acquisitions these would be for him. No, the truth is that it is we who need God. Nowadays, to banish God from one's life seems to be considered a proof of great intelligence and a high degree of evolution but, if that is so, why is it that all these intelligent and highly evolved people are permanently dissatisfied, sickly and unbalanced? Why? Because they have banished the head. If you study the Cabbalah, you will see that everything centres on the study of a venerable 'Head' and its snow-white hair, beard, ears, etc. The sacred head of God is the starting point for the whole of the Cabbalah and now we are asked to follow some witless nonentities who would have us do away entirely with this head.

Try to understand what I am saying, once and for all. This is a truth that I have experienced personally, it is not just a theory; my whole life has been based on this symbol of the circle with the point in the centre. We have to find this centre within ourselves. It is in us, somewhere, but it has been displaced, it is no longer in the centre. This is why we have to find it and put it back in the centre. All human beings possess this centre but they have allowed it to drift away to the fringe of their being, as though it were something quite unimportant, and they now give priority to their profession or to a friend, a love affair, a car. The task before you, now, is to find the Lord and restore him to the centre of your existence, because, when you do that, every aspect of your life will improve: your health, your understanding of things... everything. Even other people's attitude towards you will change; they will begin to love you because they will sense that there is a living, vibrant, gushing spring at the centre of your being. If you are not a well-spring, if nothing flows within you, how can you expect anyone to love you? Nobody loves a graveyard. Nobody loves a void, an empty hole. People only love something that is alive.

Henceforth, tread with invincible faith on this shining path which sums up all initiatic science, all the sacred scriptures. As the years go by, you will see that the events of your lives prove the truth of what I am saying. We cannot love God if we do not love ourselves, because love has to go by way of our higher selves in order to reach God. This is its appointed route. If you want to send a message by radio, you go to the studio that has the equipment you need in order to transmit your message. You cannot just shout your message into the air and expect it to be heard hundreds or thousands of miles away. You are obliged to use a transmitter. And within us, too, is the transmitter we need, our higher self, the universal soul that dwells within us. For women, this is a masculine principle; for men, it is a feminine principle. Unless our message is transmitted through our other pole it will not reach its destination. When mystics and initiates pray, they forget themselves so completely that it is no longer they but their spirits, their souls, that pray, that transmit their prayer so that it is received in heaven. Whether you think of your other pole as Christ, as your spirit or soul or as your beloved, is not important; what is important is to know that if your prayer is not sufficiently intense to be transmitted by that other pole it will not be answered.

Initiatic science tells us that we cannot discover something outside ourselves unless we have already found it within us; even when we come across something externally, if we have not already found it within ourselves, we would pass by without seeing it. The more inwardly sensitive you are to beauty the more you will see beauty outwardly, on the physical plane. Perhaps you have the impression that you could not see it before because it was not there. No, it was there, all right, but you could not see it because something was still not fully developed within you. But, once you have seen it inwardly, you can see it outwardly as well, because the outer world is simply the reflection of the inner world. Never look for something externally if you have not made the effort to find it inwardly.

Once you have found your higher self, your sister soul, inwardly, through meditation and contemplation, you will see it and hear its voice everywhere in the world around you, in the faces of others, in lakes and mountains and plants and birds. It is extremely important that people who love each other should know this truth, otherwise their relationship, their marriage, will be a disaster. If the man has already found his feminine principle within himself and the woman has found her masculine principle, and if they both want to serve it, to work for it... then let them love each other, let them get married, for their love will be a source of blessings. This is why I have explained to you that a woman must see the reflection of the heavenly Father in her beloved, for he is God's representative on earth. And in the woman he loves the man must see the divine Mother, and must love, contemplate and serve her. In these conditions, every treasure house will be open to them and they will live, day and night, in a climate of beauty, ecstasy and rapture. Otherwise, they are bound to suffer and be disappointed, and they will begin to speak of each other with disgust, simply because they have never really known each other's soul or spirit; all they have known was their ragged clothing, their shabby, worm-eaten outer garments. This is what happens to those who have refused to be instructed, who have run away from initiatic teaching and refused to listen: they bite the dust. When a man turns his back on the light which could open his eyes and light up his path, he is punishing himself.

This evening, the true meaning of all the sacred scriptures of the world has become clear to you. Why hesitate any longer? Go forward, now; may nothing stand in your way and may God be with you always.

Videlinata (Switzerland), April 8 1962

Chapter Two

TAKING THE BULL BY THE HORNS
THE CADUCEUS OF HERMES

I

Alchemical treatises explain that, in order to obtain the Philosophers' Stone symbolized by Mercury, the adept has to begin his work exactly as the Sun enters Aries and the Moon enters Taurus, for the Sun is exalted in Aries and the Moon in Taurus. Gemini, the next sign in the zodiacal circle, is the home of Mercury. Thus we have the three signs of Aries (the Sun), Taurus (the Moon) and Gemini (Mercury), which follow each other in order to show that it is the union of the Sun ☉ and the Moon ☽ that produces the child, Mercury. The trio of Sun, Moon and Mercury is found in other signs of the Zodiac as well but, for the time being, we shall consider only these three very significant signs, Aries, Taurus and Gemini.

The glyph of Mercury is composed of the disc of the Sun, the crescent of the Moon and, to indicate their union, the plus sign (+). The glyph of Mercury (☿), therefore, is simply the union of Sun and Moon.

The Sun and the Moon give birth to the child, Mercury, the Philosophers' Stone. But the true Philosophers' Stone sought by alchemists is, in reality, a symbol of the transformation of man. Alchemists work with the Sun and the Moon, that is to say, with the two principles of will and imagination and it is thanks to the work of the two principles that they are capable of transmuting their own matter and becoming, symbolically, as radiant as the Sun and as pure as the Moon. It is no coincidence if Mars is domiciled in Aries and Venus in Taurus, for it is by working with the Sun and the Moon, that is to say with the masculine and feminine principles, by sublimating his sexual energy (Venus) and the dynamic, active force of his will (Mars), that an alchemist obtains the spiritual powers symbolized by Mercury, the magic agent.

In the tradition of the Knights Templar, this magic agent was represented by Baphomet, that monstrous figure which led many people to believe that the Templars worshipped the Devil. Others called the magic agent 'Azot,' a word that is formed of the first letter of the alphabet in Latin (A), Greek (Alpha) and Hebrew (Aleph) and the last letters of the same three alphabets, Z (Latin), O (Greek) and T (Hebrew), and which signifies that the magic agent is the Alpha and Omega, the beginning and the end.

Alchemists have always taken great pains to obtain this magic agent but they often failed in their quest because they did not understand that their work with the Sun and the Moon should not be restricted to the physical plane but should be carried on, also, on the spiritual plane, that it should be a work with the two principles of the will and the imagination. This is what is meant by 'taking the bull by the horns.' For a disciple, to take the bull by the horns is to begin the interior work that will eventually give him the mastery of all the raw, anarchical, violent elements in himself. Unfortunately, in our day, instead of taking the bull by the horns, people leave it free to trample everything underfoot. This is particularly so with young people and you are going to see how many things are destroyed by the bull.

To take the bull by the horns means to bring the imagination under the control of the will. Our imagination is always linked to our sensuality and people whose imagination is not kept in check tend to be lazy and sensual: the Moon and Venus always go hand in hand. But if the Sun intervenes by bringing its light to bear on the situation and steers these forces in the right direction, then the Moon becomes extraordinarily useful, because it has the power to give concrete form to things. I have already spoken to you about the different ages of the earth's evolution, the Age of Saturn, of the Sun, of the Moon and so on, and I explained that the Age of the Sun was a period of expansion whereas the Age of the Moon, on the contrary, was characterized by a process of coagulation and materialization. The Sun and the Moon, therefore, are also symbols of the two alchemical processes, solve et coagula, dissolve and coagulate.

In the glyph that stands for Mercury, the Sun is represented by a circle and the Moon by a portion of that circle, as though it were a rib of the Sun. This, incidentally, is the explanation of that passage in Genesis which describes how God formed a woman from one of Adam's ribs. When the initiates represented Mercury by the circle of the Sun surmounted by the crescent of the Moon, combined with the plus sign (+), which, as we have seen, also stands for the earth, their intention was to show that it was this combination, this intelligent fusing of the two principles that produced Mercury. The glyph of Mercury is, in itself, convincing evidence of the profound knowledge of the initiates who composed it. One of its numerous variants is the Caduceus of Hermes (Figure 2) which is still used as a symbol, today, by doctors and pharmacists.

In modern science, the same symbol appears in the form of the laser.

The simplest type of laser (Figure 1) is a ruby crystal surrounded by a spiral flash lamp which supplies the energy required to produce the 'laser effect.' When the flash lamp is switched on, a narrow beam of extremely powerful red light is emitted from the half-silvered end of the crystal.

The beam of light emitted by the crystal is none other than Mercury, born of the combined action of the two principles. But the question, now, is to find the laser within ourselves; it is there that it becomes something really prodigious.

Figure 1   *Figure 2*

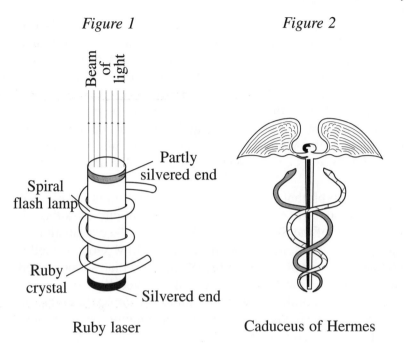

Ruby laser   Caduceus of Hermes

The truth is that, from earliest antiquity, initiates have found in themselves and used all those things which are being discovered today by scientists: radio, television, telephones, etc. Scientists are simply workers whose task is to apply in the physical world the laws that exist in the spiritual world. Everything must be given material existence. This is why today's inventors are often initiates, alchemists, magi and cabbalists from the past who have come to give material form to all those things that they have known and accomplished on the spiritual level. If these phenomena did not already exist on the spiritual plane there would be no way of discovering them on the physical plane. 'That which is below is like to that which is above' and this means that all that exists above, on the psychic plane, must be given concrete expression below, on the physical plane.

By creating the symbol for Mercury, initiates wished to teach future generations to use their will and imagination in order to gain control of their sexual energies and obtain magic powers, for the true 'Strength of all Strengths' of which Hermes Trismegistus speaks, is love. Only love can bestow life and there is nothing more important than life; it is the source and origin of all that exists. God has given us these forces of love so that we may learn to sublimate them and transform them into life, the most intense form of life and, thereby, obtain magic powers, omnipotence. As I have said, the symbol of Mercury is composed of the Sun, the Moon and the Earth. If you remove the Moon you have the symbol of Venus ♀, love. All the different aspects contained in the symbol of Mercury can be found in the functions of the god Hermes whose magic wand, the Caduceus, symbolized the powers he possessed on every level.

In the glyph that represents Mercury, the Moon, which symbolizes the imagination, is in the form of a bowl of water; the Moon, the feminine principle, has a special relationship with water. Beneath the Moon is the Sun, fire, which heats the imagination in a particular direction. And below the Sun is the Earth, symbol of realizations on the level of matter. When an initiate understands this symbol he becomes capable of creating, of helping others, of enlightening, vivifying and protecting them; he possesses all powers. Given the right conditions, he is capable of turning the world upside down because he has understood the one thing that is essential: how the will can work on the imagination. Just as a woman has the power to condense life within her womb, the Moon has the power to give concrete form to things, to materialize them, to transform them into earth, that is to say, to give them physical reality. You see: you have to make symbols speak to you; you have to seize them by the throat and threaten them: 'Your money or your life.' If you take a firm grip on them they will give up all their secrets.

A disciple must make up his mind to overpower the bull; that is, he must learn to control the untamed, brutal, violent force of his sensuality so as to make use of its strength. To overpower the bull does not mean to kill it; if you kill it you will not be able to benefit from its strength. You have to take the bull by the horns, in other words, you have to control the Moon, your imagination, for man's imagination is inseparably linked to his sensuality except in the case of those scholars, philosophers, artists and initiates who have already taken their bull by the horns and given another direction to their imagination and, thus, become capable of creating and discovering things and of enlightening others. Those who have never succeeded in taking the bull by the horns allow their imagination to run wild; it becomes a prostitute who sleeps with all and sundry and gives birth to monsters. You have to try to give your imagination some specific work to do so that it may continually produce the most beautiful, the noblest and most luminous creations. A disciple must not allow his 'wife' to walk the streets and sleep with anyone who asks her; he keeps her for himself. Yes, our imagination is our wife and she is capable of bringing children into the world.

If we pursue our interpretation of the Caduceus of Hermes, we find that it is a summary of a human being. The two serpents twined round the central staff represent the two currents flowing from the brain. Starting from the left and right hemispheres, they cross over at the nape of the neck, pass through the lungs, cross over again at the solar plexus, pass through the liver and spleen, cross over at the navel, pass through the left and right kidneys, cross over, once again, at the Hara centre and pass through the sexual glands of a man, and through the ovaries of a woman (Figure 3).

The central wand represents the spinal column, at the base of which, according to the initiates of India, slumbers the Kundalini force before it is awakened into activity. When Kundalini starts to move up from Muladhara, the Chakra at the base of the spine, it travels through a channel in the centre of the spinal column, Sushumna. Kundalini is set in motion and rises all the way to the thousand-petalled Lotus, the Chakra known as Sahasrara, when the two currents, Ida and Pingala which lie on either side of Sushumna, are stimulated by our breathing.

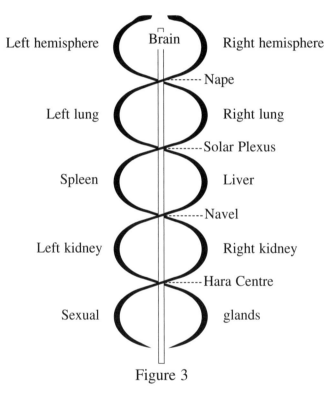

Figure 3

Yogis and initiates, therefore, who succeed in working with the Sun (Pingala, the positive current) and the Moon (Ida, the negative current), awaken the Kundalini force and send it up to the peak of their being. And here, again, we find the phenomenon of the laser: a human being is a living laser. Those who succeed in getting their inner laser to function obtain the 'Strength of all Strengths,' the universal magic agent. *(See Figure 4)*

And now, from all that I have been saying, bear in mind at least this: in order to attain true fulfilment, you must learn to work with the Moon, the imagination (making sure that you safeguard its purity for, in its true spiritual sense, the Moon is related to the purity of the imagination), with light, the fire of the Sun, with the disinterested love of Venus and, finally, with the justice of the cross, Earth. Mercury is the symbol of the perfect human being in which the two currents circulate in such balance and harmony that he bathes in an ocean of perfect peace and becomes a radiant centre, capable of stimulating others to work for good.

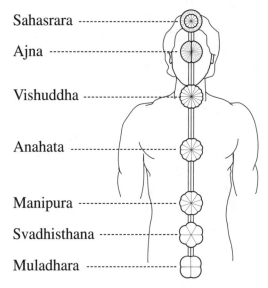

Figure 4

When the Moon lacks the impetus provided by Mars and the Sun, it encourages men's tendency to be lazy and to invent all kinds of machines and appliances that make any effort on their part superfluous. The symbol of Mercury does just the opposite: it teaches us that activity and effort are indispensable.

There is nothing wrong in having machines and gadgets of all kinds, on condition that they free men from their material tasks and enable them to undertake new, spiritual activities, gigantic labours of the will and the imagination, in order to create divine works. Unfortunately, so far, men have not started to work for this goal; on the contrary, they are bent on getting rid of both the Sun and Mars, that is to say of doing away with activity and effort – in spite of the fact that they are essential – and to keep only the Moon and Venus. They don't realize that this is the surest way to degenerate.

I feel as though I had told you nothing; in fact, I have told you everything. The ocean lies at your feet, heaven lies open before you, and you have drunk to your fill; if you are still unchanged, it is because we can only drink as much as our degree of evolution allows, no more. That is what is so sad. But if you continue to be nourished by the climate that reigns here, by all this love, by the songs, by all this light and knowledge, you cannot help but evolve and, one day, you will be capable of fantastic realizations. Even if you understand nothing, keep trying, for there will always be something luminous that will register within you.

Sèvres, December 27 1970

II

There are very few human beings who know how, why and what they should work at within themselves on the psychic and spiritual levels. Human beings are very anxious to acquire all kinds of knowledge that will enable them to practise one of the innumerable trades and professions that exist. They spend years in training as students or apprentices, but they themselves, in their inner being, remain weak, puny creatures who are bowled over by the slightest difficulty, at the first sign of trouble.

I am well aware that, in recent years, all kinds of Oriental practices such as yoga and Zen have been introduced in the West, and many people have taken them up with enthusiasm, precisely because they feel the need to do something to enhance their will-power and learn to concentrate and meditate in order to acquire psychic powers. I have nothing against these methods, which are very ancient and have given good results in the past; however, they were designed for Orientals and, although a certain number of Westerners may get good results from them, I doubt that they are suitable for the majority. Westerners need other methods, methods that suit their mentality and their way of life, and they can find such methods in the Teaching of the Universal White Brotherhood. Westerners who plunge rashly into the practice of Oriental methods without the help of a competent guide are running a very grave risk. Orientals always work under the guidance of an instructor, a Master, who keeps an eye on their progress in the same way as here, in the West, doctors keep an eye on their patients so as to ensure that the prescribed treatment is having the desired effects or, if necessary, to modify it. But those who are left to themselves, with their wholly inadequate resources of knowledge and power, are bound to be hurt. More and more, therefore, human beings are going to realize that they must explore their inner landscape but, also, that they must be very cautious about so many methods that are spreading round the world today and which are, often, very dangerous.

The initiatic work with the Sun and the Moon, that is to say, with the will and the imagination, practised by initiates, will be valid for all eternity, because the will and the imagination are two fundamental principles in man. This is why alchemical texts often mention these two figures, the Sun and the Moon, the King and the Queen, etc. Whatever form they take, the underlying meaning is always this: the Sun and the Moon, man and woman, who produce a royal child, the Philosophers' Stone, the Elixir of Everlasting Life, the universal Panacea, the Magic Wand, the Caduceus of Hermes.

Man's mission is to reproduce heaven on earth, to achieve in himself the likeness of the Creator, his heavenly Father. But before he can achieve the full splendour of this remote mission – for it cannot be achieved all at once – he must know the factors that are indispensable to his work: the two principles, active and passive, emissive and receptive, masculine and feminine, the Sun and the Moon, the will and the imagination. Only thus can he infuse all that is noble and luminous in the Sun into the Moon, so that it reflects and propagates the qualities of the Sun.

The Moon is open to every influence; she does not discriminate; anyone can manifest themselves through the Moon, for she is like water which espouses the form of whatever container it is poured into. Water, the Moon, the imagination – they are all more or less the same thing. If the Sun does nothing to influence her, the Moon may even reflect hell. This is why initiates take care not to let the Moon – their imagination, their 'wife' – stray in all directions, but to see that she receives elements of light and eternity from the Sun. In this way, the Moon becomes an extraordinary, adorable woman and other laws, divine laws, come into play to accomplish, on the physical plane, that which is formed in the imagination. This is the symbolism of the cross at the bottom of the glyph of Mercury. The cross is the cubic stone which stands for the earth. In the mind of the alchemists, the cross, the cubic stone, was the virgin earth which provided the means for the construction of the edifice.

Every day, a disciple must fix his sights on the noblest and most glorious achievements, so as to accomplish them on earth. He must begin, therefore, by working with his imagination then, by means of his heart and will, he must give concrete reality to what he has imagined. He must not be content to float in a dream world, congratulating himself on the beautiful plans in his mind; that is not enough. He has to carry out those plans in his own behaviour, in his actions on the physical plane, so that the whole world can see the things that he has created on a higher level, because they have come down and plunged their roots deep into the earth.

Whether it be the spirit that influences the soul, the will that works on the imagination, the Sun that fertilizes the Moon or a man that fertilizes a woman, the result will always be the creation of a child. But what is that child? When you light a fire under a saucepan full of water (in this case, the saucepan represents the Moon) the water is transformed into steam. And that steam, the water that has expanded, is the 'Strength of all Strengths.' The work of the will on the imagination, of the spirit on the soul, of the Sun on the Moon and of man on woman, therefore, always gives birth to a force which is the child, Mercury, and this child has the power to undertake immense realizations. On their own, the Sun or the Moon cannot achieve much – left to themselves, fire burns and water floods – but the two of them together produce a force which is capable of the greatest accomplishments: the Philosophers' Stone which has the power to transmute metals into gold. The Emerald Tablet says of this force: 'The father thereof is the Sun, the mother the Moon. The Wind carried it in its womb (the womb of the Moon), the Earth is the nurse thereof.' The earth – that is to say, the cross, the cubic stone.

The Bible says, *'Increase and multiply,'* but human beings have understood this commandment only on the physical plane and, naturally, this has led to all kinds of complications: there is not enough room nor enough food in the world, so men are obliged to massacre each other. The end result, therefore, is negative. Not that I want to quarrel with this commandment; all I am saying is that it was valid for a certain period but that people have tried to make it eternal and, now, the results are negative. Today, we have to understand it in its symbolic sense for, on that level, it is still valid.

A disciple must never neglect this work of the will on his imagination – and this applies to women just as much as to men. It is on the spiritual plane that a disciple has to fertilize his wife and produce children, thousands of angelic children, who fly off into space and work for him. You know how fairy-tales end: 'And they had a lot of children and lived happily ever after.' Well, having children is not something that can be done only on the physical plane. What is an initiate? He is the pater familias, the father of innumerable children who cluster round him, dragging at his clothes and rummaging in his pockets, but who love him so much that they are never a nuisance. When he needs them, he calls them to him: to one, he says, 'Go and take So-and-so this gift,' and to another, 'Go and tweak that fellow's ears for him,' and off they go to do his errands. These are the children of his own flesh and blood. But an ordinary human being is alone and childless; he is sad and dispirited because he has to work all alone, there is no one to give him a helping hand. This is an area that is completely unknown to some but which others know well through their own experience.

During the Christmas season I spoke to you about the birth of the Christ-child. Well, the Christ-child is Mercury. Jesus was born two thousand years ago in Palestine, you all know that, but what you have to understand is the idea behind the event, for it is an event of universal, cosmic dimensions. The birth of the Christ-child must take place in each one of us, also, for this child is the hidden force slumbering within us and which we have to awaken.[1]

Before coming down to earth man works to prepare his physical body and, as I have explained, the physical body is none other than the Caduceus of Hermes, with the two currents that flow from the right and left hemispheres of the brain and cross over on the level of the organs. Man himself, therefore, is the fruit of a work of collaboration between the will and the imagination, between the spirit and the soul, which has been given material expression on the physical plane. Insofar as he is the Caduceus of Hermes, man is capable of creation in the three worlds. At the moment, he creates only on the physical plane, but he must learn to create in the other worlds, as well.

The Caduceus of Hermes is the 'Strength of all Strengths,' life in its highest manifestation. When man succeeds in developing the Caduceus of Hermes within himself, therefore, this higher life streams from him, reaching out to all creatures and even to the stars. This is the true 'Strength of all Strengths,' this higher degree of life that is not simply vitality. Vitality is Taurus, the bull. All men possess life, to be sure, but in most men this life manifests itself as a destructive force. When people have too much vitality they are unable to keep control of themselves, they devour and rape and assassinate all around

---

[1] See *Christmas and Easter in the Initiatic Tradition*, Collection Izvor, No. 209.

them. So, this vitality has to be channelled, intensified and spiritualized in order to be transformed into divine life.

This is why you must aspire, day and night, to spiritualize your life so as to be able to give it, to send it out into the universe to vivify and enlighten other creatures. This is the idea expressed in the ancient representations of Hermes with wings on his feet. Incidentally, there are some very important centres on the feet which, if you succeed in developing them, will enable you to move freely through space, not only spiritually, but physically, as well.

The Caduceus of Hermes is life, the most sublime form of life and, when this life radiates from you, your strength becomes tremendous. If you are weak, your life will extend no more than a few inches beyond your physical body and you will be unable to do much. But if your radiance extends for miles then, to be sure, you have the possibility of influencing other creatures. The more intense your emanations and the farther they reach, therefore, the greater your powers.

I have explained how important this work is; it is up to you, now, to take it seriously and to leave aside a lot of other, useless occupations that can bring you nothing but pain. Keep working at yourselves until the 'Strength of all Strengths' begins to manifest within you.

Sèvres, January 3 1971

Chapter Three

THE SERPENT
ISIS UNVEILED

The Master reads a passage from the writings of the Master Peter Deunov:

'There is a legend that tells of how Buddha once fell in love with a beautiful maiden. He loved the divine principle in her. But, one day, as he was gazing at her, he was so entranced by her beauty that he gradually fell asleep and, as the maiden had work to do, she left him; in other words the divine principle within her abandoned her, and all that was left was her human nature, the Astral Woman, which wound itself round him, like a snake, and refused to let him go. Now, Buddha possessed great learning, but the only means by which he could free himself was humility, the capacity to grow smaller. Until that day he had learned to grow and increase in size, but in order to free himself from the clutches of the snake he was forced to shrink or die. Little by little he managed to shrink until there was almost nothing left of him. That is how he escaped from the snake.'

There are still regions of India in which serpent worship exists; it is an organized religion, in fact, with priests and priestesses, and the serpent has servants to serve it as though it were a god. On certain prescribed days, sacrifices are made to the serpent: a priestess coats her body in oil and powder made from a certain kind of rock and begins to dance before it. Gradually, the serpent pulls itself upright and the most extraordinary contest takes place between it and the priestess which ends in the serpent falling under her spell; it is the most amazing thing to see – it is as though the snake and the priestess were about to embrace. Many priestesses have died of snake bite in the course of this ritual dance, but the custom still continues.

The folk literature of almost every nation in the world has tales about a serpent or, sometimes, about a dragon, but the symbolism is almost identical. Even in Europe there are many fairy-tales in which a dragon captures a beautiful princess, a pure and innocent maiden, and holds her prisoner in his castle. The poor princess weeps and pines away and implores heaven to send her a gallant knight to set her free. But, one after another, the knights who attempt to rescue her are all devoured by the dragon, who takes all their wealth for himself and locks it up in a dungeon. One day, at last, a prince arrives, a noble knight, younger, handsomer and purer than all the others. He has learned from a magician the secret of how to conquer the dragon: he knows what its weak points are and exactly when and how it can be wounded or bound in chains. And behold, this privileged young prince, well armed and well forewarned, conquers the dragon and rescues the princess... and how sweet are the kisses they exchange. All the treasures hoarded by the dragon for hundreds of years now belong to this noble knight, this handsome prince, who has emerged victorious thanks to his secret knowledge and exceptional purity. Triumphantly mounting the dragon, the prince takes up the reins and, with the princess beside him, rides off to explore the world.

In the story that the Master Peter Deunov told us, even Buddha was almost overpowered by the serpent for, in reality, that serpent is not outside but inside man; it is the symbol of the sexual energy that we all possess and with which we all have to contend. The dragon or serpent is sexual energy; the castle is the physical or astral body of man; the princess is his soul which is waiting to be rescued and set free by the knight, which is man's ego, the disciple's true self. The sword or lance with which the knight vanquishes the dragon represents the means he has at his disposal, the will-power and knowledge he needs in order to conquer this energy and use it for his own purposes. The dragon, therefore, becomes the disciple's servant; it becomes a steed on which he can ride through space. It is all quite clear and simple: this is the eternal language of symbols.

In the ancient legend of Theseus we have a different version of the same story: thanks to the thread that Ariadne had given him, Theseus was able to find his way through the labyrinth and slay the Minotaur. The Minotaur is another symbol of sexual energy, the symbol of the potent, prolific bull, man's lower nature, which has to be harnessed like an ox, and used to plough the soil. The labyrinth, like the castle, stands for the physical body, and Ariadne represents man's higher soul which leads him to victory.

An endless variety of meanings can be seen in the theme of the serpent. The reptile known to man is no more than a pale reflection of another force, another entity that exists in nature. In ancient times, astrologers represented the Zodiac as a serpent; the twelve Signs fell into place along the body of the snake according to their correspondence with the different parts of the human body, beginning with Aries at the head and ending with Pisces at the tail.

The interesting thing about the story I read to you a moment ago is that it concerns Buddha, a truly exceptional spiritual Master, and shows us that even he had to wrestle with the serpent. If Buddha himself was not spared this trial, there is small hope that anyone else will be: every initiate has to endure it. The maiden whom Buddha loved is shown in her two-fold nature, divine and human (or astral); in this, she is like every other woman, for all women possess these two natures and, depending on circumstances, manifest sometimes one and sometimes the other. The story says that what Buddha loved in this young girl

was the divine principle. Yes, and as long as he was able to
resist the physical attraction of her beauty, as long as he remained
on the impersonal[1] level, where there is neither desire nor
lust, only wonder and admiration, he was in no danger. But,
lulled by the charm of that lovely young woman, Buddha
unintentionally allowed his lower, more personal, more egotistical
nature to be aroused and, as the story says, fell asleep. It says
that he fell asleep, because, when man's lower nature is aroused,
his other nature goes to sleep; in other words, he forgets the
counsels of wisdom and all his good resolutions and acts
according to the dictates of his lower nature. Later, he is
astonished that he could forget the promises that he had made
in all sincerity.

Since Buddha had fallen asleep, the young girl abandoned
him and went back to her work. This means that the divine
principle slipped away and, as it was no longer there to protect
him and surround him in light and splendour, the serpent was
able to bind him in its coils. Buddha struggled but, in spite of
his great learning and knowledge, he was unable to free himself.
Eventually, he realized that it was not he who could vanquish
the serpent; that is to say, it was not in his personality, his lower
nature, that he could hope for victory. Instead of trying to pit
his own puny strength against this formidable cosmic force that
has been building up within man's subconscious for generations
upon generations, he became smaller, that is to say, he became
humbler, thereby allowing the divine principle within him to
manifest itself. It was the divine principle that was victorious,

---

[1] This use of the word 'impersonal' may be misunderstood if it is not placed
in the context of Omraam Mikhaël Aïvanhov's teaching concerning the two
natures in man, the human and divine, the lower self and the higher self
or, as he terms them, the personality and the individuality. For a fuller
treatment of the subject, see Complete Works, vol. 11, *The Key to the Problems
of Existence* and Collection Izvor, No. 213, *Man's Two Natures, Human and
Divine.* See also chapter 26 in this volume.

therefore, whereas he himself, his personality, became so small that he was able to escape. What does all that mean? If I give you an example, it will perhaps help you to understand better.

Let's suppose that a disciple has already scored a few victories: he has met a lot of pretty girls without once letting himself be led astray, so now he thinks, proudly, 'I'm strong. I have overcome temptation.' It is when he believes this that the danger is greatest, for traps of such subtlety will be laid for him that he cannot help but fall into them; his lack of humility makes his downfall inevitable. He is so proud of his strength and attaches such exaggerated importance to his tiny achievements, that he has begun to rely only on himself. He still has no idea of how wily the serpent is. *Genesis* says *'The serpent was more cunning than any beast of the field which the Lord God had made.'* It is just when we are feeling really sure of ourselves that the serpent lies in wait to surprise us. A true disciple knows these things; when he has won a few little victories, he begins to be afraid of what is in store for him: 'What's next, I wonder? It's much too soon to cry victory.' Not only is he on his guard but he knows that he cannot stand by himself: he begs the Lord to be with him and to give him the means to fight and conquer. As you must have noticed, fairy-tales never say that the knight is victorious all on his own; there are always others to advise him and give him the weapons he needs.

The most interesting point in this story about Buddha is that he escaped from the grip of the serpent because of his humility, not because of his strength. If it were only a question of human strength, the serpent would always be stronger, because he is so deeply rooted in the whole of nature. You must understand, therefore, that if you always come off second-best in your battles with the serpent, it is because you have been struggling alone and trying to become bigger, whereas you should be making yourself smaller. This is such an important point and yet so few people know it. It never occurs to someone to get smaller, to shrink, the only creatures that understand this are certain insects: they know how to trick their enemies and escape from their clutches by pretending to be dead. Yes, the insects know this secret... although it doesn't always work because, of course, their pursuers know that they are shamming and are not really dead.

But, let's talk about the other interesting point raised by the story which says that what Buddha loved in that girl was the divine principle. I have already told you, over and over again, that men and women should see each other as bearers of the divine principle. When they manage to do this, instead of being constantly in danger, they will have wings, they will transcend themselves and discover the world, they will be creators. When you see things in this way, it changes everything. This is why you should learn to see nature as a means of approaching the Creator, as a ladder – Jacob's ladder, perhaps – and every object or person as a rung by which you can climb up to the Lord.

Since nature as a whole contains such an indescribable wealth of treasures: flowers, precious stones, trees, birds, butterflies and fishes, etc., and since, through them, we can understand something of the Creator's design, why is it that the question of man and woman is so confused? Think of the rule that was drilled into Christians for centuries: that men should shun the company of women, that they should not even look at them, above all, that they should never look at and admire them in the nude. To be sure, if such rules exist, it is because of men's weakness. That is the whole point, in fact: the degree of evolution reached by the individual. To someone who is highly evolved, it makes no difference whether the woman he sees is clothed or naked; he will remain untroubled and in peace, in heaven, because he sees the Divinity within her.

The Mysteries teach that an initiate must attain the vision of Isis unveiled; his purity and wisdom must be such that he is able to contemplate Isis, that is to say, the divine Mother,

mother nature, everywhere and in all her manifestations. It is Isis, herself, in fact, who gives him the joy of knowing her in all her mystery, in all her beauty, purity and light. Ideally, symbolically, every woman who stands naked before her beloved, represents Isis unveiled before the gaze of an initiate. But people simply don't understand: they spend their lives repeating the mysteries of initiation, the mysteries of Isis, without any understanding of what they are doing. Why is a bride veiled? And why, on her wedding night, does she take off her veils and allow her beloved to gaze on her nakedness? Hardly anyone understands the deeper meaning of these customs; instead of preparing themselves to understand one of the greatest of all mysteries, they only see the lower, cruder, more material aspects. People don't prepare themselves; that is why so many things turn sour later on. Newly-weds go off together on a honeymoon and, for many, this is a period in which they are expected to indulge in the pleasures of sex to the point of nausea. What a monstrous caricature of the eternal symbol of the initiate preparing to approach Isis, his betrothed, to celebrate their nuptials.

The *Apocalypse* speaks of the *'Marriage of the Lamb'*; this is exactly the same initiatic mystery but on a higher level of knowledge, which has little in common with marriage as people understand and practise it, today. In marriage as it is understood today, people find neither light nor knowledge, neither learning nor liberation, neither joy nor peace; on the contrary, it is when they marry that peace deserts them. If they persist in such gross misconceptions, they might as well give up any hope of finding what they are looking and longing for. I ask someone where her newly-wed daughter is: 'She's gone to Venice with her husband. They're on their honeymoon.' There you are: the honeymoon. And what are those two poor ninnies going to do? Knowing nothing about anything, they are going to glut themselves with pleasure until they are disgusted with it and each other. As they are both blind, neither will see the true beauty of the other; neither will see the other's soul or spirit, the splendour that dwells within. All they will see will be their bare flesh, their limbs, their physical matter; nothing else. Poor, wretched humanity! An initiate is not interested in orgies; he is interested in preparing himself for the Marriage of the Lamb, for union with his betrothed, for ecstasies that others know nothing about.

When man finally understands these mysteries, everything else will fade in comparison. The misguided notions that fill the heads of religious people will all be swept away by the powerful light of knowledge; the whole of mankind will, at last, breathe an air that is pure and rejoice in the Marriage of the Lamb. All men are predestined to experience that joy. 'Even old people?' you will ask. Yes: especially old people. Old people are better equipped than the young to live with a partner they love, because their love is different; also, their thoughts and ideals are on a higher level, so they are better prepared to relish the joys of divine love.

When men become capable of contemplating the divine principle in a woman, whether naked or clothed, they will no longer feel the urge to pounce on her; they will no longer lose their heads. Instead, they will say, 'Oh, divine Mother, how beautiful you are. Now I understand why everyone needs you and tries to find you; you are the source of life.'

At one time or another, you have all seen how powerful the two principles are. Is there a woman in the world who can swear that she has never been bowled over by the face of a man glimpsed in the street, in a train, in a film or, even, in a book? Can you show me a man who has never been bowled over by the face of a young woman? No, there's no denying it; it is as clear as day that the two principles are powerful and active and that the influence they have on each other is for a purpose: the purpose of creation. As I say, everyone knows this. Yes, but what they don't know is the necessary degree, proportion and distance that must be respected, and the attitude they must have towards each other in order to create a divine state of harmony, instead of living in a perpetual state of turmoil, failure and regrets. Who can deny that both principles, the masculine and the feminine, are potent forces? The world itself is set in motion by the energy that is released when they come in contact with each other. Each exalts the other, and the power of the laser, that I have already spoken to you about, is based on this exaltation.

Initiates have always known about and used these two forces, the masculine and feminine principles. In fact, it was thanks to this knowledge that they were able to create immensely powerful batteries in order to achieve the results they sought. The batteries I am referring to were men and women who were consciously and harmoniously united. Men and women still have no inkling of the tremendous forces that nature has given them. When they are used correctly, these forces can project beams of light so powerful that they are capable of producing phenomena of cosmic importance. But this can only be done by beings who are pure, luminous and enlightened, otherwise the results can only be catastrophic.

Reasonably and carefully, we are going to work to clear the ground, open up our consciousness and, above all, reach a much broader understanding of purity. People believe that young girls and boys are pure simply because they know nothing about the relations between men and women. But if you could see what goes on in the minds and hearts of some young people, you would be horrified to discover that they are more debauched and vicious than adults. The imagination is far more active in adolescents than in adults. Some of them are pure, of course, but so ignorant and vulnerable that they are likely to fall a prey to the first comer. Purity that is ignorant cannot last long. Purity is far more than not kissing or being kissed. Purity is a question of light; where there is no light there can be no purity. It is light that makes everything pure. You must begin by having light in your head before allowing your feelings to come into play; only then will your feelings be pure.

But, let's get back to the question of nudity. The initiates speak of knowing the naked truth and the naked truth is Isis, whom every initiate must contemplate without her veils. The veils correspond to the seven planes: physical, etheric, astral, mental, Causal, Buddhic and Atmic. Only when the seventh veil is stripped away, can the divine Mother, mother nature, be contemplated in all her nakedness, that is to say, in her purest, subtlest matter that has become one with the spirit. If you want to know someone in this life, try to know him, himself, and not his clothes or veils. If you want to know your Master, it is not enough to watch him eating and drinking, to look at his outer wrappings; you have to strip away all his wrappings until you get to where he truly is; you can only know him in that inner abode. I am not Isis; I am Osiris veiled, and if you persist in seeing only my veils, my outer aspects, you will soon get tired of them, whereas, if you discover the self behind the outer appearances, you will never tire of it; you will have discovered an inexhaustible source of joy.

This is what I do when I see you. If I did not look at you from this point of view, I would have had enough of you ages ago. I would have thought to myself, 'There's nothing interesting there; just the same old faces all the time.' Well, fortunately, I don't think that and the reason is that I 'undressed' you all a long time ago – just as men 'undress' every woman they meet. Now, don't misunderstand me. No one has ever properly understood this impulse on the part of men to undress a woman and gaze on her. It is nature herself who has given men this instinct in order to incite them not to be content with outward appearances, but to look further and higher to where a woman is truly naked, in the realm of perfect purity, light and glory. There is nothing shameful on this higher level, for the object of our contemplation is not a woman's physical body, her hair or her breasts, but her soul, the inner Divinity. Human beings don't know how to interpret the language of nature correctly; they sense certain instincts in themselves but they are content to go no further than their crudest manifestations. They give up the struggle and become mired in their lower nature and that is the end of them.

So, when I say that I have undressed you, don't misunderstand me: I simply mean that I am not content to know you only on the physical plane. I want to know you on another level, on the divine level of your being and, when I look at you, I see you as sons and daughters of God and everything is transformed, my joy is untroubled and the forces of life flow within me. If it were otherwise, I would have packed up and left you a long time ago. Don't you think that you should learn to do the same where I am concerned, instead of seeing only my outer appearance? That may satisfy you for a time, but don't let it last for centuries, for you won't get much benefit from it. I tell you this for your own good, so that you may find true life, that inexhaustible source of joy. Physical form is necessary, of course, but you must not expect it to satisfy you for long; it is only a starting point. It is like a bottle: its only value lies in the fact that it protects the precious perfume it contains, the quintessence of life.

What you should look for is the vibrant spirit that radiates life and light, that creates worlds. If you do that you will never know disappointment; otherwise, sooner or later, you are bound to be disappointed. Physical form cannot satisfy you if it is not animated. If it is animated, that is another matter; in that case it may satisfy you but, whether you know it or not, your satisfaction actually comes from the life contained in it. When you look at a beautiful painting you can be enraptured by it because it contains life; yes, even in a painting there is life, the life of the creator who put something of himself into it when he painted it. Men and women are paintings, too, paintings that contain life, the life of the Creator and it is this life that we must look for. If we never acquire the habit of seeking that life, the inevitable outcome will be quarrels, divorces and tragedy.

And now, if you are wondering why initiates are so full of admiration at the beauty of human beings, I will tell you. Although true initiates, who are always in search of the harmony and perfection of the world above, know that it is reflected everywhere, in stones, animals and plants, in mountains, lakes, rivers and oceans and in the stars, they also know that that perfection, that harmony and beauty, is nowhere more perfectly represented than in the human body. Everywhere else it is scattered and fragmented: the oceans are a part of the cosmic Body; the rivers are another part; mountains and the sky are yet other parts. Only men and women reflect the whole cosmic Body. God has condensed the entire universe in man and woman. This is why, when an initiate sees a human being who reflects the splendour of the universe more perfectly than others, he delights in contemplating that beauty and uses it to strengthen his attachment to the beauty of God. He says to himself, 'Here is someone who speaks to me of the virtues of God himself.' When he contemplates her or him, he is in communion with divine beauty. But ordinary men and women, instead of being filled with wonder at the beauty of heaven reflected in those they love, misuse them and despoil that beauty. They are like wild horses galloping through a meadow full of flowers: their hooves trample and crush all that beauty. If they were initiates, they would admire the beauty of their beloved ten times more... and think what strength and inspiration this would give them and with what energy and determination they would continue their work.

While I am on the subject, I want to mention a very interesting point. You know that the limbs and organs of the human body correspond to certain lines of force flowing through the cosmos.* Each organ of our physical bodies was created with a special link to a specific force and you may remember that some of you were astonished when I told you which regions of the cosmos corresponded to a woman's breasts. Everyone

---

* See the supplementary note at the end of this chapter.

thinks that the only function of the breasts is to suckle children. That is their physical function, to be sure, but they have another function that no one knows about. I told you, then, that the left breast was related to the moon and the right breast to the Milky Way and that women's spiritual evolution would be greatly enhanced if they knew this. Most women are totally unaware that they are in communication, in this way, not only with nature as a whole but with other human beings as well. But, even if they know nothing about it, this etheric, magnetic communication still exists; their breasts still give and receive something. Not long after I had revealed this to you, I visited a museum in Spain and came across a painting by a relatively unknown artist which portrayed a nude woman with a moon on the left breast and the Milky Way flowing from the right breast. I must say that I was both astonished and delighted to see this illustration and confirmation of an initiatic truth. The painter must certainly have been an initiate.

The human body is a condensation of the universe and a disciple must learn to have the right attitude, an attitude of awe and respect, towards it; above all, he should see it as a starting point in the work of linking himself to the sublime world above, in order to give glory to the Lord and advance on the path of evolution. In this way, he will discover all the secrets of nature for, when Isis sees that she need no longer fear the rape or abuse of her body, she will reveal herself to him. She will say, 'This being is considerate and loving; he respects and admires me, so I shall reveal myself to him.' Thus, truth will reveal itself, for Isis is truth. Truth will reveal itself to the spirit of the disciple in all its nakedness, that is to say, as it is above, no longer hidden by the veils of illusion, of maya, as it is here, below. Truth, therefore, reveals itself to those who have the right attitude towards the mysteries of love.

The Bonfin, July 24 1962

Supplementary note:

Some people have very strange notions about the state in which man finds himself in heaven. They believe that only his head goes to heaven, nothing else, because the liver, stomach, intestines and, above all, the genitals, are not very dignified organs. But I say that man goes to heaven whole and intact; in fact, you would be astounded to see the splendour, the beauty and purity of his body, just as God created it in the beginning. He has lungs, but in a different form, a brain, ears and eyes, but all in a different form or, rather, of a different quintessence, for forms no longer exist in the world above; there are only currents, lights and forces. Everything in man is organized and functions as though he had a stomach, arms and legs, nothing is missing, it is all there, but as virtues, qualities and faculties. For the organs of our physical body are, after all, simply condensed representations, reflections of qualities and virtues. If you could see human beings in that Heavenly state, with all those colours and lights continually flashing and radiating from them, you would never tire of looking at them.

Official science is a long way from any real understanding of what human beings are and how God formed them in his workshops in the world above. Only the great clairvoyants, the great Masters, have been able to go there and see these things for themselves, and they tell us that, in that world, a human being has no form; he consists of forces, currents, energy, light, emanations, and that it is the condensation of these elements that produces the physical organs that we know. The stomach, liver, spleen, brain, eyes and ears, legs and arms, therefore, represent higher forces. And when a man acts in contradiction to reason, he begins to extinguish his lights, to lose all his virtues, and the organs that correspond to those virtues begin to deteriorate. This explains all physical disorders and disease.

Le Bonfin, August 1 1975

Chapter Four

THE POWER
OF THE DRAGON

In the Christian religion the dragon represents the Devil and the Devil, as we all know, smells of sulphur or brimstone. The dragon is any combustible material such as oil, petrol, gasoline, gunpowder or gas, that produces flames and a revolting stench. And the dragon exists in human beings; it is a fuel, a fire, that is capable of carrying man out into space. If he does not know how to use it properly, however, instead of being projected to tremendous heights, he will be thrown down and engulfed in the depths of the earth.

We all have this dragon within us. There is an individual dragon, therefore, and there is also the collective dragon of which St John speaks in the Apocalypse, saying that it will be bound for a thousand years and cast into the bottomless pit. This means that the day will come when this collective sexual force, which drives human beings to things that are far from divine, to wars and assassinations, will have to be educated, domesticated and sublimated. What else could be done with the dragon? Could it just stay down there, in the pit? No, it is going to be properly trained. It will have magnificent teachers who will give it an excellent education; there will even be chiropodists, manicurists and dentists who will take care to trim its teeth and claws and make it harmless, fit for polite company.

You must not slay the dragon, you must educate it... unless, of course, you prefer to eat it. That makes you laugh, perhaps, but you should read what the Talmud says about it: it says that Leviathan, the great sea monster that symbolizes evil, lives in the depths of the ocean and that, in the last days, it will be caught, cut up and pickled in brine and served as a banquet for the Righteous. Just think of the treat in store for us all... on condition, of course, that we are numbered amongst the Righteous. I don't know what the others are going to eat, but we, the Righteous (well, we have to say it for ourselves. Nobody is going to say it for us, are they?), we must be prepared to feast on the flesh of this monster. I suppose that there will be a few problems involved; if it is as tough as an old boot and you are toothless, for instance, what will you do? Perhaps there will be all kinds of sauces and clever ways of cooking it to make it tender. Then, there is also the question of the cut: there will have to be maps of how to carve it up. And some of it will have to be tinned. What a glorious prospect: hundreds of factories busily engaged in putting the Leviathan in tins. It's just as well the monster is so huge, for there will be thousands of people to feed. So, let the Righteous rejoice for their future is assured.

As you see, evil can be used in many different ways. The important thing to remember is that you have all this fuel, all these formidable forces, within you and that you can use them to propel you to a higher level. As long as you don't know that these forces can be used, they will consume you and reduce you to ashes or cast you down into the depths of the earth. Henceforth, you must see sexual love as the dragon, the strongest motive power in man. It is always this force that moves men, that incites them to work; it is always love, whether good or bad, and not, as many people think, money, that sets things in motion. People only want money because they can use it to get what they covet, whether it be the love of a woman or a precious object.

You must learn to use this extraordinary driving force, therefore, and there are many examples in daily life that can show you how to do so. What does a cook do when she wants to boil some water? She puts the water in a saucepan before putting it on the fire, otherwise the fire would be extinguished or the water would evaporate. In other words, there has to be a barrier of some kind between the two elements. In every motor-driven vehicle the same principle applies: the fuel is kept in a container so that it can drive the car, the boat or the plane without burning the occupants. In the same way, a disciple has to discover the secret of how to love without burning the heart or soul of the one he loves. Many young girls have a beautiful, romantic notion of love but, once they have had experience of a man, it does not seem so poetic or divine; they are disgusted and disappointed. This is certainly because the man used methods he should not have used. When human beings lose all that is most wonderful in their souls, it is because love is a consuming fire and they have let it burn them, instead of being exalted, renewed and vivified by it and using it to advance on the path to heaven. Why does love so often contribute to the destruction of what is good when its role is, on the contrary, to amplify and strengthen it?

The first thing to understand is that there are two kinds of love. There is a purely sensual love in which tenderness, intelligence and delicacy of feelings have no part. A person is hungry, so he behaves like a wild animal and throws himself on his prey, then sits back and contentedly licks his chops. The fact that his victim has been devoured is not important; what matters is that he has satisfied his own appetite. In the other sort of love, however, a person tries to forget himself; even if he is hungry and thirsty, his first care is for the one he loves. His only thought is to protect and enlighten her, to give her peace and riches. When two human beings love each other with this kind of love, their possibilities for growth know no limits; like the fire of the sun, their love vivifies and resuscitates them and gives them eternal life. The heavens lie open before them, for they have discovered the meaning of life; something so luminous and subtle emanates from them that other people stop and look at them as they go by.

Since you are in this school of the Universal White Brotherhood, the least you can do is learn a better way to love. Now that you have been introduced to the dragon, don't forget that he is tremendously powerful, that he possesses fantastic energy and that, if you can master and subdue him, he will carry you where you will in the universe.

Sèvres, April 4 1968

Chapter Five

SPIRIT AND MATTER:
THE SEXUAL ORGANS

I

We are seeing, today, the birth of a new culture, a universal culture of the collectivity, of brotherhood, in which all the human beings in the world will learn to love and understand each other and to form one family. When I speak of forming one family, I don't mean that everybody will have to sleep in the same bed – or even the same dormitory – but that everybody will discover how magnificent it is to be together to work, sing, meditate and pray.

Nature has instilled in each human being the instinct to avoid solitude; they see it as a burden, as something to be feared. That is all well and good, but we have to know the best way of escaping solitude. There are so many young men and women who are very unhappy because they have no solution for this problem. Try as they might, they have failed to find a partner with whom to sing a duet and the result is that they wilt and fade away. But why have they got it so firmly into their heads that their duet must necessarily be on a physical level? Is there no other way of doing it? There are all kinds of ways of escaping solitude; why persist in trying to do so in the old-fashioned way, by possessing another human being?

Women, especially, have this urge to possess someone; they want to be able to hold someone, if only a child, in their hands. They know that they can never hold on to a man, that he will always slip from their grasp, so they cling to a child. As long as her child is young and needs her protection, a woman is happy because she can keep him. Then he, too, grows up and slips from her grasp and she is miserable again, because she is left with nothing. A woman's need to possess complicates everything. You will say, 'And what about men? Don't they have this possessive instinct?' No, a man only wants to 'have' a woman – in the crudest sense – on the physical level. A man's idea of possession, is to 'love them and leave them,' whereas a woman's first thought is to tie her man down before giving him all the rest. A man will say, 'Don't worry, we'll get everything organized later; first, let's have our fun.' But women are not so stupid, they know very well that, once he has got what he wanted, he will leave her, so she says, 'No, first you have to sign this,' and she makes him give her a contract, a commitment.

All the different ways in which men and women manifest themselves and all the mysteries of the physical, emotional, moral and intellectual aspects of their lives, stem from what are called their 'private parts.' These organs represent a summary of man and woman. Every human being carries his own personal summary with him, wherever he goes, without realizing that it contains all the answers, that the geometrical structure and the functions of these organs explain even the most deeply philosophical questions. It is amazing to see how men manage to carry with them all wealth and all the keys they will ever need, without ever realizing that they are rich, that they possess all science, all criteria, everything.

It is in the nature of woman, therefore, to be acquisitive and provident, whereas man is a natural spendthrift. We have all seen this but, although the thing is obvious, people don't recognize the origin of these characteristics; they don't make the connection. These natural traits of character in men and women are due to the form and function of their sexual organs. Woman has to be possessive, otherwise no creation would be possible. Her role is to collect, to hoard, to preserve and protect. In Bulgaria, we say, 'It is because woman hoards that the store-room is full.' To be sure, there are women who are wasteful, but they are not true women; they are men in disguise. Cosmic intelligence had a very good reason, therefore, for giving woman her acquisitive, retentive tendencies: she must not be wasteful, otherwise there would be no children. If a man is wasteful, on the other hand, it does not matter much; there will always be plenty of raw material. A great deal of seed is needed to produce a very small harvest. Nature understands that man has to give generously in order to ensure at least one birth, otherwise his seed could be lost or fall on barren ground. If woman were as generous as man the result would be sterility; this is why she hoards so carefully the little she receives.

This physical tendency to acquire and hold on to things is also found in woman's character in the form of a serious failing, that of jealousy. The situation in which the wives and concubines of many kings and, especially, of oriental sultans, found themselves is a case in point. Every woman in the vicinity, whether at court or in a harem, had only one idea: to monopolize the affection of the sovereign, to be the favourite, the best-loved. To reach this goal, no effort was too great and calumny and conspiracy were frequently resorted to in a relentless battle amongst the women... of which the prize was the king or sultan. And why did they all want to possess him? Because of the advantages this gave them: a woman was flattered to be the chosen one, to think that she had captured the sultan's attention. All her dreams were fulfilled, a great emptiness, an eternal void within her was satisfied. This is why every woman would go to any lengths to get rid of her rivals.

You will, perhaps, say that all that is a thing of the past and that, in any case, it was only the Turks who behaved like that. Not at all; wasn't it exactly the same in France? History tells of countless court intrigues of this kind. What about Louis XIV and XV? There were always dozens of women just longing to captivate them.

It is natural for a woman to want to be an ornament for a man who is worthwhile, but the terrifying thing is that she never accepts that other women should have the same advantages, the same favours. Rather than trying to overcome this fault, women have done everything possible to reinforce it. It seems that they cannot live without jealousy; it torments them but they cannot do without it. It is as though, without jealousy, there were nothing to stimulate them, they were bored, whereas jealousy drives them to embark on all kinds of clandestine activities and then life seems really exciting.

Women always have a tendency to envy the good points of other women which cause them to be noticed and admired. There is virtually not a woman on earth who will forgive a man for showing a little tenderness and love to anyone but herself; in her fury she will invoke every moral and legal argument to convict him. But if it is to her that he shows tenderness... Ah, that's another matter; that's only right and just; she will find him blameless. When a woman is furious with a man it is often because he has not given her what she hoped for and has given it to another. When a girl detests a boy, you can be sure that it is because she wanted him to kiss her and he has preferred someone else. You will object that this is a very cruel analysis; not at all, my analysis is faultless. Can you show me a woman who would be sorry to be loved. No, that is the only thing she wants, the only thing she is waiting for. And, if a man prefers someone else, she will exaggerate and distort everything he says or does in order to accuse and condemn him, almost to assassinate him. This is why women must work at developing generosity and learn to rejoice in other people's happiness.

And, now, let's talk about a more philosophical aspect of this question of the sexual organs of man and woman.

If the invisible world sometimes imposes limitations and constraints on certain people, it is in order to awaken their will and their desire to overcome their limitations and free themselves. This is what happens with gunpowder: you compress it and put limitations on it and, then, when you put a match to it, it blows everything sky-high. But, if you give it lots of room and then put a match to it, it will just fizzle out. And the same goes for man: if his life is easy, he will just fizzle out, but if he suffers and is constrained, the spirit within him is glad, because he is going to have to exert himself to break out of his limitations. The man moans that he is suffering, but his spirit rejoices. The same phenomenon can be seen in intercourse between a man and woman: why does the man need to be held tightly, to be confined and restricted while making love? Because this is what causes something within him to rejoice. If the woman gave him unlimited space he would not feel anything.

You have never thought about these things and yet you imagine that you know all there is to know in this area. It is not the physical manifestations that interest me, it is what lies behind them: the profound, philosophical, divine aspect hidden behind those manifestations. It is always the woman that has to envelop the man, to enclose and encircle him, while he is lost somewhere in space, like the spirit that loses itself in matter. The entire philosophy of creation – the relation of spirit to matter – can be read in these organs which all men and women possess and which they use, night and day, without understanding anything about them. You must try to understand.

Human beings are up to their necks in physical love; they do nothing else, day and night, but they don't understand the first thing about the really sublime truths contained in this act. They are so completely submerged in their sensations that they have neither the time nor the lucidity to understand anything. But those who don't practise this kind of love have time to understand what the others practise without understanding. How do you think that I have had time to understand the greatest mysteries of creation?

The Bonfin, August 8 1963

II

Why do men and women seek each other out? For the sake of their physical bodies? No, for the sake of something else, something subtle and alive that we call love. And, when they receive this they are happy and fulfilled. If it were really the physical body they needed, they would have to cut off a piece so as to eat and drink it. But their physical bodies remain intact, and this means that they are simply a means through which they receive something else, an emanation or fluid. Human beings, as you see, are not very enlightened: they don't even know what they are looking for. If it were really the physical body, why is it still intact after their desire has been satisfied?

The truth is that, by means of their physical bodies, men and women are simply conductors, conductors either of heaven or of hell. This means that these organs are not predetermined, they can be used to stir up hell or to touch the fringes of heaven, depending on what the men and women who use them have in their heads or their hearts. If you have a knife, for instance, you can wound or, even, kill someone with it but, with the same knife, you can release a prisoner from his bonds or save a man's life by operating on him. In the same way, the use of the sexual organs is not necessarily either good or evil. A person can be soiled and contaminated by contact with you but, equally, they can be saved: it all depends what is in your heart and soul. This is why, with the same man or woman in your arms, you can reach either heaven or hell; you can reach demons who will plunder and devour you and never leave you in peace again, or you can reach angels and heavenly entities. This is something no one ever thinks about. They do everything blindly, mechanically; they feel the urge, the need to do it and they never think about what it means; they never pause to reflect that, behind this act, there is an immense, a prodigious science. Heaven has given human beings these organs for the accomplishment of a specific work, they are destined to achieve fantastic things; at the moment, however, they use them only in ways that stir up the astral regions and do harm to themselves.

There is much more that could be said about this subject, so immensely rich, vast and essential. Yes, essential, because this is where life comes from but, instead of obtaining life, people lay waste to it. I am going to leave you to meditate on the question, now, and perhaps you will discover some things for yourselves. I cannot tell you everything; in fact, I am not allowed to tell you everything. These truths are so sacred that to give them to you all at once, without the necessary precautions, could have very regrettable consequences. If you are not sufficiently evolved, if you do not have the highest possible ideal, even the truth can be very prejudicial. When someone receives a truth for which they are not ready, it can become an obsession: although they are incapable of making use of it, they cannot stop thinking about it, and that is dangerous.

But, let me add a few words which might be very helpful to you. One day, a young girl came to talk to me about something that was troubling her greatly. She was in a great state because, wherever she looked, she kept seeing the male sexual organs and the more she struggled against that image, the more it became an obsession; she was at her wit's end to know how to free herself from it.

I told her, 'Listen, young lady, it is not really so terrible. Since the world began, a great many women have been in the same situation at some point in their lives. And men, too, sometimes see certain parts of a woman's body. There is nothing catastrophic in that; don't panic. The trouble is that no one has ever told you that the phenomenon was perfectly natural or taught you to understand it properly; that is why you are so upset. Nature has given the gift of imagination to boys and girls in order to prod them into action, to get them to work and to find things for themselves; without this stimulus mankind would come to an end. Unfortunately, the health of many young people is undermined because of the absurd education they receive. If you follow the advice I am going to give you, you will be cured. And not only will you be cured, but you will make great progress spiritually. It's very simple.

'What does this image you keep seeing represent? It represents nothing less than the eternal, active, dynamic principle of the heavenly Father, the spiritual principle that created the world. It is a stimulus designed to lead you towards a wonderful, infinitely powerful reality. Why not take the opportunity, as soon as this image comes into your mind, to put yourself in touch with the heavenly Father? Within a few minutes, you will find yourself catapulted to sublime heights and will have forgotten the cause. There you are: instead of being panic-stricken, you can learn to put everything to good use. The worst thing in such a situation is to dwell on the mental image and worry yourself sick instead of using it to climb very high and very far. That is the only real danger.'

And now, let me repeat this for all of you: everything in nature is simple; it is human beings who complicate things and make themselves ill. What do they find to object to in the sexual organs? Have you any idea how long it took for nature to create them? What profound meaning and beauty they contain. The whole of life is there. What makes you want to destroy God's work and replace all that splendour with your own complicated ideas? Perhaps you will object: 'Yes, but if I want to be pure, I must try not to think about these things.' What purity can there possibly be in opposing the natural order? You have always been told to fight against your sexual impulses but the methods we teach, here, are different. They consist, simply, in learning to see the beauty and intelligence that exist in every single thing.

Nowadays, people discard all the rules but can you show me someone who has gained freedom by doing that? The new method is both easy and intelligent: it generates neither conflict nor stress nor neurosis. If you use this method, you will be lost in admiration at the way in which nature has created men's and women's organs for, when you reflect on these things, you gradually work your way up to their source. This method will help you to feel so much in harmony, so full of light and peace, that you will burn with eagerness to pour out all that joy on the whole world. So, this is how you can become more evolved instead of sharing the fate of most people who have never managed to solve their sexual problems and have become soured and bitter. When you begin to understand me, the whole of creation, all created things, will give you untold joy; you will see the splendour of the Lord in everything and you will live in perfect purity, for you will ask for nothing more; your only desire will be to distribute that overabundance of joy within you.

Videlinata (Switzerland) March 22 1975

Chapter Six

THE MANIFESTATIONS OF THE
MASCULINE AND FEMININE PRINCIPLES

I

In the presence of the masculine principle, even at a distance, the feminine principle immediately reacts and is set in motion. Similarly, the presence of the feminine principle triggers an immediate reaction in the masculine principle. These two principles are powerful forces and, as soon as they are brought face to face, they begin a specific work together. In most men and women, however, all this is unconscious and purely instinctive. They walk or run in response to a stimulus, seeking each other out and embracing, without ever trying to understand why nature designed these mechanisms and how they could apply them in other areas.

The masculine and feminine principles, therefore, have a specific effect on each other; even if a man and woman don't notice it, this interaction always takes place: the masculine principle becomes active, dynamic and assertive whereas the feminine principle becomes receptive. This happens automatically in all normal creatures. But initiates, who go much further in their understanding of all phenomena, know how to use this law in their spiritual life in order to awaken certain qualities. At this point, it is no longer a question of men and women but of divine principles. When an initiate, who is a man, wants to acquire the feminine qualities of receptivity, gentleness, humility and obedience, he has to make contact with the heavenly Father;

only in this way can he attract the virtues of the opposite principle. Conversely, if he wants to acquire the masculine qualities of authority, strength and power, he makes contact with the divine Mother. An initiate advances on the path of perfection by a harmonious development of both the masculine and feminine qualities.

How often we see this in everyday life: the feminine principle makes a young man chivalrous and brave. Even the most cowardly creature tries to put on a brave face in the presence of a girl. You will say that he is just bluffing. Perhaps, but why does he feel the need to bluff? Why does he pretend to be a hero? Because of the girl. Look at what happens when a man goes home in the evening and tells his wife how one of their neighbours insulted him. 'What?' says his wife, 'And you let him get away with it? Go over to his house right away and give him a black eye.' 'You're right,' says her husband, not wanting to show how chicken-hearted he is, 'I'll teach the So-and-so,' and off he goes. But, on the way, his courage forsakes him and he decides to go home and tell his wife that the man in question was not at home. And his wife believes him and feels very proud of her heroic husband.

Why do men need to boast and put on an act in front of women? Because they know, instinctively, that that is how to win their respect. Because women are weak and need the support of somebody strong, they admire strength. In the tournaments of the Middle Ages, it was often a woman who rewarded the victor with a rose or a smile. In those days, women were very impressed by heroism and showed their admiration for a knight who returned from battle covered in glory. You will find the same attitude in animals. When two males fight for the possession of a female, she always chooses the winner. A female prefers the one that shows himself to be stronger and braver. Women don't like weak men; there are exceptions to this, of course: some women are so charitable and protective that they are drawn to someone who is weak.

Now, let's look at a few aspects of life and see the signs of differentiation that cosmic intelligence has placed in the two principles: in the way they behave, the way they look at things, the way they work and talk, etc.

All deep, hollow forms in nature represent the feminine principle; all vertical forms represent the masculine principle. When they speak or sing, however, men have deep voices and women have high voices. Why? The answer is simple: that which is on a lower level has a tendency to look upwards, whereas that which is on a higher level tends to look down. When you are already at the top, you cannot look up: if you are at the summit there is nothing to look up at, you are obliged to look down; whereas those who are down below look up. As a matter of fact, you can see this in everyday life: the poor strive for wealth, the ignorant for knowledge, the weak for strength, etc. And woman – who represents the depths, the abyss, emptiness – strives for fullness, sending her gaze upwards, towards heaven, towards her beloved. And he looks down towards her; this is why his voice has become deeper. It is by their voices that the two principles express the most basic tendencies of their nature.*

Let me give you another example: have you ever noticed that, when a man and woman embrace, the woman puts her arms round the man's neck, whereas the man tends to put his hands lower down? If I call your attention to this, it is not because of any lewd implications it may suggest to your imagination; what interests me is the philosophical aspect and I find some very significant details in the gestures that men and women make instinctively. Woman reflects the tendency of matter to evolve, to move onto a higher plane, whereas man reflects the tendency of the spirit to descend and explore the depths.

There are also differences to be seen in the activities of men and women: man is primarily creative whereas woman is

---

* See the supplementary note at the end of this chapter.

primarily formative. In bringing a child into the world, for instance, it is the father who is the creator, who supplies the seed, the spirit, and it is the mother who supplies the materials with which to form its body. Man creates, therefore, and woman forms. The creator of a house is the architect who designs it and draws the plans; the house is not yet visible or tangible, you cannot live in it, but it has already been created in someone's mind. It only remains to give it form with the help of various materials. Creation always precedes formation and takes place on a higher level, in the mind, on the mental plane.

When God created the world, it was done instantaneously. It was the process of formation that took time; in fact, it was during the course of the formation of the world that time first appeared. This is why we talk of the six days of creation. Those six days are symbolic, of course; they represent the time that it took for the world to be formed, whereas creation is instantaneous; it is eternity.

And why, again, when she kisses a man, does a woman have a tendency to put her tongue into his mouth? This is simply a way of showing that what happens below, on the physical plane, is the reverse of that which happens above, on the astral plane. On the physical plane, man is emissive and woman receptive; on the astral plane, it is man who is receptive and woman who is emissive. Man is the one who receives on the astral plane, because he is weaker on this plane and woman is stronger; a woman is stronger on the level of sentiment. On the higher level, woman gives and, on the lower level, she receives. Man gives on the lower level and receives on the higher level. This reversal of polarity on the different planes is a great mystery. In fact, it is the reason why so many people misinterpret the realities of the invisible world: they don't know that they should reverse things; they get the different planes all mixed up. Clairvoyants say that figures and numbers are reversed on the astral plane. As a matter of fact, this phenomenon is quite well known: people who have been saved from drowning at the last minute, for instance, have told us that, on the threshold between life and death, they saw their whole life passing before their eyes in reverse. This is because they already had one foot in the next world, where everything is reversed.

'That which is below is like to that which is above'; that which is above, in the head, the mouth with the tongue and the two lips, is like that which is below, the genitals. The words used by Hermes Trismegistus, 'below' and 'above,' give only a vague indication. In every domain, we need to know exactly what this 'above' and 'below' are and how they correspond: heaven and earth (or heaven and hell), the brain and the genitals (or the brain and the stomach). That which is below is like to that which is above, but in reverse. Even in the anatomy of men and women we find this reversal: in a man, everything is external and visible whereas, in a woman, everything is internal, hidden and mysterious.

Now, imagine that a supposedly naïve, innocent young girl, gets a young man to sleep with her (quite unintentionally, of course), what is her reaction going to be, afterwards? She is going to shed bitter tears, saying that she didn't really want that, that he has wronged her, and the wretched young man, who wants to do the right thing, tries to make up for it by committing himself: he promises marriage – or some such arrangement – and the girl is secretly triumphant, because that is exactly what she wanted. Sometimes of course, the boy abandons her anyway, leaving the poor girl pregnant, but that is not what concerns us today.

In reality, if you study the structure of the female sexual organs, you will see that they are designed in such a way as to hold the man and make him her prisoner. The man imagines that it is he who is the conqueror and that the poor little woman is his victim. Not a bit of it. The truth is that it is she who holds on to him, who constricts him and fences him in; he is her slave and it is he, therefore, who is the victim. On the surface of it the woman seems to accept and submit to the man but, in reality, she is bent on possessing him so that, for the rest of her life, he will be there to satisfy her and work for her, etc. Besides, look at another aspect of this: it is the man who is diminished, he who is deprived of something, while she gains something, she receives the seed of life and a marvellous work begins within her. Yes, things are not always what they seem on the surface. The man seems to be proud of himself and the woman much less so but, deep down, it is she who is prouder than he; it's just that he is more gullible.

This is how everything works in nature. If you want to catch a bird, an insect or a butterfly, you have to surround it, get a grip on it. Human beings, for instance, are surrounded and dominated by nature. Nature is all round them, like a house; if you walk into a house, the doors can close and shut you in and, then, you are a prisoner, a victim. The one who is in control of a situation has the other one at his mercy, and this is what happens between a man and a woman: it is she who is the stronger because she has control of the situation; for a few moments, at least, he is at her mercy. Women need men and, in order to attract them, they assume the role of victim, making themselves seem weak, delicate, tender and fearful. They know instinctively that a man likes to believe that he is stronger, that he is a hero, a champion, a conqueror. But she only does this in order to possess him the more surely, to get what she wants from him.

Actually, there is nothing to choose between them: they both plot and scheme; it's just that they set about it differently. The ordinary kind of love is a war, a battle in which both try to conquer the other. On the outside, we see only friendliness but, beneath the smiles and kisses, a relentless war between the sexes is being waged. Of course, it is not open warfare, it has to be carefully camouflaged because a great deal of diplomacy is needed in order to conquer one's adversary, and it is only years later that one can see which of the two was more cunning. You will protest, 'That's a terrible thing to say.' It's the truth, nevertheless. Except, of course, when the man and woman have a philosophy, an ideal, when they both want to work for the Kingdom of God. Then, instead of being adversaries in disguise, they are true collaborators: each of them collaborates consciously, bringing to their joint venture the particular qualities that nature has given them.

If, outwardly, man seems to be the aggressor and woman the victim, it is because men are active and assertive; they are not good at hiding things. Everything that goes on in them is visible. Women, on the contrary, are built to dissimulate; you cannot tell what is going on inside them. This is why women are untroubled by dissimulation; they don't see anything wrong or dishonest in it. A woman can be waiting for a man, for instance, and when he turns up she pretends not to see him or to be taken by surprise. You can never tell what a woman thinks or wants, because she manifests herself in conformity with her intimate structure, in which everything is turned inwards. That which is external in a man, is internal, reversed, in a woman and, when she dissimulates or even lies, she is only obeying the laws of her nature. Men, too, obey the laws of their nature which prompts them to be direct and frank about things, even, quite often, to be brutal and clumsy.

So, there you have a few little anatomical, physiological, psychological and diplomatic details. They are details, perhaps, but they are of great importance in helping us to understand the character of men and women and how they manifest themselves.

And now, to conclude, let me tell you that men and women must work to develop their complementary principle within themselves. Women must develop the masculine principle in themselves, and men the feminine principle. When I was in India, I went into a great many temples; in almost all of them, even the smallest, I saw a lingam, which is the symbol of the union of the masculine and feminine principles. On several occasions, in fact, I had an opportunity to talk to some yogis and I would ask them, 'Do you really understand the meaning of this symbol?' They would stare at me indignantly. How could a European have the impertinence to question their understanding of a symbol that has been part of their tradition for centuries. 'Well,' I would say, 'If you understand it, why do you do the exact opposite of what you have understood? Why are you married? There's nothing wrong in being married, of course, but it means that you are looking for the other principle, the feminine principle, outside yourself, in a being who is separate and foreign to you, whereas this symbol shows you that the two principles must never be separated. The lingam is a symbol of the perfect, androgynous man, who possesses both principles within himself. If you are still looking outside yourself for your complementary principle, it means that you have not understood this symbol.' When I spoke to them like this, they would look at me as though they were hearing these truths for the very first time; some of them would reflect about what I had said, but others were almost angry.

A disciple must work to manifest the qualities of both principles: the strength, will-power, endurance, steadfastness, activity, ambition and dynamic energy of the masculine principle, which seeks to lead and dominate others, to impose his will; and the flexibility, delicacy, docility, self-sacrifice and charm of the feminine principle. The disciple who possesses the two-fold nature of man and woman is that perfect being known in initiatic science as an androgyne. It was the goal of all initiates, whether alchemists or cabbalists, etc., to be androgynous and, like God, to possess the fullness of both principles. In God, the two principles are united, that is why he loves all his creatures, why he indulges them and answers their prayers. God has always been presented as a terrifying Father, as a consuming fire, but this is false: God is both Father and Mother.

The Bonfin, August 27 1967

Supplementary note:

A great many musicians, even those who have studied the theoretical aspect of music, have never paused to reflect on the underlying significance of sharps and flats. The flat lowers a note by half a tone, whereas the sharp does the opposite: it raises a note by half a tone. Sharps and flats are also an image of the feminine and masculine principles, matter and spirit, which are responsible for all creation. The spirit descends; the masculine principle constantly looks downwards. The feminine principle, which is below, looks upwards and is obliged to rise, to climb. This is why the feminine principle is associated with the evolutionary process whereas the masculine principle is associated with the process of involution. The sharp and the flat are symbols of the feminine and masculine principles because of their form, which reflects that of the sexual organs of men and women, but primarily because of the role they play in a scale, by raising or lowering the notes by half a tone.

The spirit lowers itself in order to encounter matter, that is to say, in order to caress it, to irrigate, vivify and resuscitate it. And this is what the man does in the act of love: he lowers himself towards the woman and, in doing so, of course, he loses something; he is weakened and drained. Whereas the woman is raised – the sharp – and rejoices because she has received something, she is fulfilled.

Sèvres, May 30 1965

II

I would like to add a few words to what I was saying this morning.

I told you that a man must know how to become a woman and a woman a man; not outwardly, of course, but in their inner attitudes, thoughts, feelings and reactions. If you know how to be positive or negative, emissive or receptive, active or passive, depending on the circumstances, you will be in a position to solve a great many problems.

Let me show you how this happens in a family: the husband comes home in a furious temper because his boss has treated him unfairly and, on the slightest pretext, he is ready to vent his rage on his wife. Seeing this, if she is wise, she will immediately become passive and receptive; in other words, instead of answering aggressively, she will remain quite calm. In this way, a magnificent exchange takes place between the positive and the negative and her husband will soon calm down. If she knows how to polarize herself, the wife can absorb and even transform all those energies and give them back to him in a form that is capable of enlightening and uplifting him. In the same way, when it is his wife that is in a fury, the husband should be capable of polarizing himself negatively. Unfortunately, neither of them knows that this is possible and, when one of them gets angry and violent, the other responds in kind, and the resulting quarrel often ends in blows and a separation.

Disciples, whether they are men or women, must know how to be both.

Take another example: you go to see your Master when you are feeling emissive; you are full of things to tell him and explain to him as though it were he who was ignorant and you who had to instruct him, and your Master is obliged to listen to you. But it should be just the opposite. When you are in the presence of your Master or any truly outstanding person, you must be receptive, you must keep quiet and listen, so as to receive some of the treasure that is theirs. When you are with people who are dishonest, vicious or weak, you must be positive; in this way, not only will you receive nothing from them, but you will be able to drive out what is negative and give them something positive. But, when you are with a source, a Master, you must be just the opposite; you must be receptive. A great many people have come to see me and have had so much to say that I could not get a word in. They used me as a receptacle in which to empty themselves and went away happy, but I had not been able to help them; they were so full of themselves that I had been unable to find even one little opening that would have allowed me to give them something. An initiate understands immediately that there is nothing he can do for people like that; he can neither use them nor enlighten them. So, you must learn how to use the two principles and know when to be positive and when to be negative.

You can be sure that, if you are unhappy and unsuccessful, it is because you don't know how to work with the two principles. If you have all kinds of misfortunes, it is because you bring them on yourself: you are polarized in such a way as to attract them. If you want to repulse them, therefore, you must switch your polarization. You must learn how to reject the evil that you have attracted and attract the good that you have so often repulsed, without realizing that it was good for you.

God has put before us, in nature, the solution to all our problems but, as we have never learned to read and decipher nature, we fail to find that solution.

The Bonfin, August 27 1967

Chapter Seven

JEALOUSY

Jealousy is something that is often found in lovers. In the rich, too, for the rich want to keep their wealth for themselves; the idea of having to leave it to their heirs is painful to them. They often come back, after death, to look at their estates and houses; they are so attached to the possessions they have left behind them that they still worry about them and try to look after them. They are unable to break free and rise to higher regions, because the roots that bind them to the earth are too strong; they are incapable of cutting them, and this means that they often suffer dreadfully as they continue to prowl round their house and their money, enviously watching the new owners.

The jealousy of lovers is even stranger and it is the cause of much misunderstanding and many misfortunes; it makes life hell. Many couples come to me, the husband accusing his wife and the wife accusing the husband of being unfaithful. And then, when I examine the situation, I find that the whole thing exists only in their imagination. What is really at the bottom of all this commotion? People are afraid of losing the one they love, and yet, what a lot of pleasure they get from nagging and tormenting them. 'It's because I love you, that I torture you, darling.' Strange logic! Many women, in fact, are dissatisfied and unhappy if their husband is not jealous. A woman may have a husband who shows that he loves her, who gives her whatever she asks for, who gives her all the freedom she wants and, instead of being grateful and happy, she is worried and suspicious and thinks he must be keeping a mistress. Does she want him to keep her chained to the home? Does he have to behave like a dragon to keep her happy? We have already seen women in the clutches of a dragon and they are far from happy. Believe me, it is impossible to satisfy human nature. If a husband gives his wife complete freedom, she complains, 'Why doesn't he keep me for himself? Why does he give me so much freedom if not because he has another woman, somewhere?' And if he is a tyrant, a despot, she weeps and moans and tries to find another man to set her free.

When you want to own something as your private property, you are afraid to share it with others, you are afraid of losing it, and here we have the root cause of jealousy: the fear of losing something which supposedly belongs to you. But who has ever decreed that your husband or wife should be your private property? You may have known them for two years or ten, but they were created long before you ever knew them. They have parents and a Creator; they have existed for millions of years; they don't belong to you. A husband will say, 'She's my wife and I can kill her if I want to.' Yes, she is your wife, but for how long? Only God knows that. You are simply associates. If you want to avoid serious misunderstandings and misfortunes, look on her as your associate or business partner – whether willing or unwilling, who knows? You are partners in a specific task, in the building of a house, for instance. To bring a child into the world is to build a house; the child is a spirit that comes from a long way away and you build his house for him, brick by brick.

The fear of losing something that belongs to you, therefore, is the cause of all misunderstandings. You are afraid of losing the person you love and you imagine that they belong to you, but they don't; they are not your property. You use every means you can think of to hold on to them, you torment and ill-treat them and force them to do what you want, but all this creates disorder. And, when it comes down to it, what are you actually holding on to? Suppose that you have a very pretty wife: can you prevent other men from looking at her and admiring her or, even, from following her? There is no lack of opportunity: other men will look at your wife in the street, at the theatre and in restaurants, when you are with friends, everywhere, and, if you are unreasonable about it, you will suffer continually. You are like a man with a garden full of flowers: he cannot prevent their perfume from filling the air and being enjoyed by everybody. What you are actually clinging to with such jealousy is the body of your beloved, that is to say, an envelope, a shell. That which constitutes the essence, the true value of a human being, are his thoughts and feelings and you cannot imprison them. It is the greatest possible illusion to think that one can dominate a human soul. It is as though one tried to tie up a bundle of sand or change the direction of the wind. The soul can never be subjugated. The physical body can be held captive, but not the mysterious being that inhabits it.

Some people have attempted to win a man's or a woman's affections by means of magic. It is possible to do this; there are all kinds of magic formulas and practices that can be used to put a spell on someone, but I certainly don't advise anyone to do so. Why not? Well, suppose you do force a woman to love you, to be madly in love with you, even... it could happen. Yes, but when that woman embraces you and gives you what you wanted from her, you don't know what else she will give you, at the same time. You don't know what entities live in her, what spirits you may have evoked. For, don't forget, she will necessarily be inhabited by spirits that have been attracted by the power of your formulas; it is not she herself, her own spirit, that loves you but a host of inferior entities. In fact, if you could see them, your hair would stand on end and you would implore heaven to deliver you. No, to cast a spell on someone is not a good method. To be sure, you may get what you coveted but it will not be love that you taste on her lips, it will be a poison that will gradually destroy you. It is possible to call up entities from the astral plane and impose one's will on them, but the Spirit is free and can never be bound or imprisoned.

How can the fear of losing a shell, someone's body or house, be compared to the joy of winning a spirit, of having that spirit at your side? You will say that you would rather have both, the body and the spirit. Yes, that is understandable, but there are other ways of winning them. You cannot win them with anger or violence; on the contrary, you will only lose both of them, that way. You are going to have to adopt quite a different attitude if that free spirit is to become so attached to you that nothing will ever tear it away. This is where the science of love begins. There is only one absolutely harmless way of getting someone to love you freely and without coercion, and that is never to think anything negative about them, to send them only the purest and most luminous, the most splendid thoughts. Even if they are cruel and hard-hearted, be very patient; put up with everything, however hard, and continue to love and help them. If you truly love them, sooner or later, they will begin to love you in return, with a pure, divine love.

Jealousy is a very difficult feeling to conquer. It cannot be done simply by struggling against it. As I told you, yesterday, there is nothing you can do about a force that has already been unleashed; the pressure is too great, it overturns everything in its path. Don't try to dam up a river once the floodgates have been opened, it is too dangerous: it will sweep everything before it. The only thing you can do is avoid opening the floodgates; that is the only way to remain in control of the situation. Intelligence is the only thing that can overcome jealousy. It is all a question of thought, of reason.

Perhaps someone will say, 'That's all very well, but if I don't keep a jealous guard over my wife, she will go and get herself into trouble.' Don't you believe it. On the contrary, it is when a woman is guarded jealously that she is most likely to get into trouble. Have you ever been inside her head or her heart, to find out what goes on in there? A woman is such a good liar she could almost deceive the Lord himself... how can a jealous husband be fool enough to imagine that he can hold her? If there is one thing that I don't believe, it is that a man can hold a woman. She can hold herself, yes, but her husband cannot. He can lock her up in a tower, but she will summon the Devil himself and amuse herself with him in order to revenge herself on her husband.

Jealousy always brings disaster. If a woman continually hears her husband accusing her of being unfaithful to him, she may well be driven to thinking, 'Perhaps it's not such a bad idea, after all. Why don't I try it; it might be fun.' Until then, she has always been faithful and never tried to deceive her husband; it is his constant suspicion that ends by creating the right conditions on the astral plane and, once she has made up her mind to deceive him, not only does she do so, but she shows extraordinary skill in putting his suspicions to rest: 'Darling, you can be absolutely certain: I'm telling you the truth.' And, although he refused to believe her when she was telling the truth, now that she is lying, he believes her.

Jealousy is a lack of intelligence. Someone clings desperately to his property because he does not see that the soul and spirit of the person whose body he possesses so jealously are absolutely free. If you begin to realize that there is something else to a human being, something subtler, which must regulate your relationships, you will be less rigid and more willing to use gentler, more intelligent methods in dealing with the one you love. And they, when they see that you are capable of being reasonable, that you are not going to use violence and that they can really trust you, they will become far more deeply attached to you. When fear disappears, you will relax and be less crude, brutal and vindictive; you will be more peaceful and more able to find solutions to your problems.

And what if your wife does stop loving you? Remind yourself that her soul is free, that she will not be with you for the rest of eternity, in any case, that she has loved hundreds of husbands before you and will love many more after you. Why be upset if she does not love you any longer? What about you: will you always love her? Have you loved her ever since she was created? No. Stop worrying, then, and get it into your head that it is unfair to demand everything of her while you consider yourself free to do whatever you please.

Jealousy is a terrible sentiment that casts a shadow on the light of the spirit. It is hell's most evil counsellor; it drives people to do senseless things that, when it is too late, they regret. A man kills the woman he loves in a fit of jealousy and then mourns her and kills himself.

I want to add something, now, that you may never have noticed, and that is that jealousy drags men and women down to a very low level at which their sensuality is unleashed. A scene of jealousy is always followed by an outburst of love more violently sensual than before. If you don't want to be enslaved by an extremely sensual kind of love, therefore, be sure not to manifest jealousy, otherwise, you will end by being trapped and bewitched, and you will never even know how it happened. So many men, after making a terrible scene of jealousy with their wife or mistress and swearing to leave them for good, are driven by an irresistible sexual impulse to grovel before them and abandon every vestige of self-respect in the hope of being allowed one caress.

A disciple must have nothing to do with jealousy. It is a disgrace for him to continue to be beset by such worries, such anguish. If his wife leaves him, he should reflect about it and tell himself, 'It is really sad that I have lost my wife; I'm going to miss her dreadfully, but I still have heaven, God, the light, the Teaching, the Master... I'm rich.' If you only have one loaf of bread you are not going to be very generous, but if you have dozens, you will give some of them away, because you know that you will still have some for yourself. Jealousy is a sign of poverty. He who is inwardly rich is not afraid of being left alone; even if everybody abandons him, he senses that hundreds and thousands of spirits will continue to keep him company.

One of the best ways of freeing oneself from jealousy is to learn to love on a higher plane. Why does a woman who loves a man for his intelligence and learning, for his noble spirit and great kindness, want the whole world to know him? Why is she happy when she sees that everybody comes to him? Because her love is of a higher kind, far superior to the commonplace, physical love with which most women love a man because he has an adorable little moustache or marvellous muscles. The important thing, therefore, is to learn how to transform your love; you must realize that, if it is very sensual, it will inevitably be accompanied by jealousy. The more physical your love, the more you will want your beloved to belong exclusively to you and you will be jealous. The more spiritual your love, the more you will want to share it with others.

I must tell you, too, that a woman should never marry a man who is much younger than herself; this is bound to lead to unhappiness. It is more in accordance with nature for a very young girl to love a mature man, because men do not change physically as quickly as women. But when a woman is so unwise as to take a husband younger than herself, sooner or later, the young man she is clinging to will begin to neglect her and start hunting for more tempting game – and she will be in a continual state of torment. You must not let yourselves get caught up in such situations.

Don't be surprised if I often talk to you about the same things. It is not a theoretical but a practical understanding that you need, so I shall keep telling you the same things until you are capable of putting your knowledge into practice. For seven years, I have been talking to you about the same things – although from different points of view – and, particularly, about love, because I see you still wrestling with the same difficulties. When I see that you have solved your problems, I will go on to other things. If I see that your collective consciousness has reached a higher plane, I will make new revelations to you but, until then, you don't need to know anything else. Take a lecture in which the principles of the Teaching are explained and really work at those principles; if you do this, your whole life will be illuminated. As long as you continue to be content with theoretical knowledge, you will always have the same old problems to contend with. The time has come for you to put all that theory into practice; when you do this, you will see a whole new world opening up before you.

Sèvres, March 24 1945

Chapter Eight

THE TWELVE DOORS
OF MAN AND WOMAN

I have already spoken to you, in the past, about the twelve gates of the heavenly Jerusalem, and shown you how they represent, symbolically, the twelve gates or doors of the human body. Where are the doors of the body? The seven first doors are in the head: two ears, two eyes, two nostrils and one mouth. All these doors are open and in working order but, so far, in most human beings they only function on the physical level. It is time, now, to begin using your ears, eyes, nose and mouth on the spiritual level. When you begin to be clairvoyant and clairaudient, when you begin to be sensitive to the scents and flavours of the divine world, when your speech begins to be creative, it means that you will have begun to open the first seven doors.

What about the five remaining doors? Two of them are on the chest: in a woman, they are open and serve to suckle her children but, in a man, they are closed. The navel is also a door on the level of the solar plexus and, in most people, this door is closed; those who have opened the door of the solar plexus spiritually, are in communion with all the heavenly regions. There is no need for me to name the two last doors, everybody knows them but here, again, only their physical function is known; they still have to be opened spiritually. You all know, also, that, in a man, one of these doors serves both for procreation and elimination. From an initiatic point of view, however, it has five, still unknown functions; this one organ, therefore, has a total of seven different functions and, as you will see, it can be used to solve certain problems and accomplish other kinds of work. You will say, 'Five unknown functions? Oh, this is fascinating... tell us more,' but it is very difficult to talk about this, because most human beings have been brought up from their earliest childhood with such distorted ideas that, for the time being, it would be dangerous to reveal these things to them.

What I can tell you, though, is that it is possible to do tremendous work with these doors, for nature had grandiose plans in mind in creating man and woman; she is only waiting for human beings to become sufficiently mature before she reveals these new ways of being creative to them. Men and women do not know that they already hold the keys to all mysteries, the instruments they need to accomplish fantastic creations. They don't know how to set about this work of creation yet, but it will all be revealed to them as soon as they are capable of understanding. Mankind is predestined to reach a profound and intimate understanding of these twelve doors, to explore them and find all the riches that lie behind them.

When we speak of a door, it always implies the existence of a passage, of access to something else. No one makes a door without a reason, if there is nothing in front of or behind it... except in the theatre, of course. In theory, a door or gate allows one to enter a new region – a temple, a palace or a city – and to discover the riches and buried treasure, or the terrifying sights, that lie behind it. Many fairy-tales mention doors; in some of them the hero has to open a certain door, in others, on the contrary, he must never open it for fear of being assailed by all kinds of monsters that threaten his life. In real life, too, there are doors which must not be opened prematurely.

The Cabbalah speaks of fifty Gates. The twelve gates of the heavenly Jerusalem, that I mentioned earlier, correspond to the twelve signs of the Zodiac but, in the Cabbalah, the fifty gates are the Gates of Understanding found in Binah. They relate to the Sephirotic Tree of Life[1], and each one corresponds to one of the five regions of each of the ten Sephiroth, thus giving us fifty Gates. An initiate who attains perfection is able to open the fifty Gates and make use of all the treasures of the universe that have been stored up for all eternity. But it is said that, before opening the fifty Gates, one first has to travel the full length of the thirty-two Paths of Wisdom and this, of course, requires time, strength, considerable spiritual qualities and the help of a guide. There are twenty-two Paths linking the ten Sephiroth with each other. The first Path, for instance, which corresponds to the Hebrew letter aleph א, links Kether and Chokmah. To these twenty-two Paths we add the ten Sephiroth themselves, thus reaching the total of thirty-two. To travel the length of a Path, therefore, means to go through certain experiences that enable one to understand its name and its properties. One can travel along these Paths one after another or simultaneously, but it is said that it is the thirty-second Path that is the most terrible.

Now, let's get back to the twelve gates or doors of man and woman and, in particular, to the sexual organs. I told you that if you knew the five other functions of these organs, you would be capable of fantastic creations. For the time being, though, I am obliged to be silent about these things. As a matter of fact, initiates have always veiled these mysteries and the reason why they advised men and women to keep these parts hidden had nothing to do with either modesty or hygiene; it was an indication that they should be concealed because they were too significant, the powers they contained were too tremendous. There is a great deal more that I could reveal to you, if I wished, but I will say just one little thing to put you on the right track. Some initiates in the past, who knew how to use these divine

---

[1] See *Angels and other Mysteries of The Tree of Life*, Izvor Collection, No. 236, and *The Mysteries of Yesod*, Complete Works, vol. 7.

forces, did so, not for their own pleasure, but for the good of others and, especially, in order to produce an abundant harvest; although the whole population in their countries lived in abundance and prosperity, nobody knew the real reason. What a difference between this conception of things and that of most human beings. The majority can think of nothing better to do with these organs than to deprive themselves, becoming always poorer and more unbalanced by wasting all their wealth for the sake of a few moments of pleasure.

You will say, 'Is that really true: is it really possible to do another kind of work with these parts of the body?' Indeed it is; in fact, they are at the origin of much of the greatest work that man has ever done. 'But, they are shameful, ugly, diabolical...' Really? But if that is so, why do children come from there? Didn't God give those 'shameful' parts of the body the power to create life? A power that he did not give to the brain, nor to the lungs, the eyes, the arms or the legs. This proves that these parts conceal a great mystery, for is there any greater mystery than the mystery of life? Why would God, who is all wisdom and intelligence, amuse himself by putting the most precious, most sacred thing that exists in such a dreadful place? The time has come to correct these mistaken notions, for it is they that are the root of all the anomalies and psychic unbalance that plague human beings.

The sexual organs are the source of all life, all dynamism, all inspiration; the physical and psychic equilibrium of human beings depends on them. They are the factories in which all that is most necessary to human life is manufactured and yet men and women despise and misuse them more than all their other organs, constantly doing stupid, filthy things with them. It should be just the opposite; they should be lost in wonder and say, 'Dear Lord, what riches, what treasures you have given me. How can I use them for the good of the whole world?' The first step towards this changed attitude is to replace the words 'pleasure,' 'voluptuousness' and 'gratification,' by the word 'work.' You will ask, 'Yes, but will there still be a little joy and pleasure in that work?' Indeed there will. Your joy and pleasure will be twice, three times, a hundred times greater.

I have not been given permission to make revelations about these truly sacred subjects yet for, indeed, there is nothing more sacred. These are the Mysteries: the Mysteries of Egypt, India, Greece and Thrace. There are no others: it is they that give access to all the other Mysteries. They are the Alpha and Omega of the sacred science. Most alchemists don't even know what their traditional texts are referring to when they speak of the Elixir of Everlasting Life, the Magic Wand or the Philosophers' Stone. They are going to have a shock, one day, when they discover that these three symbols refer to realities related to sexuality. Some of the ancient writers hinted at these things, because they were familiar with the symbols but they never said anything openly. Incidentally, the Arabs, who were highly skilled alchemists – especially those who lived in Spain and created schools in which they handed on their art to Europeans – had a very significant word in their language for the Philosophers' Stone, tack, which is the word for the male testes as well as for stone or rock. And it is these two 'stones' that are the foundation of everything. In fact, if I were not certain to be misunderstood, I would tell you how to interpret the words of Jesus, when he said to Peter, *'You are Peter* (Pierre – Rock), *and on this rock I will build my church.'* If you only knew the alchemical value of that rock and the meaning of the words 'my church'.

And women, also, know nothing of the deeper meaning of certain parts of their bodies or of what they are related to. They do not know, for example, that an invisible form of energy emanates from their breasts and that one breast is related to the Milky Way and the other to the moon (there was once a painter who was inspired by this subject). Do these things surprise you? They were well known to the Ancients. In some women, this current is so pure, intense and luminous, that which emanates from them is so enchanting, that all eyes are drawn to them.

In others, on the contrary, however lovely the full, gracious curves of their breasts may be, there is nothing to move one, nothing emanates from them. And if this is true of the breasts, why should it not be true of the rest? Some people's emanations are absolutely repulsive while, in others, they are a crystal-clear spring.

I have already explained in other lectures that, even when there is no physical contact, women must be aware of the currents emitted by men which they can receive through their sexual organs. Things are always mixed; everything contains a mixture of good and bad, purity and impurity, so they must learn to use a spiritual filter and filter the currents that enter them. The currents that a man emanates and projects from these parts are not always very pure; women must be on their guard. I must also add that the organs God has given women can become so sensitive and intuitive that they can function like radar and inform them of the nature of imminent events and of anyone that approaches them. Some women, who are sufficiently evolved, notice that their organs are beginning to warn them of coming danger and give them time to take steps to avoid it. Others, poor things, only notice that their organs are sensitive when they are in bed with a man.

Now, I would like to say a little more about the door that we call the solar plexus. The door of the solar plexus is very important and it is vital that it be opened, because it is through this door that we are in communion with the womb of nature, that we receive nourishment from nature. Like babies in their mother's womb, who receive all the materials they need through the umbilical cord, we are in the womb of nature. You will say, 'Yes, but we have already been born. The umbilical cord has been cut.' Ah, but there is another cord that has not been cut; we are still in the womb of nature. We have been born on the physical plane, I agree; but on another plane we are still unborn, we are still nourished through another cord, we are still immersed in unconsciousness. When we are born on this other plane, we shall have another consciousness; this will be the second birth. The first birth consists in cutting the umbilical cord that links us to our physical mother and, while waiting for the second birth, we are still linked to mother nature through our solar plexus. When I think of how much I have learned through the solar plexus. For years, now, I have done a great deal of work with the solar plexus and it has revealed many things to me.

Everybody knows that a man and woman play complementary roles in procreating a child: the man provides the seed, the germ of life, and the woman provides the necessary matter in which to wrap the seed, causes it to grow and gives it form. Everybody knows this, true, but they know nothing about woman's role on the spiritual plane. On the spiritual plane, too, women provide a necessary matter but, on this plane, it is a fluidic matter that makes divine realizations possible. By their fluids and emanations, women contribute to the concrete materialization of ideas; they give them tangible reality in exactly the same way as they give a child its physical body. It is obvious that all those ascetics and hermits who fled the company of woman had never understood her importance. Woman is the key to all material realization. Every woman possesses the power to emanate the quintessence with which to envelop and give body to a sublime idea.

Woman's role is grandiose. This is why I have such a high regard for women, for the sisters here, in the Brotherhood. While maintaining that precious distance between us, I receive this quintessence from them, through their glances and smiles, and I use this subtle matter to populate the world with thousands of angelic children. I am not afraid of woman; I look on her as a divinity, not as the daughter of the Devil. Only women can give me the matter I need with which to do divine work. Men are different, they cannot give me that matter, but they give me something else, something that women cannot give. The purity of those who chose the path of chastity was such that, if they had possessed this knowledge, they could have accomplished extraordinary things. But, one day, they will come back for another incarnation and, then, they will receive this light. Why flee from woman? Instead of running away from her, you must understand her. This is what I try to do: understand her.

In conclusion, I will add just this, and it is something you must never forget: not a single form, not a single function or activity exists in the universe that is not present in a condensed, synthesized form in the masculine and feminine principles. They are the summary of all that exists. Whatever you do, whether you travel, gaze on the beauty of mountains and rivers, explore caves, visit your friends, talk, listen, eat, pour out a glass of water, drink, build a house, sew, paint, write, play the violin – I don't care what it is – there is no activity, no science, no technique, that does not correspond, either in its structural or functional aspect, to the male and female sexual organs. You will say, 'You must be totally depraved; you keep bringing everything back to that.' It is not I who keep coming back to that; it is the Creator who decided that every manifestation of life, everywhere, in all forms and in every domain, should be in the image of these two functions. God has taken them as the model on which all his creatures are fashioned. If you don't like it, you'd better go and complain to him. Tell him that his way of doing things shocks and upsets you. Believe me, God will not really care if you are upset; this is how he has organized things and if it does not correspond to the principles that have been drilled into you, he is not going to let it worry him.

You are beginning to understand, now, why the initiates saw these two symbols as the most sublime, the richest and most profoundly meaningful of all symbols: the whole of creation is summed up in them and all other symbols are drawn from them. To me, they are sacred and I never stop marvelling at the intelligence that managed to bring the entire Tree of Creation from these two little seeds. I encourage you to rise to a great height so that you, too, can contemplate this splendour and understand how and why God created these marvels.

When Hermes Trismegistus said, 'That which is below is like that which is above,' many people thought that 'below' referred to the earth or to hell. That is not false, but he meant something else as well, something that you are now in a position to understand. 'That which is below,' is as intelligent, as sublime, as divine as 'that which is above,' in heaven. The significance of this first sentence of the Emerald Tablet is absolutely prodigious, but only those who possess the light of initiation can decipher it.

Sèvres, January 3 1965

Chapter Nine

FROM YESOD TO KETHER:
THE SUBLIMATION OF SEXUAL ENERGY

In the Sephirotic Tree,[1] purity is represented by Yesod, the region of the angels, or Kerubim, who work with life. This is why, in representations of Adam Kadmon, cosmic Man, the genital organs are shown to be linked to Yesod, purity, because it is these organs that create life. Of course, for the moment, at least where human beings are concerned, purity and the sexual organs do not often go together, but they must go together if life is to be sanctified. Sanctity is linked to a proper understanding of sexual problems. A man becomes a saint when he attains the mastery of his sexual energies, not before; it is no use looking for sanctity anywhere else.

At the other end of the Sephirotic Tree, is Kether, the Sephirah in which dwell the Seraphim, that angelic order of beings so pure, so holy, that it is they that have been given the privilege of glorifying the Lord. Day and night, says the *Apocalypse*, the Lord is glorified by the voices of the Seraphim, singing, *'Holy, holy, holy, Lord God Almighty, Who was and is and is to come!'* Sanctity, which we always think of as belonging 'above,' depends, in fact, on 'below.' Kether, the Crown, represents the full flowering, the sublimation of sexual energy. Sanctity is the sexual energy that an initiate has sublimated through purity, and it manifests itself in the form of a golden light shining above his head. Sanctity does not stay

---

[1] See *Angels and other Mysteries of The Tree of Life*, Izvor Collection, No. 236, and *The Mysteries of Yesod*, Complete Works, vol. 7.

down below, it always rises and this is why we think of it as belonging to the world above whereas, in fact, it comes from below.

The Sephiroth represent the organs of the Cosmos and Yesod, therefore, represents the sexual organs of the universe. This is why, when everything is functioning harmoniously in the Sephirotic Tree that is man, when he has purified himself below through the purity of Yesod, the sexual energy that mounts to his head, to Kether, becomes a halo of light. Kether is not the head; it is the crown above the head, the aureole, the halo of sanctity that one sees illustrated in churches, shining above the heads of the prophets, apostles and saints.

True initiates are those who have realized, within themselves, the purity of Yesod. They possess the same organs as everybody else; they manufacture, perhaps, the same matter as everybody else, but that matter is sublimated, it rises and nourishes all their higher spiritual centres and shines over their heads in the form of radiant light.

Sèvres, February 2 1969

Chapter Ten

A SPIRITUAL FILTER

I'm sure you all feel the extraordinary purity of the atmosphere this morning, don't you? Are you wondering why I keep talking about the weather? Because I think that, if I don't, you might not pay much attention to it. Look at all those colours, at that light, at the transparency of the air. The purity of the sky always makes a deep impression on me.

Look at that helicopter; it is a privilege for the pilot to pass overhead. Without knowing it, he will take something good home with him that he has received from the aura, the cone of light that surrounds us. If he was in a harmonious frame of mind, if a door was open, all manner of good things will have flooded into him and he will be able to distribute the seeds he has received. It is as though we had given him a sack full of letters that, without realizing it, he will distribute to others. Believe me, this is the reality.

Sometimes, when you walk down a street, you may pass close to the scene of a crime, of evil. If at that moment you are inwardly attuned to the vibrations coming from that place, you will pick them up and be influenced to do something evil, yourself, without realizing that it is because of the etheric, fluidic emanations that you received when you were close to that place. You have to learn to shut out everything negative and open yourself only to that which is harmonious and luminous. The question is how to do so. I think you will be very surprised by some of the things I can tell you about this.

To me, the masculine and feminine principles are a key which allows me to open a great many doors; this is why I keep talking to you about them. As I have often told you, the nature of the masculine principle is to be emissive, and that of the feminine principle is to be receptive, and this should help you to understand that, through her sexual organs, a woman is liable to pick up dark, impure emanations, without realizing it. This is why, by her thoughts, she must equip herself with a filter so as to keep out many of the currents that attempt to get in to her and receive only those that are good and beneficial. This is something that women never think about; besides, no one has ever explained to them that, in a certain part of their bodies, they are like sponges that soak up every fluid. It is time that women became more aware of these things and ceased to be receptacles for all the filth that men leave lying about. Many men stare at every woman they pass in the street, imagining all that they would like to do with them, and the women, sensing this, are pleased and flattered, because they have no idea of the dirt they are picking up.

Women cannot remain pure if they do not protect themselves; this is why they must be more conscious of the role and importance of the instruments nature has given them. They must reflect, meditate and pray so that these instruments do not pick up impurities and elementals which, sooner or later, lead to all kinds of psychic and, even, physical disorders. As a matter of fact, if so many women suffer from problems with their sexual organs, it is because they have not known how to protect them with a fluidic filter which would have prevented impurities from slipping in and creating havoc. They go and consult doctors but doctors cannot help them, because they don't know that the remedy is to be found on the fluidic level.

The situation is different for men because men, by nature, are not receptive; they are emissive. The problem is that instead of being conscious of this and taking care to emit only vivifying, luminous, harmonious forces, more often than not they project dark, negative currents, priding themselves on being seen as beautiful male animals. And the filth that men project with such pride on the astral plane is absorbed by women – who are equally proud of themselves.

Nature has organized woman's body in such a way that, as in man, her sexual organs have six other functions in addition to their purely physical function. At the moment, women know how to vibrate only on the level of the last and least subtle string of their instrument. The other strings have never been awakened but, one day, women must set all their strings vibrating in unison with all the most subtle currents in the universe. Then woman will be the Aeolian harp which vibrated in response to the least breath of air. When women are more highly evolved spiritually, they will find that they react to every event and every presence with their sexual organ. They will find that it is a highly accurate instrument that informs them of the nature, good or bad, of those around them, thereby making it possible for them to take any necessary precautions. Forgive me for saying this but, at the moment, it is only when she is having relations with a man that a woman notices the reactions of her organs. Those who are more highly evolved, though, sense that they possess an instrument that gives them information about all kinds of things. It is very worthwhile, therefore, for women to place a fluidic filter in this part of their body, so as to prevent anything harmful from entering.

I am touching on a subject, today, that is virtually unknown. Doctors study the anatomy and physiology of human beings but they know nothing of the fluidic dimension of the body, which is, after all, the most important. Sooner or later, they are going to be obliged to explore this aspect, for the path they are following, today, will take them no farther: it will come to a dead end. A study of man's subtle bodies will be the only avenue open to them. Nowadays, the structure and function of the male and female sexual organs are well known but it is only the outer husk, the material support, that inspires interest and admiration;

the one thing that is essential about them, the currents and forces that animate them, are totally neglected. Initiates, on the other hand, know a great deal about these forces – but, then, nobody is interested in what initiates know.

As I have said, it is in man's nature to emit, to project and, for this reason, he is less spiritually vulnerable. The current that flows in him repulses impurities rather than attracting them, as in woman. Man attracts above, with his head, whereas woman attracts below, so that is where she must put her filters. I sense that the sisters who are listening to me are asking within themselves, 'How do we make this filter you are talking about?' By your thoughts. You must pray and meditate and ask the divine world to send you a protector, an entity who will keep watch over you and deflect the impure currents formed by the desires, passions and covetousness of human beings. If you succeed in attracting a luminous entity from the divine world to protect you, you will experience a joy, purity and innocence such as you have never known and, little by little you will become a receptacle for the divine Spirit, the temple of the Living God.

Practise this, therefore; reflect and meditate. Your physical and psychological health will be improved by this work and you will begin to understand what true purity is; you will understand that intercourse between men and women is always a question of vibrations, give and take, interpenetration on every level, and that this intercourse must take place on a very high level, in the most complete purity, and not only on the lower levels. In this way, your life will become more and more like that of the angels. The angels ceaselessly mingle and fuse together like rays of light and there is not a trace of impurity in their loving intercourse. They live continually in this love for, in the world above, only love exists. An angel's life consists entirely in this fusion, this exchange of love in absolute purity. When human beings become capable of vibrating with their seven strings, they will be like the angels. And the music will be beautiful beyond words. Blessed are those who understand me.

Meditate on this subject now, in the greatest possible purity and light, and try to rid yourselves of obsolete notions that prevent you from understanding and advancing. In this way you will become true sons and daughters of God.

Of course, there is a great deal more that could be said about filters, for the need for protection does not apply to only one organ in woman. A disciple is conscious of the fact that he is immersed in the cosmic ocean and that he forms his bodies, his physical, as well as his subtle bodies, with the materials, whether good or bad, that he receives or picks up from this ocean. His principal problem, therefore, is to know how to draw only good things into his heart and head and how to repulse what is bad. Actually, the most effective filter, the one filter which includes all the others, is the aura.[1] If you really want to be protected, therefore, meditate on your aura. Imagine yourself surrounded by colours, purple, blue, green, golden yellow, etc., in the form of an immense, intensely powerful, vibrant, radiant aura all round you. This is the ultimate filter. Not only can nothing impure, nothing harmful or evil, get through that aura, but also, thanks to its influence, you will begin to see the splendour of the divine world. You will eat and drink, breathe and bathe in that cosmic ocean of love and beatitude.

However, in order to form a strong aura, it is not enough to imagine yourself surrounded by colours; the aura will not last if it is not sustained by qualities and virtues. As each different colour symbolizes a particular virtue, the colours of your aura will fade if they are not nourished and supported by the corresponding virtues. This is why the initiates have given us precepts and methods that can help us to develop the virtues which manifest themselves as colours and light. The spirits in the world above are used to looking down on the earth and

---

[1] See *Harmony*, Complete Works, vol. 6, chap. 12: 'The Aura'.

seeing nothing but darkness so, when they see, in the midst of that darkness, beams of light radiating from an initiate, a disciple, they draw closer to help him; they water him like a flower, and give him light and nourishment.

So the thing to bear in mind, today, is that our aura is our best protection.

The Bonfin, August 16 1962

Chapter Eleven

LEARN TO LOVE BY
LEARNING TO EAT

I

For centuries, the Church has been telling us that man was conceived in sin: there's nothing we can do about it; we were all conceived and born in sin. Well, for my part, I don't agree with this attitude; firstly because, by spreading this notion and emphasizing it so much, one makes it impossible for mankind to improve; it deprives men of hope and the will to extricate themselves from the morass they are in. 'We are all in a state of sin; there's no way out, no point in trying to do anything about it.' To be sure, there is an element of truth in this, but we need to see exactly where. Man is conceived in sin in the sense that he receives from his parents a heritage that is already tainted. It is because the thoughts and feelings of their parents are neither luminous nor pure that children are conceived in sin. But to say that, ever since Adam and Eve, original sin must necessarily be handed on from generation to generation... No, I don't agree. Of course, if human beings continue to be so thick-headed and stupid and so grubby, the sin of Adam and Eve could well be handed on from parent to child for billions of years. But, if they draw nearer to light, if they become wise, intelligent and pure, whether Adam and Eve committed a sin or not will be unimportant; everything will be changed, transformed.

It is not good to drill into the minds of human beings ideas that crush them and pin them down in their guilt and imperfection without a glimmer of hope that, one day, their situation can improve. We are sinners, it's true, but we are not obliged to remain sinners for the rest of eternity; we have to make progress. Besides, heaven has more faith in someone who has sinned and repented than in one who has never done anything wrong. There is always a risk that someone who has never done anything wrong will do so one day: having had no experience, he has not had a chance to strengthen himself and is liable to set off blindly in the wrong direction and to stumble and fall. Whereas he who knows what it means to be in the grip of the Devil, who has already suffered atrociously and who has succeeded in breaking away and devoting his energies to doing God's will, will attract the attention of the invisible world. They will say, 'At last, here's someone we can trust. We cannot trust the others.' Of course, this does not mean that you have to do all kinds of terrible things now, so as to make a spectacular conversion later; you never know how many hundreds of years that might take. In any case, mankind has already committed quite enough horrors. It is about time it decided to reform and start to serve heaven.

Take the whole question of love, for example.

In the course of the centuries, to be sure, man's conception of love has evolved. Primitive and savage people behaved with great violence and brutality and indescribable sensuality in this domain; no element of thought, care, kindness or consciousness was present in their manifestations of love. It was as though they were in the grip of a furious storm at sea or a volcanic eruption. But gradually, as time went on, with the awakening of men's consciousness and the slow development of the spiritual life, new elements of tenderness, refinement and delicacy began to manifest themselves. And yet, even today, in most cases, love is still a primitive manifestation. The passionate, instinctive kind of love that has been practised for thousands of years is so deeply engraved in man that he does not know how to make it finer and nobler. Actually, there is nothing more difficult, and yet, at the same time, there is nothing easier... nothing easier, that is, as long as you have a certain number of rules and apply them in all your activities, instead of keeping them only for when you hold someone in your arms, for a law is applicable in every domain.

Love is divine life which flows down to permeate, irrigate and vivify the lower regions. It is always the same love, the same force, the same cosmic energy, that manifests itself everywhere and in every possible form. But, as human beings don't realize this, they do nothing but waste this energy in the belief that it is no more than an instinct, a source of pleasure and a means of propagating the human race. Initiates who have studied the nature of this divine force of love in the world above tell us that it is the same energy as that which comes from the sun, the same light, the same warmth and the same life but that, like a river, it has been polluted by the impurities of all the regions through which it flowed in the course of its descent. But this does not mean that, when it sprang from its source in the mountain tops, it was not pure and crystalline. This energy that we call love comes from the heavenly regions; it is exactly like the light and heat that flow from the sun, but it has become unrecognizable because of its descent into the lower regions, amongst human beings.

The great question is this: since this energy is divine and, therefore, the most powerful and the most vital, how can we restore it to its original purity? Before anything else, we have to understand that there are thousands of different degrees of love and, knowing this, we must work very hard on ourselves, by means of conscious thought, sustained attention and intelligent control so that, instead of spreading ruin and destruction, this energy becomes once again as limpid as the light of the sun and does good wherever it goes. There are a few rules to be learned, therefore, but you must not wait until you are holding your beloved in your arms to apply them. You must learn to apply them in all your everyday activities, even before the processes of love are set in motion.

Every day, you prepare your food and eat it. But you don't eat everything; you sort out what is edible and what is not. Whether you are preparing fish, cheese, vegetables or fruit, you always have to wash or throw away the parts that are dirty or indigestible. Man, who is more highly evolved than the animals, sorts his food whereas animals do not but, when it comes to thoughts and feelings, he never sorts or sifts anything: he swallows whatever comes his way. Why does he allow all kinds of poisonous elements to enter his heart and mind? Why doesn't he start by cleaning the food he is preparing to eat? Why, when lovers embrace, do they never think about what they are going to eat so as to discard the impurities in advance? It is because they don't do this that their consciousness is incapable of recognizing and eliminating the seeds of disease and death that slip into their feelings as well as into their kisses. Yes, death always manages to slip into a stupid, inferior kind of love, into a love in which there is no consciousness, no control, no light. And this is the love that everyone acclaims, praises and glorifies. No one knows any other kind of love and, if you venture to mention it, people look at you and wonder if you have not gone mad.

Everything begins with nutrition. Before sitting down to a meal, people wash their hands and, in the past, anyway, they would say a prayer to invite the Lord to share their meal. There may be some peasants in the world who still do this but educated people have abandoned traditions of that kind... which just shows what intelligence and culture lead to. The custom of washing one's hands and inviting the Lord to share one's meal was full of profound meaning; the initiates who introduced it were saying to their disciples: 'Before loving someone, before embracing them, wash your hands and invite the angels to share your banquet with you, that is to say, purify yourself so as not to soil your beloved, so as not to give them your illnesses, your discouragement, your sorrows.' But look at what happens in most cases: the man is feeling unhappy and discouraged, he feels the need to be comforted by holding his sweetheart in his arms, but what does he give her? He takes all the strength and inspiration she has to offer and, in exchange, gives her his own impurities. At times like that he should avoid embracing her; he should think to himself, 'I'm too poor and dirty and depressed today; I must wash and prepare myself first and, then, when I'm in a better state, I'll go to her and give her all the treasure I possess.' Today, no one ever envisages things in this way but, in the future, they will understand and be ashamed and sickened to think of the ugly way in which they loved others. You will say, 'But when you're feeling miserable you need some consolation; everybody does this.' Yes, but the fact that everybody is stupid and selfish is no reason to be the same. In the future you will learn to love as the sun loves, as the angels and great Masters love, for they know how to love without stealing, they know how to love by giving instead of taking.

There are days when you feel that you are poor; on days like that, stay away from your sweetheart, otherwise the law will want to know why you have robbed her. People are really extraordinary: when they are feeling on top of the world, they distribute their riches to others and then, when they are dejected and desperate, they go and despoil the person they love. They are thieves; nothing but thieves.

The first rule in love, therefore, is the same as in nutrition: never eat what is put before you without sorting the good from the bad. In order to do this, you have to be able to recognize the difference between two feelings, to distinguish between a selfish feeling and a disinterested one, between a feeling that hampers and one that liberates, between a feeling that creates discord and one that harmonizes. And this discrimination is not possible if one is not very vigilant. If you allow yourself to be carried away, if your attention wanders, you will not be on guard at the frontier to see the enemy when they try to slip in to your kingdom. Vigilance, attention and control are all necessary so as not to be carried away. But to be carried away is exactly what human beings want in their love life. To their way of thinking, a grand passion is not possible if you think too much, if you are fully conscious, if you are not a little drunk. Apparently, if you are not drunk you won't feel much. But what do they know about it? Have they ever tried to be on their guard, to be selective or to put themselves in touch with higher currents and see what joys they experience and what discoveries they make? If they have never tried, how can they be so sure of their opinion?

I told you that the lower kind of love, passionate love, brings death; to make this clearer to you, let me give you a few notions based on astrology. As you know, the Zodiac that astrologers speak of is a living book which is reflected in all that exists on earth and in which initiates can read the great truths of life and of the world. All earthly forms of existence were created and fashioned by the twelve constellations. If you need the answer to a philosophical question, you only have to consult that great Book of nature above us, the Zodiac – in fact, I have often done this in front of you. Today, let's take this question of love and death and ask the Zodiac which signs speak of love. Actually, many of the signs have something to say about love, but especially Taurus and Libra, because these two signs are both ruled by Venus. If we analyze Taurus, we see that it represents a primitive, sensual love, the fecundity of nature. In worshipping Apis, the Bull, the symbol of fertility, the ancient Egyptians attempted to draw down into Apis the forces contained in the constellation of Taurus, so that the earth would produce an abundant harvest. By means of magic rites, the Egyptian priests succeeded in fixing this abundance. Libra, on the other hand, the other sign that is ruled by Venus, represents a purer, higher love. This does not mean that all those who have the planet Venus in Libra in their birth chart necessarily manifest a very spiritual, divine kind of love (there are so many other negative elements that have to be taken into account) but, generally speaking, Libra indicates a love that is spiritual and sensitive to beauty, poetry and music. The love of Taurus needs to touch and taste whereas the love of Libra is content to look and listen.

Taurus and Libra, however, must be studied in relation to their opposites: Scorpio, for Taurus, and Aries for Libra. Scorpio is related to the genital organs (this is a further indication of the sensual nature of Taurus) and is at home in the eighth astrological House, the House of death. All of this shows that in primitive forms of love, in which men swallow whatever presents itself, without discrimination, the seeds of death are present, to begin with, in the form of arguments and divergent points of view and, progressively, in the form of wars, revolutions and destruction. Libra, on the other hand, is linked with Aries which represents the head, that is to say, audacity, courage, the will to advance and explore, to scale the heights, to surpass and sacrifice oneself. This is why Christ is represented as a lamb, Aries. Aries represents the head and, symbolically, instead of manifesting itself with passion and lack of control, it shows moderation, reason and wisdom. Aries represents germination, life that sprouts and grows. If a plant grows, it is because it has received the light, it has learned discernment: harmful elements are rejected whereas life rises and flows through it.

Aries linked to Libra, therefore, represents a spiritual form of love in which the powers of thought are wide awake and on guard so as to prevent the intrusion of any impurities. This is why Aries is the first sign of the Zodiac, the sign of Spring, the season in which everything is reborn. Aries is love, the love of the sun, the love of an initiate which begins to radiate in the form of light, warmth and life. And this love is pure because thought is present. Customs officials have been posted at the frontier to prevent any harmful elements from getting in. While you are embracing your sweetheart, your mental faculties are wide awake, you see exactly what is happening in yourself as well as in her, you are in touch with the sublime intelligences above and you make great discoveries and become truly powerful. Is it really worthwhile sacrificing all this for the sake of being drunk and losing control?

But it seems that everybody is eager to lose control of themselves, to be, as it were, wiped out; it is in this extinction that they find happiness. They will tell you as much, themselves: 'If my mind is in control I don't feel anything.' They don't know that they are signing their own spiritual death warrant. More and more, this is the accepted thing, it is what everybody does. If a man is vigilant, if he keeps control of himself and allows nothing to intrude into his love that is not luminous, poetic and beneficial to his partner, she looks at him in disgust, thinking, 'He's no man. He's still perfectly lucid; I haven't managed to make him lose his head.' But if his eyes show that he is about to lose his head, if he breathes hard enough to shake the whole earth and forgets all about his convictions, his plans for the future and his good resolutions, then she will say to herself, 'Aha, wonderful! There's a man for you!' Actually, it is not so much that she thinks he is wonderful but that she is proud to have this power over him; she thinks that she has got him eating out of her hand. She is pleased, triumphant, in fact, to see him troubled and defeated, and says to herself, 'He seemed so strong, but now he's done for; I'll be able to do what I like with him.' It is her lower nature that triumphs, because she sees that she has the power to dominate him, to lead him by the nose and get him to satisfy all her whims. Yes, but this triumph is not very lovely; it is a disguised form of cruelty. No woman should be pleased to see her husband or lover so utterly subjugated by her; on the contrary, it should be a cause for concern.

There is no law against enjoying intense sensations but you have to be careful about the quality of these sensations; you have to keep control and be capable of steering them in the right direction. We all know that, with a very powerful mechanism such as a rocket, it is important not to lose control when you launch it into space. Similarly, in human beings, love can be a fantastically powerful rocket, but it always has to be guided, steered in the right direction, purified and kept from spinning out of control so that the divine work can be accomplished. And if a child is conceived in a union of this quality, it will be an angel, a genius. There are so many highly evolved beings on the other side, waiting for just such conditions to reincarnate.

You must be watchful; that is, you must switch on the light so as to see what is happening and keep any undesirables away. It would take another complete lecture to show you the effects of light on the astral and mental planes and how it staves off undesirables. If you project a beam of light on to them when, in the hopes of eating and drinking all your forces and energies, they try to sneak into your love, you will frighten them away: they won't dare to show their faces, because they know that they will be seen and attacked. These unwanted intruders prefer the dark, because then they can slip in wherever they like; this is why, if you keep all your lights of vigilance switched on, you will be protected from them.

If, before making love to your sweetheart, you call on light – exactly as, before sitting down to a meal, you call on the Lord to share your meal with you – you will be capable of giving her divine elements that she has never received before and her soul will be eternally grateful to you, because your love will be disinterested. Your desire is to illuminate and vivify her, to link her to Christ and the divine Mother, and that is the only kind of love that is constructive. You will say, 'That's all very nice, but how can it make us happy to get Christ and the divine Mother all mixed up in our love-making? It's impossible.' On the contrary, that is the only way to be happy, because it is the only way to be sure that your love will last, that it will never again be marred by bitterness, boredom, regret or anxiety.

Disinterested love is the only kind that never entails these troublesome elements. In any other case, you are like a thief who steals some money: to begin with, he is jubilant but, later, he starts to worry about whether somebody saw him and whether the police are going to catch him. He never knows a moment's peace again. If your love is of the inferior, selfish kind, you will never be at peace, either. Perhaps you will say, 'That's not true; I'm completely at peace.' In that case, all I can say is that you must be an animal; animals are always perfectly peaceful. Look at the peaceful expression of a cat as it licks its chops after devouring a mouse... But when someone is just a little more advanced he cannot be at peace.

You will say that I am asking the impossible of you. Yes, I know. But to know the truth, the ideal solution to a problem, is in itself a step forward, even if you don't achieve anything very wonderful. Once you are in possession of a truth, it begins to work within you and you gradually come closer and closer to attaining it. If you don't know it, obviously, you can never attain it, but if you do know it, half the battle is already won, because there is a bond between you and that image of ideal, poetic perfection. Tremendous possibilities are in store for you, even if there are still many other aspects that need to be developed. Love will be the great question for future generations. Every other question will pale beside this one; everyone in the world will be concerned with this one, vital question of love: how to love and how to become a divinity by loving. If man's relations with love are in order, it means that his relations with God are in order.

When Jesus said to his disciples, *'I still have many things to say to you, but you cannot bear them now,'* what do you suppose he was referring to if not this question of love? He could not talk to them about it, because they were still too full of prejudices inherited from the religion of Moses. Look at what St Paul says, for instance, about the clothes and adornments that he considers suitable for women and how they should be subject to their husbands. Nowadays, everybody laughs at St Paul and thinks him ridiculous but, one day, I will explain the cabbalistic reasons behind the rules he gave and then you will see that they are not quite so ridiculous as you thought.

There: that is just one of the interesting questions that are still in store for you. Oh, I know what you are thinking: 'Tell us now; tell us today.' No, I can't talk about it today, for even on this one subject I don't know which aspect to choose. So many things are crowding in on me... I have to do some sorting, too. It is as though a flock of birds were coming at me from every direction and I have to push them aside.

Jesus did not reveal everything to his disciples, therefore, although he certainly talked about a great many things. The communion of bread and wine that he gave them was, already, an initiation into the science of the masculine and feminine principles but the Church is still a long way from understanding the deeper dimensions of this question. Jesus said, *'He who eats my flesh and drinks my blood has eternal life.'* But where can we find this flesh to eat and this blood to drink? These are the great mysteries that will, one day, be revealed to the children of God.

The Bonfin, August 14 1961

II

When a man and woman make love, they must not cut themselves off from the Whole, from the universe, the cosmos, from God himself. They must always hold on to their link with the Whole and constantly think about it and direct their energies to it. If they think only of themselves, their energies will be directed downwards and will be swallowed up by their personality. In this way, although they may believe that their love nourishes them, they will always be half-starved. Why do men and women seek each other out? Because they are driven by hunger. They are hungry and are looking for something to eat. Love is both food and drink, comparable to the bread we eat and the water we drink. To love is exactly the same as to eat, it is subject to the same laws and rules and it reflects the same processes.

The fact is that hunger can express itself in regions other than the physical body. There are people, for instance, who always eat until they are full and yet, when they get up from a meal, they still feel hungry; they would like to go on eating but are incapable of doing so; their physical body is sated but their astral body continues to crave for food. Normally, the two agree: the astral body is satisfied as soon as the physical body has eaten enough. But the balance between the two can be upset and, in this case, when the physical body still needs food, the astral body may be satiated, or the physical body may be satiated while the astral body still feels hungry. In other words, there is an imbalance, an anomaly.

The same imbalance can exist in the area of love; it can happen that someone is physically satisfied, replete, while his astral body craves for more. This is a terrible situation: the physical body has done all it can, but the astral body continues to clamour for more; its appetite is never satisfied. Some people suffer a great deal, therefore, and are very unhappy, because the needs of their physical and astral bodies no longer coincide. This imbalance can also exist on higher levels, even on the mental plane.

You are, perhaps, surprised by this comparison between love and nutrition, by the fact that I speak of hunger and thirst, food and drink, in relation to love. But the laws are the same. I have already told you more than once that, when you are eating, you should forget everything else and concentrate on linking the process of nutrition with the whole cosmos so that your physical body should not be the only one to be nourished by all those energies, but that they should be directed to a higher plane. In these conditions, the food you eat will be good and divine, and it will have divine results: you will have other, higher thoughts and feelings; other impulses will motivate your actions. If you have never understood the processes involved in nutrition, you will not understand those involved in love, in the intercourse between men and women, either. As long as you continue to eat mechanically, for pleasure, and never do any spiritual work while you are eating, you will be incapable of doing that work while you are making love and will continue to be as limited and obtuse as you are today. Whereas, if you begin with nutrition and learn to eat according to new rules, you will also learn to nourish yourself on the divine plane, with the fragrances, the emanations, the currents flowing from the springs of heaven. This is a prodigious science which human beings will soon begin to study.

If I have insisted for years on this one small point, the way to eat, it is because I have a very precise goal in mind. I have told you this over and over again, but you have still not understood, you still don't do what I ask. You continue to eat without thinking, without meditating, without making contact with heaven or even giving thanks for your food. My fervent wish is that the nutritional process should take place, here, in a truly initiatic way, for it is this that will make all the other, subtler kinds of nutrition possible; it is this that will enable you to find nourishment in the stars, in mountains and rivers, in plants and trees, in perfumes, sounds and music and in the light of the sun. All this is nourishment; all this is nutrition, with the same laws, the same correspondences.

Unfortunately, human beings don't believe that the way they eat matters; to them, so many other things in life are far more important. But this attitude makes them neglect the treasures that nature has spent millions of years preparing for them. They know that they have to eat in order to live. Yes, but they eat in the wrong way, they eat automatically, mechanically, unconsciously; they don't understand what they are doing and the process fails to achieve its goal. We have to eat, yes, but instead of keeping all the energies we get from our food for ourselves, the important thing is to direct them heavenwards because, in that way, we cultivate generosity and disinterestedness. From now on, give the energies and forces you gain from a meal to the Lord. Say to the Lord, 'Lord God, come and eat with me, come and nourish Yourself with me.' And invite the angels and archangels to share your meal with you, also. If you adopt this attitude it will lead to tremendous transformations. When you understand how to do this – for you still have not really understood; I cannot see any of you doing it properly – you will have a solid base from which to make progress in other realms, in the realms of feelings and love. Instead of trying to monopolize everything and keep it all for yourself, instead of being selfish, violent and cruel, you will be doing some real work and will sense a new light within you; new possibilities will be given to you to progress further, but always in line with the same divine rules.

In order to nourish themselves properly, instead of feeding the diabolical, animal principle within them, men and women must learn to nourish their divine principle. But as things are today, when they are together, walking, talking, embracing and creating children, they forget the divine principle and abandon it completely. It is the least of their concerns. This is why their exchanges not only fail to bring any blessings on them but are the cause of worry and distress, anger, arguments, physical and emotional disorders, even suicide. No wonder the whole of society is disrupted, for everything hangs together; everything is connected; the least little things have repercussions all the way to heaven.

So, learn to eat, first and foremost, and then you will know how to nourish yourselves on other planes. When men and women begin to nourish themselves with love in a divine manner, it will always be beautiful and untainted. Heaven itself will look on in wonder and take part in their love; divinities will come down to earth and walk amongst men. How can you expect to attract sublime entities and intelligences if you are brutish, ignorant and selfish, if you have a closed mind and are incapable of seeing any of this? That is a terrible thing to say, I know, but it is the truth; I am obliged to tell you these things: that is what I am here for. If I never said anything, heaven would not be at all pleased with me. They would say, 'What use are you to anyone? What do you think you're there for? Go away; we don't need you.' You will say, 'That's all very well, but it's not very pleasant to hear all that.' Well, it is better for you to put up with this little unpleasantness rather than having to endure far worse.

Nutrition, as I understand it, reveals all the secrets of the universe to me. To me, it represents the world, an infinite world. As long as you are always in such a hurry that you cannot spare one hour in order to eat properly or meditate, you will be deprived of immense possibilities for understanding life and, above all, for transforming your sexual energies into energies of light, intelligence and splendour; you will continue to stagnate on the lowest levels. As long as you fail to link what you do to the whole cosmos, you will eat all the wrong way, you will love all the wrong way and you will never get any good results. Whereas, if you link yourself to the divine world, to the universal soul, every time you embrace your husband or wife you will be sowing sparks, seeds of light, in their soul and, twenty or thirty years later, those seeds will still be alive, still produce fruit. And all this simply because, instead of linking the one you love with your own selfish little personality and sucking him dry before discarding him like an empty lemon peel, you will have linked him with the Whole. The power of love is infinite, the power of love lasts for all eternity when it is understood divinely, when it is understood in relation to the Whole and for the good of the Whole.

The Bonfin, August 12 1962

Chapter Twelve

WOMAN'S ROLE IN
THE NEW CULTURE

The Bible tells us that Solomon had seven hundred wives and three hundred concubines. Usually, people have no idea what he did with so many women; they imagine that he kept them for his own pleasure, that he spent his life in debauchery. In actual fact, Solomon was a great sage and magician who was capable of making the spirits of the invisible world obey him. How could he have possessed such powers if he had lived a life of debauchery? This is just the point: his relations with all these women was of a totally different order. You still have no idea of the role a woman can play in relation to a man who is enlightened and illuminated and who practises a truly divine form of magic. Later, to be sure, Solomon succumbed because he was unable to master the forces he had unleashed and keep them under control. But, at the peak of his reign, his material and spiritual power was such that he built the truly amazing Temple of Jerusalem, rendered judgements of the most extraordinary wisdom and ruled over a kingdom of such splendour that his name became famous throughout the world.

Of course, the reign of Solomon did not attain the spiritual splendour for which the greatest initiates strive and this is why they do not consider him to be in the highest category. He worked too much for himself, for his own glory and renown. He was a little like Louis XIV; his magic was not true theurgy. There are different degrees of magic and very few magicians have ever reached the highest degree, the point at which they are no longer really interested in magic itself, at which they no longer practise magic rites or command spirits, elementals and genii in order to achieve their own ambitions. The truly great magi were not interested in all that; they worked exclusively for the Kingdom of God; they devoted all their powers, all their energies and all their knowledge to bringing about the Kingdom of God on earth. These were the true theurgists, that is to say, beings who practised the most sublime, divine form of magic; their work was utterly disinterested. Of course, in order to reach such heights they must have been beings of exceptional selflessness and purity, without the slightest desire to seek glory or pleasure for themselves, whose one desire was to transform the earth so that God would come to dwell amongst men.

Solomon was unable to attain this level; his knowledge was immense, however, and, in particular, he knew that women were capable of providing the primary substance, the matter which the divine Spirit, the divine Principle, can use to create concrete forms. The divine Principle produces the germ, the spark, the fire, the power, but these essences are so subtle that they cannot be fixed; left to themselves they disappear into the infinite. The collaboration of the feminine principle is needed in order to obtain solid, stable, real, tangible forms on the physical plane. This is why only woman is capable, thanks to the fluidic, etheric matter that emanates from her, of producing the primary substance needed to give concrete form to the divine ideas, plans and goals of a theurgist. For a theurgist makes use of all the emanations that, without realizing it, women release into the atmosphere; thanks to them, he can achieve his sublime plans for the Kingdom of God. Without women, the Kingdom of God cannot be accomplished.

Women, therefore, possess this indispensable matter and diffuse it into the atmosphere around them but, if the spirit, the divine principle, were not there to use this matter, they would be sterile, utterly useless and barren; they would produce nothing.

They, too, need something: in order to create children – the invisible children of their thoughts, spirits, souls and hearts – they need this divine principle. And then their children will be angels and will bring showers of blessings to the whole earth. This has always been the work of the great theurgists. Solomon practised his magic thanks to the energies of all those women who surrounded him, and it was successful, to be sure, but it was not divine magic. Divine magic is wisdom. Magic and wisdom are one and the same thing: divine light. Very few human beings have ever risen to that level. All, or almost all, have used this sacred knowledge to practise witchcraft, to obtain money, glory, women and material possessions. Every magical practice, whose purpose is to satisfy the inferior desires of the personality, is witchcraft or sorcery. Many well-known occultists are still at this stage; they are far from being theurgists.

The most sublime form of magic consists in knowing how to use everything, absolutely everything, for the Kingdom of God; in knowing how to use water, the earth, the air, plants, rivers and rocks, in knowing, even, how to use all that emanates from men and women, all those extraordinary energies that flow from them and waste themselves in space because no one knows how to use them. Or, if a few people know how to use them, they do so for their own, personal satisfaction. This is what Solomon did and, because, as I have often told you, the personality is in contact with the forces of hell, he began to be infested by diabolical spirits looking for food. Try as he might to drive them away, they kept coming back and, in the end, he weakened and succumbed to them.

Now, if you don't mind, we'll forget about Solomon and get back to essentials. The really essential thing in all this is that women should understand that they must consecrate the subtle matter that emanates from them, that they must dedicate their whole being, their very existence, to the divine Principle above, so that the angels and archangels may use this unique, precious substance in order to prepare the forms of the new life. Instead of always being at the service of human beings, women must be at the service of the Deity. This is the ideal I am offering them. How many women will manage to realize this ideal, I don't know, but I am there to invite them to do so.

For centuries, men have misused their authority over women; they have shown themselves to be selfish, unjust, violent and cruel, and now, of course, women are beginning to wake up. But they are not awakening to the light, or not, at least, to true light; they are awakening to revenge and this is no improvement, even for them. Women must, on the contrary, forgive men. Since woman is mother; since she has greater love than man and, since her nature makes her more inclined to be kind, indulgent, generous and ready to sacrifice herself, she must not seek revenge. The time has come for women to awaken to greater virtue, to rise above their personal interests. All the women of the world must unite in a work of construction, a work on the children they bring into the world and on men. Instead of thinking to themselves, 'I know how pretty and attractive I am; I'm going to take advantage of my charms...,' and seeking to satisfy their vanity by seducing men with their looks, they must attract them in such a way that they begin to collaborate in a work for the regeneration of mankind. There is no denying that, for good or for ill, nature has given great powers to women. The only question is how they use those powers: they are perfectly capable of becoming the tormentor in their turn and using their powers to persecute men.

God has given great powers to both men and women, but their powers are different. Women can do things that men cannot do and men can do things that women cannot do. Woman provides the matter and man provides the spirit, that is to say, life. Everybody knows that this is so on the physical plane but human beings are still ignorant of these great mysteries on the divine plane. Henceforth, all the women in the world must unite to form a single, collective Woman who will create the new life in humanity. Without this matter, the divine Spirit cannot incarnate. The phenomenon is well known in spiritualistic seances during which a medium lends the spirits that wish to appear to the participants some of her own matter, her emanations. The spirits wrap themselves in this matter in order to become visible and tangible and, once they have it, they are capable of displaying tremendous strength on the material plane and can move and even destroy heavy objects. If you weigh a medium during a seance, you will find that she loses weight, sometimes several pounds but, at the end of the seance, she will be back to her normal weight. This fluctuation depends, of course, on the amount of matter she lent to the spirits.

Now that you know these laws, you should understand how important it is that you dedicate yourselves to the divine forces so that they may find nourishment in you. If the Scriptures tell us that man must offer himself as a burnt offering to the Lord, it is so that he may nourish the Lord himself. This is symbolic, of course. In ancient religions, animals were immolated in order to nourish certain entities of the invisible world and, nowadays, we light candles, burn incense and put flowers on the altar because the light, smoke and scent are a nourishment for luminous spirits. But man can go further than this and offer himself in sacrifice so that God may come and find nourishment in him, in his thoughts and feelings.

The Lord cannot accept our invitation to come and find nourishment in us unless we have some delicious fruits to offer him. We are trees and plants and he will not eat the tree, of course, only the fruits; the tree will remain intact. Our fruits are our thoughts and feelings and God will pluck and eat them only if they are really delicious. This is how initiates provide food for the divine world; they are the fruit trees in the orchards of the Almighty and he plucks their fruit for his own nourishment. As for those who produce no fruit, they are like the barren fig tree that we read about in the Gospels. You all know the story, of course: one day, when Jesus was hungry, he saw a fig tree by the road and going up to it found nothing on it but leaves.

Then Jesus cursed the tree, which immediately withered. The incident, obviously, is not just about an ordinary fig tree; Jesus would never have been so cruel to a poor tree. No, the tree symbolized the Sanhedrin. When Jesus, the great Gardener came to harvest the fruits he had a right to expect from the People of Israel, he cursed them because they had produced none. And this is also why Jesus wept over Jerusalem, saying, *'O Jerusalem, Jerusalem, the one who kills the prophets and stones those who are sent to her. How often I wanted to gather your children together, as a hen gathers her chicks under her wings, but you were not willing. See. Your house is left to you desolate...'* And this prophecy was fulfilled. The same thing could happen, today, to European civilization if it makes no effort to produce any fruits for the Almighty. But such an idea never occurs to anyone.

Women must begin to understand the gigantic work that they have the power to accomplish. They are a reservoir of extraordinary substances capable of realizing heaven's designs. At the moment, women are busy realizing the designs of every whippersnapper, every imbecile, every criminal on earth... never those of heaven. They understand no better. But, once they decide to dedicate themselves to heaven so that all that marvellous substance may be used for a divine purpose, then we shall see pockets of light bursting out over the whole face of the earth, and everybody will speak the language of the new culture, the language of the new life, the language of divine love. What are women waiting for? They always pick on tasks that are too low, too ordinary. From their earliest childhood they prepare themselves to 'settle down' and bring up a brood of children. They prepare such a drab destiny for themselves and then they complain about it: 'It's a dog's life!' But it is their own fault; why didn't they adopt a higher ideal? Their whole destiny would have been different.

What I am revealing to you, today, is one of the greatest secrets, one of the greatest arcana of initiatic science. All those initiates, prophets and ascetics who fled the company of women, who failed to understand the importance of woman's role and refused to work with her, never accomplished anything, because it is only through women that ideas can be incarnated.

This is why, today, I am asking that all the sisters of the Brotherhood, at least, dedicate themselves in full consciousness to heaven – not to me, to heaven. In this way, heaven, using me as its intermediary, will be able to carry out its plans, for what counts is this sublime consciousness, not the physical aspect. I ask nothing more of the sisters than their presence, their smiles and glances, their emanations, their good thoughts and feelings and, then, with all that material, I can do the work that is mine. For the work of creating beautiful forms in the divine world requires the masculine principle; nothing else can do this. A woman cannot be a magus, her nature does not allow it: she is receptive, clairvoyant, a medium, a pythoness, at times, even, something of a magician or witch. But to be a magus, one has to be tremendously active and dynamic, one has to be in possession and in complete control of the masculine principle in all its fullness and perfection. Can a magic wand be effective if it is bent and folded in two or three places? It would not be a wand any more. If someone possesses a magic wand, it means that he is active, that he has a will of such potency that he is capable of scaling the highest peaks so as to reach and fuse into one with the universal soul.

How can anyone who is flabby, impotent and ineffective reach and fuse into one with the universal soul so as to be capable of creation? It is as though someone who was sexually impotent wanted to have a child. The laws are the same on all levels – and if you are shocked, you can hide your face or block up your ears.

The Bonfin, September 11 1962

Chapter Thirteen

NUDISM AND THE
INITIATIC SIGNIFICANCE OF NAKEDNESS

I

A couple of years ago, some people who ran a camp for nudists invited me to visit them so that I would have some idea of what it was like. Amongst all those naked people it was I who was the oddity: I was the only one with any clothes on. Gradually, the campers came up to me; there were young girls, older women and men, and the extraordinary thing is that when one finds oneself with so many people who are naked, one has no particular reaction. I must say that I was quite surprised. I looked at all those people and thought to myself, 'There's really nothing to be shocked about.' Everything seemed perfectly simple and natural. We sat down and talked to some of them for a few moments and several of them asked me questions and listened to what I said with great attention. The curious thing was that many of them said, 'One can sense, from the way you look at us and talk to us, that you are a Master. If only you could give us a few lectures and teach us something.' I was surprised to hear that from nudists but, unfortunately, I was in a hurry and could not stay.

Now, I know that you are going to ask me if I am in favour of nudist camps and the answer is that I am neither for nor against them but I noticed a great many things that were not as they should be. I had been told that nudists were more advanced than others, because they had already freed themselves from certain complexes and that nudism gave them a better chance of being healthy, well-balanced and, even, pure. I wanted to see if this were true and I found that it was not entirely true. In the first place, they were bored, because there was nothing much for them to do but, above all, as they had no initiatic knowledge of the power of the elements, they did not get any great benefit from them. I could see, too, that they were full of desires and passions that their nakedness allowed them to satisfy. Their nakedness, therefore, did not make them any purer. Purity is much more than being able to take off one's clothes without any sense of shame.

Last year I gave you a series of lectures about purity in which I explained what true purity was, how to purify oneself, the advantages of possessing it, the power it represents and so on. Most people think that purity applies only to the area of sexuality. Not at all: purity embraces every dimension and every area of life. When purity enters a man's intellect, he understands; when it enters his will, he becomes powerful; when purity reigns in his physical body, he is healthy, and when it enters his heart and soul, he becomes clairvoyant. This is what Jesus was saying when he said, *'Blessed are the pure of heart for they shall see God.'* It is not enough to limit purity to the area of sexuality.

Nudism is spreading, nowadays, all over the world. A great many books and articles are devoted to the subject but, as the knowledge people have in this domain is insufficient, it will not be as beneficial as they imagine; the few experiments that we see today will not go very far.

The main thing to be said in favour of nudists is that they have understood how important it is to be in communion with the forces of nature, with the air and the sun. The trouble is, though, that unless they learn far more about the structure of human beings, even this will degenerate. Do they even know how to expose themselves to the sun? No, they don't; their physical pores may be open but their spiritual pores are closed, because they do not really know what it is to expose oneself to the forces of nature. So, even when they live freely in the midst of nature, they don't really get much benefit from it. Only our Teaching can really bring light, balance and fulfilment to all activities and every area of life. Without a Master, without the guidance of one who is heir to this science, this light, it will be a long time before human beings grope their way into the great mysteries of nature through their own experience.

There is nothing wrong in being naked; everybody gets undressed at home, to have a bath, and so on. It is considered perfectly acceptable to be naked when one is at home, alone; it is when one is with others that it is considered unsuitable. As human beings are not strong enough to control themselves nor very pure nor intelligent, they have had to invent rules for their own protection. But, in itself, there is nothing wrong in being naked. Ask any pretty woman what she thinks about it; she is so delighted with her own nudity that she spends hours in her bathroom looking at herself. It is when a women is plain that she does not want to look at herself and becomes modest and virtuous. Yes, simply because she is so plain. But if a woman is beautiful she forgets about morality; she is eager to show herself so as to be admired and contemplated.

Almost all women have the need to show themselves in the nude. This is not the case with men; on the contrary, men are inclined to be embarrassed to undress in front of others. But they like to see women in the nude and women like to be seen. This is something that nature has given them, because Truth desires to be seen in all its nakedness. If women identified themselves with Truth, if they became as pure as Truth, there would never be anything wrong in their showing themselves in the nude. But, as long as they have not managed to identify with Truth, it is better that they should be dressed in the presence of other people.

There is no doubt that women have a natural tendency to undress; it does not embarrass them to do so. In fact, when I went to that nudist camp, I was astounded to see the innocence with which some of the young girls showed themselves. Their faces and their whole being expressed such purity. In spite of the fact that, for centuries, women have been told that nudity was contrary to modesty and purity, it is obvious that many of them have never assimilated that notion. They may wear clothes in obedience to the rules but, in their hearts, they have never been convinced; this idea does not correspond to their deepest nature, which remains innocent and chaste in nudity. Very often, it is not from vice or depravity that women want to be seen in the nude but because that is their nature and they see nothing evil in it. The evil came later: when women saw how weak men were, how easily they were bowled over by their nudity, they realized that they could turn this to their advantage and now they use their charms in order to dominate and exploit men or to revenge themselves on them.

It is not woman's natural impulse to show herself in the nude that is reprehensible, it is the use she makes of her nudity. It has become so widespread that there is hardly a woman on earth, today, who is not aware of the powers of her physical body and who does not try to use them in order to lead men by the nose. This is why our Teaching also has the task of instructing women so that they may recover their true innocence. No one can possibly object to women being beautiful and having a lot of charm but, instead of using the powers that nature has given them to tempt men and make them grovel in the dust, they must use them to uplift and inspire them. The power of woman is immense and can be either a good or an evil influence; it all depends on how she uses her charms, on her goal, her ideal.

But let's get back to the question of nudists.

Men's and women's physical bodies are equipped with antennae which enable them to be in touch with nature. This is why they pick up the forces and messages of nature much more easily when they are naked. If, when they wish to communicate and do some spiritual work with the earth, water, air and the sun, they go into a forest or to the seashore and expose their bodies, they will be more likely to pick up and emit waves and, therefore, to get results from their work. Sorcerers, particularly witches, have always known the power of nakedness and used it in their magic rites. Occult literature tells of many instances in which witches undressed before conjuring up spirits or casting spells, curses and so on.

As nakedness attracts evil forces as well as the forces of light, it is dangerous to expose one's naked body if one is not sufficiently conscious and in control of oneself to close one's doors to the forces of darkness and open them only to the forces of light.

And now, by means of the science of eternal symbols, I will reveal the true significance of nakedness to you. To be naked is to be stripped of all false conceptions and all cupidity. Only Truth is naked. In order to achieve true nakedness, therefore, one has to free oneself from all that is opaque, drab and crude, all that is impervious to the divine world. Once one has attained true nakedness one can rise to great heights and receive messages, guidance, wisdom, love and help from heaven.

If human beings often get so little out of their meditations, it is because they try to rise to sublime heights before taking off their dirty, tattered old clothes – symbolically speaking. In these conditions how can their antennae pick up anything? We have to come before heaven naked, that is to say, stripped of all cupidity, self-interest and false ideas. If we denude ourselves, we can go higher, and the more we denude ourselves the higher we can go. Afterwards, when we come down again, we put on our clothes and go on with all our schemes and projects. For the world this is necessary, but not for heaven. Heaven appreciates only those who are 'naked.' You can see, now, what a magnificent image the initiates bequeathed to us when they spoke of the naked truth, of Isis unveiled.

Because of the disorder and anarchy that reign in every area of life and culture today, many powers and entities that have been confined to the subterranean regions for centuries have now been released. You only need to look at what has happened to present-day standards in life and in the arts. Men have opened the doors of the subterranean world and now they are being overrun. If you want to protect yourselves from these forces, you must be sure to maintain your links with light, with the Lord, with the heavenly powers; you must analyse and control yourselves and not let yourselves go, otherwise you will inevitably become an 'open house' for undesirable entities that will enter you and create havoc. If you don't want to believe me, life itself will show you that I have always told you the truth; you will experience the existence of hostile, destructive forces for yourselves. Open your heart and soul only to what is intelligent, reasonable and luminous; if you allow yourselves to be seduced by the follies of the world, it will be the end of you.

The Teaching is something absolutely extraordinary. But if you don't put it into practice, it will still be wonderful, but you won't. If you don't apply it to your lives it will not do anything for you. But if you apply it, if you establish it firmly within you, it will protect you from every evil, from all misguided options and, instead of always walking in darkness and accepting things that are harmful and dangerous to you, you will choose only the best and every possible blessing will be showered on you.

The Bonfin, September 12 1967

II

If nudism starts to spread all over the world it is going to make many people reflect, but it is also going to make many others angry. But why try to prevent people from exposing themselves to the sun in the midst of nature? Why try to stop them from freeing themselves from obsolete traditions? Even in a country as strait-laced as Bulgaria, apparently, nudist camps exist. Well, it's only to be expected: Bulgaria, too, wants to be up to date. But even if more and more young people do go in for nudism, is that a reason to be indignant and tear your hair? One thing you can be sure of: the young won't give two hoots for your indignation. You will probably think, 'Aha, he's preaching nudism so as to prepare us for it, too.' No, not at all – not yet, anyway. But a few centuries from now, when mothers know how to work on the children they bear and produce divinities, then it will be time for beauty to come to the fore. Why hide what is beautiful and pure? But you must not be in too much of a hurry because, as things stand today, instead of coming closer to heaven, people are getting further away. In the meantime, therefore, get to work. Mothers must learn to form children of such purity and beauty that, whether clothed or naked, mankind will always be absolutely pure. Besides, if you ask nature if it enrages her to see human beings strolling naked through the forests or on the beaches, she will tell you, 'I couldn't care less; if it does them good to go about naked, let them. In any case, when I sent them to earth they didn't have any clothes on. It was they who thought about it and decided that, as a protection against cold weather and cuts and bruises, or in order to conform to some strange ideas of their own, they would do better to wear clothes. But when I made them they were naked.'

One day, therefore, if mothers work to improve future generations, human beings will be able to be naked all the time. Towns will be heated thanks to solar energy, which will be in use everywhere, and men and women will go about their business free and unencumbered, in a continual state of wonder. In fact, I can tell you now, in the light of the new heaven, that the initiates of ancient Greece understood that, if man's sexual energy was sublimated, it became a source of inspiration. This is why Greece produced the greatest sculptors, architects and philosophers that the world has ever known – even today there are none to equal them. And all this was possible simply because they knew how to sublimate their sexual energy. The initiates instituted holidays during which the purest and most beautiful young girls danced through the streets, clothed in a single transparent veil. And the men watching them were lost in wonder and admiration at their grace and beauty, at the subtlety of their movements and gestures, and this wonder, this energy, would build up within them and surge up to their brain and manifest itself, later, in the form of wonderful creations. Even in the past, therefore, human beings were familiar with the new heaven but they abandoned it. Perhaps you think that I am going to say that you should revive the customs of ancient Greece. No, I would not advise that; human beings are so backward that it would not be beneficial. One has to be very highly evolved to get results in this domain, otherwise one can be torn apart.

This is how the Vestal Virgins came to be: they were pure, lovely young virgins who danced naked before the initiates, and the initiates found inspiration from looking at them without ever touching them. To keep these mysteries from the masses who would have been incapable of understanding them, the story was put about that the function of the Vestals was to tend the sacred flame and see that it never went out. But is it reasonable to suppose that a host of young girls would live in the temple simply to tend a flame? No, the flame that the Vestals tended was the sacred flame of these great Masters. You will ask, 'But did they really need that flame?' Indeed they did: the flame is indispensable; without it, even initiates would be powerless to accomplish anything. Those initiates of ancient Greece were old men and they never so much as touched a Vestal Virgin, but they used their emanations for a work of the highest kind of white magic.

The power that mother nature has given to woman is so effective, especially when she is young and pure, that even initiates have no substitute for it. They need it in order to kindle the fire within them. With this fire, therefore, the initiates of old prepared a subtle form of nourishment which they projected to a higher level in order to win blessings for their whole country. It was in order to do good, to accomplish a divine work and not for their own pleasure that they projected this force. Of course, it is very likely that they did find pleasure in this work, for it is impossible to separate the two, but they did not do it for the pleasure involved. When pleasure is your goal, your energies are swallowed up by the earth, whereas, when your purpose is to work, it goes without saying that you also experience pleasure, joy and a sense of expansion but your energies are directed upwards, towards heaven, and the joy you experience is even greater than if it had been your only goal. This kind of joy does not degrade you, it can only make you more noble. The only problem is that, in order to understand these things, we need a far greater understanding of the psychic world.

This conception of the sublimation of sexual energy is very ancient. Unfortunately, as time went on, many of those who tried to practise it were incapable of maintaining the necessary degree of purity and it degenerated into sexual magic. Being incapable of self-restraint, they would go too far and, instead of limiting themselves to homoeopathic doses, they would take an allopathic dose. But the effect of an allopathic dose is not at all the same. Whereas a homoeopathic dose affects the psychic level which, in turn, influences the physical body, an allopathic dose affects only the physical body. In the future, human beings will be taught how to take love in homoeopathic doses and then it will no longer drain and exhaust them; instead of defiling them, it will uplift them and raise them to heaven. All those who have succeeded in this have reached great heights, because their love endowed them with tremendous power.

I could teach you how to nourish yourselves with homoeopathic doses but I don't know how you will understand me. I am sure that some of you will be shocked to learn, for instance, that I have often watched women on the beach. They will think, 'Someone like that can't be an initiate; he can't possibly be a Master. Even we don't spend our time looking at women in bathing suits.' Well, I do; and I do so deliberately and without shame, with a specific purpose in mind. In fact, I have often taken some of the brothers with me. I told them, 'Try to understand how I do this and why and which women I look at.' In this way they understood that it is a science in itself to know how to look at someone. Why are all those women there? To be looked at, of course. But people don't know how to look, and yet everything depends on the way you look at things.

I will teach you how to look. I will teach the brothers – and the sisters, too, because they don't know how to look, either. Their heads have been stuffed with false notions sufficient to freeze and inhibit them for ever – and then they are told that marriage will be their salvation. A great many women are inhibited and condemned to suffer because they do not know how to understand these things, what to think about them; they don't know what attitude to have towards them or how to make everything serve the glory of God. They spend their time meddling in other people's affairs, criticizing everybody and becoming more and more vindictive, embittered, jealous and even hysterical. Women must be saved. And men, too, need to be saved but no one can be saved with antiquated ideas. The only merit of these antiquated ideas is that they provide plenty of work for doctors and psychiatrists; they never improve the situation. And yet the whole thing is really very simple: everything would be improved if people changed their way of understanding and looking at things.

The thing is to know how to look at beauty and be grateful for it without destroying it. Beauty was not made to be eaten, only to be contemplated. In contemplating beauty you launch out into space and everything is given to you: purity, nobility, patience, understanding; you soar to the heights and become a source.

Always seek true beauty; it is this that will save you, because it will teach you to choose that which is purest and most luminous. If you have sometimes seen paintings of naked women you will have noticed that, when the bodies are perfect, you do not feel desire, only admiration. Many artists have had this experience. It is when beauty is imperfect that it is more likely to arouse desire. People say that nakedness is chaste. No, it is beauty that is chaste, whether clothed or naked. But nakedness itself? Well, when people strip themselves naked it is precisely for reasons that are the opposite of chaste.

Do I need to say any more? Do you feel that you are beginning to have an idea of what purity really is? Purity lies in beauty. You have to love beauty in order to attain to purity, for the love of beauty will prevent you from getting lost in regions of darkness.

Sèvres, January 1 1967

Chapter Fourteen

THE MASCULINE AND FEMININE PRINCIPLES:
A RELATIONSHIP OF EXCHANGE

I

Everyone knows that, where the mutual behaviour of men and women is concerned, it is generally the man who takes the initiative in approaching the woman. I say 'generally,' to be sure, because, if you notice what goes on today, you will see that it is more often the woman who makes the advances. The normal thing, however, is that woman stays still and that man, like a hunter, goes in search of her. You will say, 'But a man goes to a woman because she has attracted him.' That is true, she attracts him; she throws her net over him and draws him towards her. If the man approaches her, it is because he is already a captive, he has already been snared. The woman is like an angler; all she has to do is stand on the bank of the river and reel in the fish. This is woman's normal behaviour: she does not stir from her place; it is the fish that is drawn to the bait. You will say, 'But a man can also be attractive; I have often heard women say that they felt attracted to a man.' Yes, that is true; man also throws out something invisible, but his behaviour is that of a mountaineer, a rock-climber: he throws a grappling-iron up to the top of a cliff and then climbs up. The difference between them is that a man throws out something that he then uses to move towards a woman, whereas a woman throws out something that invites a man to move towards her. They attract each other mutually; it is a form of warfare in which both use different tactics but in view of the same goal: to be together in a relationship of exchange.

Have you ever noticed that, when boys and girls go to a party, for instance, they are happy, simply because they are together and can exchange glances and a few words with each other? Their happiness comes from the tension between them, which gives them a feeling of lightness and clarity. And yet nothing actually happens, they don't even touch each other; their intercourse is confined to the subtle level of emanations. When men and women descend to the heavier, denser regions of sexuality, the physical act is simply a crystallization of the subtle exchange that has already taken place between them on the etheric plane and of which they were not even aware. For men and women are only aware of love when it is expressed physically; then, to be sure, they realize that something is going on. But before that point is reached their consciousness is not aroused; they don't notice anything.

When someone is speaking, he is emissive, that is to say, he is positively polarized, whereas those who listen to him, whether male or female, are receptive, that is to say, negatively polarized. The words he speaks penetrate them and fertilize them divinely or diabolically, depending on whether they are good or bad. Nature operates according to the same principles on every level, but human beings pay attention only to the densest, most concrete levels; they cannot see, still less understand, the subtle and invisible realities which give rise to all concrete realizations; they are simply unaware of them. It is precisely in this respect that they need to be enlightened, that their horizons must be expanded, so that they may glimpse all the splendours that nature has prepared for her children once their consciousness awakens.

Man is emissive with the whole of his body: with his eyes, his brain, his mouth, his hands and, above all, of course, with the organ which was specially designed for giving. And woman is receptive, also, in every part of her body but, especially, in the part that was specially built to receive. And there is nothing anyone can do to prevent etheric intercourse between them. Why do you suppose that everyone, both men and women, like to get dressed up and go out? To look at the shops and watch the passers-by? Not only for that. Although they don't realize it, there is a deeper reason behind this taste for going out: if they like to stroll through the streets and parks of the city, it is precisely because they need this intercourse, this exchange, with other human beings and with nature; it is absolutely necessary to them, it is indispensable to life.

You will ask, 'What about all those ascetics and hermits who shut themselves up and never see another man or woman?' They have decided to renounce certain forms of exchange in order to open their souls and spirits to other, less tangible, less physical influences. As soon as one shuts out one kind of influence, one automatically opens oneself to another kind. If you decide not to see or hear anything any more, other eyes and ears will open within you and receive other kinds of impressions. As soon as you cease to be emissive or receptive through your five senses, other senses awaken to make you emissive or receptive in your soul and spirit. If certain initiates counselled their disciples to live in isolation in a forest or on top of a mountain, it was not because they wanted to prevent them from being emissive or receptive, but in order to help them to move onto another plane and continue to be emissive and receptive on a subtler level. We are obliged to be ceaselessly emissive or receptive[1]; anything else means death, and in death there is no intercourse, no exchange. Exchanges are the very foundation of life and to know how and with whom to effect them in the most ideal manner is to possess the science of true life.

I have already talked to you about the exchange we have with solid matter in the form of food, with liquid matter in the

---

[1] See *Harmony*, Complete Works, vol. 6, chap. 4: 'A Disciple Must Develop his Spiritual Senses.'

form of drink, with air and gaseous matter through respiration and, finally, with heat and light by means of the skin, which absorbs heat, and the eyes, which absorb light. But the possibilities for exchange do not end there; there are many more on other levels.

Unfortunately, men and women have gone no further than the first rung of the ladder and exchange with each other only on the physical plane. On this level it is not possible for intercourse to be truly divine; by its very nature, it is the crudest form of exchange. The entire science of intercourse on all the different levels is contained in the symbol of the Aeolian Harp, the harp whose seven strings vibrate in response to the wind. A human being, whether man or woman, is a harp of seven strings and they have to learn to make each string vibrate and resonate. For it is no use imagining that, by concentrating exclusively on the lowest string, they will ever attain perfect happiness, fulfilment and power. Men and women should not be single-stringed instruments; they must learn to set their six other strings vibrating for it is from them that they will receive other sensations, other joys and a fulfilment far superior to the pleasures obtained from purely physical contacts. But this is something that cannot be explained; you cannot explain the sun, light and colours to someone who is blind. If people have never seen or experienced certain things for themselves, it is not possible to explain them.

When men and women are together, a tension builds up in them and this is normal; nature planned it this way. The only question is whether that slight tension should necessarily make them disperse and squander all their strength. This is the point at which wisdom – or stupidity – begins. If they waste these most precious of all energies by doing something stupid, it shows that they have not understood anything. It was not nature's intention that they should get rid of that tension as quickly as possible and in whatever way they could. Her intention was to get them to reflect on the why and how of it so that they would discover what it meant and how to use it for some magnificent work, so that they would project it up to every part of their body and that every single cell would be irrigated, impregnated and fertilized by it. The fact that you have certain sensations does not mean that you have to dwell on them to the exclusion of everything else. No, you should either leave them alone and busy yourself with something else, or send them somewhere else, send them up to the brain.

If nature has created this tension, it is not so that it should be destroyed. People can't bear to feel any inner tension or turbulence but, without it, there would be neither desire nor impulse of any kind; without this tension man is listless and apathetic. From one point of view, there may be some advantages in this but one has to be able to apply certain methods, otherwise the results can have a bad effect on one's evolution. The fact is that tension is necessary in order to pump the water up to the top floor of a skyscraper. But this question, which is of first importance, can only be solved if one studies human beings, bearing in mind that it is not only their physical body that must be satisfied. Since nature has given man the capacity to experience this animal sensation of relief and enjoyment, it is obviously necessary to him, but not to the point of sacrificing everything else to what is, after all, a purely biological sensation. Most human beings don't know that this tension is indispensable in order to carry their energies up to the top floor and, as it torments them, they seek release by gratifying it as soon as they can, whereas initiates do their best to maintain it for as long as possible – for a hundred and fifty or two hundred years. Yes, because it is tension, not release, that interests them. Release can be very harmful. If you don't know how to channel the energy that you release and use it to set your inner wheels in motion, it will run away in all directions and cause great devastation.

But let's get back to the question of intercourse. In the great Book of living nature it is written that you cannot be pure if all you do is take. Purity begins with the need to give, to overflow. It is only in a movement of liberality, of open-handed giving, that you can be pure. For this, the law will never condemn you. It will only condemn you when you take from others, because that means that you are a thief. Human beings call this love, but it's not: it's robbery. A young man feels hungry, so he pounces on a girl, saying, 'I love you, I love you,' and everyone here says, 'That's normal. He loves her.' Well the invisible world above says, 'He's a thief; he has taken everything from her.' If you take something, simply in obedience to your needs, you are a thief. You should not need to take, only to give.

Actually, there must always be the two poles, emissive and receptive; this is what makes the circulation of energies possible. When a man and woman make love, the man gives the woman an energy which she receives into herself and which rises the length of her spinal column as far as her head; by means of her mouth, she then projects this energy into the man's brain which thus becomes receptive. Man receives above and gives below, whereas woman receives below and gives above. Woman, so tender, weak and delicate, is the one who gives above; if women knew this they would be able to transform men by means of their thought. During their love-making, the woman is far stronger, on the level of thought, than the man, who easily loses his head. You can see proof of this in the fact that if you surprise a boy and girl embracing, the poor boy will stutter and stammer, whereas the girl will be perfectly cool and give you all kinds of plausible explanations; she does not lose her head so easily.

In reality, physical intercourse between men and women is not evil or unlawful in itself. If it were, would nature have shown us nothing else, in all species, since the beginning of creation? If the act itself were reprehensible, how could nature tolerate it? How could heaven have refrained from exterminating all those who practise it? No, the act in itself is neither good nor bad; the only thing that renders it either sacred or evil is the intention. Take a simple comparison: which is more important, the water or the tap from which it flows? What if the tap is made of gold but the water is dirty? The important thing is the purity of the water, and an evil intention is like dirty water, whereas a good intention is water that is crystal-clear and vivifying. In love, therefore, there is no guilt attached to either the physical gestures or the organs themselves. What counts is the quality of the energies, emanations and quintessences released in the act, the nature of the psychic forces that the man and woman project when they are making love.

If a man who has never worked at making himself purer and nobler and whose intentions are selfish and dishonest, decides to marry and accomplish this act, his friends may approve and applaud his decision, his family may hold a reception in his honour, the magistrate may give him a license and the Church her blessing, but nature will declare him guilty. For what is he going to give to his wife? Nothing but disease, vice, pernicious influences. The world may approve what he does, therefore, but the laws of living nature will pronounce judgment against him because he will be defiling his wife. And conversely, the world may criticize you for not marrying, but if you have poured heaven into the soul of the woman you love and she has become a divinity, all the angels on high will be filled with wonder and delight.

So, this is something you must know, my dear brothers and sisters: the question of whether your actions are good or evil does not depend on whether they conform or fail to conform to certain conventions, but on the nature and quality of what you give through them. Initiates are not interested in knowing whether the union of a man and woman is licit or illicit; they are only interested in what each is going to give the other for their mutual welfare, edification and evolution. Their judgment is based on these criteria, for this is what is essential. Initiates know how much work human beings need to do on themselves before marrying, how much they need to purify, harmonize and perfect themselves so that if they have children, one day, it will be possible for heaven to manifest itself through them. In fact, although many initiates never marry, they, too, work tirelessly to become purer and more luminous in order to become divinities; they are not disturbed by the opinion of those around them who criticize celibates. In point of fact, they are not really celibates. I will say more about this question another time, but I can already tell you that many initiates have had exchanges with nature spirits, with very pure beings such as sylphs, salamanders, nymphs and devas – marvellous, extremely subtle exchanges which gave them indescribable happiness.

In fact, I will tell you of a personal experience I have had in this connection. Several times, I have been woken in the night by the presence of unreal, diaphanous creatures of extraordinary beauty. They were all round me, looking at me in such a way that I felt myself melting in indescribable love. They did not touch me, just stayed there, looking at me, and all their power was in their eyes. I have never yet seen such an expression in the eyes of a human being. It seemed to come from a great distance and a great height. The experience lasted for hours. I learned, later, that these creatures were devas and I understood that they had visited me in order to show me that there existed in nature a beauty beyond anything one could imagine. I was allowed to experience this state so that I would, at least, know that it was possible. Those devas opened up a new world within me. I cannot describe that absolute purity, that light, that radiance, those colours. The divine Mother, who knows where my heart, my soul, my ideal belong, sent these creatures to me for my instruction. It is they who have revealed so much to me concerning love, the true love that does not need to manifest itself physically.

You will say, 'Yes, but that is a world of illusions.' What do you know about it? But, even if they are illusions, I prefer these illusions to what you call reality and which is often so ugly. It is far better to live in a world of beauty in which the things we learn and feel surpass the imagination. Nothing is more desirable than to live in purity and be constantly in admiration before such splendour, without coveting it carnally. A single glance can give you greater happiness than all the rest. He who is content with no more than a glance is nearing perfection.

One day, when I was still very young, the Master Peter Deunov told me, 'For you, a glance is enough.' At first I was very surprised, I did not understand what he meant by these words, but I observed and analysed myself and I saw that it was true. The Master had seen the roots, the structure, of my deepest nature and had summed it up in a single phrase: I need only a glance, a look. Later on, I often used a glance and I discovered some important laws or, to be more accurate, I discovered how to look in such a way as to sanctify oneself, how to be filled with wonder, to feel elated and fulfilled with only a single glance. I worked at this for years; it is a science in itself but I have not revealed it to you yet.

I have one absolute need and that is to contemplate beauty; I will never deprive myself of that. I don't care what anyone tries to tell me, my only response is: 'Do whatever you please, but leave me alone; I have a different path to follow. I don't deny that you are a saint, I respect you as a man who is blameless according to the old tradition, but leave me alone; I have a path to follow that you know nothing about. I have found my own path.' And, without listening to anyone, I shall continue to contemplate beauty. There is so much beauty on earth, what a pity it would be not to see it.

As I have said, we must not pounce on beauty in order to devour it but it is a crime not to look for it and contemplate it. If human beings use beauty to lure each other into the abyss, it is not that beauty is at fault but that men and women are not ready for it; they stir up a fire in each other and, because of all their impurities, the fire smokes. Beauty should not cause people to fall; on the contrary, it should lead them to the Deity, project them heavenwards. For my part, I would like to be nourished only by beauty. In fact, I tell you, if God were not beautiful, if he were only wise, omniscient and almighty, I would not love him. It is because he is beautiful that I love him and want to be like him. The only thing that attracts me is beauty, but pure, spiritual beauty, not just any kind of beauty. For I have my own idea of beauty; very often, where other people see splendour, I see only ugliness and where they see nothing in particular, I see a hidden splendour.

At the beginning of this talk I told you that, when young men and girls are together, enjoying each other's company at a party, the young men unconsciously project into the atmosphere rays and etheric particles which the girls, being receptive, absorb equally unconsciously. The intercourse between them takes place, therefore, on the etheric plane long before anything happens on the physical plane, and this is enough to make them happy. The only thing is, though, that men must become conscious of this phenomenon so as to be sure to project nothing but very pure particles, capable of healing and vivifying others. As for women, they must take care to use filters so as not to absorb any psychic 'dirty water.' Some women are absolute sponges: they soak up everything. There are many rules to be learned in this area for, if women suffer from so many disorders in these parts, it is because they have neglected to use a filter and have absorbed too many harmful influences.

Since this etheric intercourse is a reality, why not work to be sure that it is done divinely? Neither saints nor prophets nor great Masters can prevent the great laws of nature from manifesting themselves in them. Even the purest and most saintly beings experience certain reactions; the only thing is that they are conscious of what is happening and that which emanates from them is divine. The sole preoccupation of an initiate is to emanate the Deity for the benefit of the whole world. You cannot prevent the spring from giving water or the river from flowing; the only thing you can do is make sure that the water is pure.

Sèvres, January 2 1967

II

You will gradually begin to understand that when I speak of the different degrees of love I am speaking always of the same force, a force which manifests differently and gives rise to different sensations. To kiss a woman gives you a certain sensation, but if instead of kissing her you gaze at her with tenderness, the sensation will be different, less strong perhaps on the physical plane, but more intense and more fulfilling on the subtler planes. And it will give you indescribable joy. Yes, a smile or a glance is capable of transporting you.

One day, when I had been working and meditating very intensively, I relaxed by going for a walk along the Paris boulevards. There were hundreds of people about and, naturally, as we passed in the street they looked at me and I at them. At one point I saw a couple coming towards me, a young man and a very young girl, and as we passed each other the girl gave me a glance... but a glance that was totally indescribable. Heaven itself was in her eyes. The light, the love, the beauty contained in that glance were staggering, completely overwhelming. Who was looking through the eyes of that girl? It was certainly not she who looked at me that way. She was a channel for someone else. It often happens that beings of the invisible world want to show you their love. Perhaps it is your soulmate who, although she may not be reincarnated, is always with you and can occasionally glance at you through the eyes of another.

For days I could not forget the look that young girl had given me. You will perhaps wonder if I spoke to her or tried to see her again. No, for there are certain things I know and you do not. If I had found her in the hope of receiving the same look again, I should have been disappointed, for it was not she who had looked at me. Her look could never express what that unknown heavenly being had given me through her.

Believe me, my dear brothers and sisters, if ever you receive such a divine look you must cling to the impression and not try to pursue the person who gave it to you in the hope of recapturing it, for no one can create it of himself. You are still unfamiliar with the subtle realm of the human soul: no girl on earth could have given me a look so celestial, so divine. Naturally, I would love to receive such looks all the time, but it was too beautiful to happen often.

There is no man or woman on earth capable of remaining unmoved by such a celestial look. Or if there are any such, they are made of stone. Even if they consider themselves initiates, they are stones; they are dead. A genuine initiate is alive: he feels and understands what is beautiful. An initiate does not lose his head when he encounters beauty, but he is sensitive to it. To be pure does not mean to be made of stone. There are many theories and mystical practices marked by deviations and corruptions, but they are anomalies.

You must learn to exchange with others by means of a look, but your look must not be an invitation, it must be simply amicable and undemanding.

Sèvres, January 1 1970

Chapter Fifteen

EMPTINESS AND FULLNESS:
POROS AND PENIA

There is a law which anyone who wants to be capable of acting intelligently and with efficacy in life must respect, and that is the law of polarity, which is based on the existence of the two poles, masculine and feminine, positive and negative, emissive and receptive.

You are all familiar, of course, with the very ancient custom that requires someone who goes to see a king, a prince or a sage to take him a gift: fruit, cattle or a work of art, for instance. In India, when you go to see a guru, you have to take him a gift of fruit; a single orange or mango will do, but you must never appear before him empty-handed. And, of course, you remember the three Wise Men from the East who took gifts of gold, frankincense and myrrh to the Infant Jesus. They, themselves, were kings and sages but they knew this law and they came to Bethlehem their hands full of gifts.

A person who is mobile and active, represents the masculine principle, whereas he who stays still, waiting for others to come to him – the Child Jesus in his crib, for example, or a king on his throne – represents the feminine principle. It is always the masculine principle that bestirs itself in order to approach the feminine principle and this means that it has to have something to give, it has to possess an abundance of gifts. The masculine principle represents abundance, plenitude, and the feminine principle represents the void, the emptiness that the masculine principle must fill to the brim with its gifts. This is the meaning of the tradition of bearing gifts, which dates from the very earliest times and which stems from a profound understanding of the laws of life.

As a matter of fact, Plato mentions this in his Symposium, in which Socrates relates how a rich man called Poros (Abundance or Resource), who was a guest at the marriage feast of Aphrodite, encountered the beggar-maid Penia (Need or Indigence). Poros and Penia met at night, in the garden, and fell in love and, from their union, was born a child who was none other than Eros. Love, therefore, is a result, a product, a child of the two principles: fullness or wealth and emptiness or poverty. It is always fullness that decides to bestow its wealth on emptiness, the void. The void is an abyss, a chasm that is waiting to be filled and it is fullness that approaches it to give it what it longs for.*

Suppose, therefore, that you are going to visit someone: this means that you are playing the part of the masculine principle and must possess abundance. Your hands must be full of fruit, flowers and gifts or your soul full of good thoughts and kind feelings; it does not matter which. The only thing that matters is not to be empty. The feminine principle is never enchanted or charmed by something that is empty, something inert, naked or destitute. Woman (matter) is only moved to admiration by those who possess wealth, fullness, strength. Imagine a man who goes out for a walk and passes a woman in the street: do you suppose that she will be charmed or attracted by him if he gives her a dull, sleepy look? Oh, of course, it is always possible; some women are so bizarre they might fall in love with him because of his 'moony' expression. But, generally speaking, women prefer a man who bowls them over with a

---

* See the supplementary note at the end of this chapter.

look full of passion. They say, 'There's a man for you.' A man, that is to say, riches, fullness, power, activity, dynamic energy. Isn't that the way things are? Yes, and this is the Book of Life... but you have to learn to read it.

If you are empty-handed, physically or symbolically, when you go to see your friends, they will end by losing all affection for you. They will say, 'What kind of a man is he? He is always empty when he comes and, by the time he leaves, he has emptied me, too,' and they will begin to be wary of you and keep you at arm's length. In the long run, they will close the doors of their heart and soul to you completely. This is how stupid people lose their friends: by always trying to take advantage of them. Don't go and see your friends, therefore, if you are really empty, if you cannot even take them a smile, a kind look, a few warm words, a gift that is alive. If you understand the profound meaning of this custom of bringing gifts to your friends, you will immediately be able to improve the way you behave.

But, let me take this a little further: when you go to a well or a spring with a bucket, what are you doing? You are playing the part of the masculine principle; you walk, you move from one place to another, whereas the spring is motionless; it stays where it is. But, once you get to it, if you don't switch your polarization, you will be unable to fill your bucket. For a time, therefore, you identify with the feminine principle, you become receptive and your bucket is filled with water. The spring, which is feminine in its immobility, is masculine in the water that flows from it, whereas you, who began by being masculine because you walk towards it, are also feminine in that you take your empty bucket to be filled. The water flows and fills your bucket and you go away, satisfied. You will say, 'All that is really too simple, too obvious.' Yes, but wait for the conclusion that can be drawn from this example.

What is your attitude when you approach God? God does not move, he stays where he is, so he represents the feminine principle. It is you who climb towards him, you who go in search of him, so you represent the masculine principle. At this stage it is you who must be full, who must take gifts to lay before him, you who must offer him your heart and soul, saying, 'Lord God, all I have is Yours.' Once you have given God everything, you are empty, you become the feminine principle, and it is then that God, who is an ever-flowing fountain, fills your soul and heart and you find yourself enriched, enlightened, full of strength and power, and you return home filled to overflowing. This is how polarization works. You must begin by being active, dynamic and full of initiative, that is to say, by meditating, thinking and concentrating. Then, when you have succeeded, like a bird that soars swiftly into the air and then, suddenly, floats on motionless, outstretched wings, you cease to be active, you make no further move, you simply float in peace, light and silence. At that moment you will feel that strength and blessings are pouring into you and filling you to overflowing.

Activity and passivity, two states whose different possibilities I have often experienced and which you, too, must learn to use. Someone who is perpetually in a state of activity is always tense and strained and incapable of achieving this euphoric state of repose and peace, this sensation of floating in a new world. On the other hand, you cannot achieve this second state without, first, actively triggering and stirring up currents. And if you say, 'Oh, it's not necessary to do that; I'd rather be receptive,' you will be like so many mediums who are too sensitive and fragile and who end by being ravaged and laid waste, because they have never learned to protect themselves. Not having known how to develop the masculine principle in themselves in order to defend and orientate themselves consciously and learn the ways of the invisible world, they expose themselves stupidly to every danger and fall a victim to all the chaotic, anarchic forces of nature. In order to avoid being exploited in this way, you have to begin by manifesting yourself as a man – active, energetic and dynamic – and only later, armed with this will-power, can you safely allow yourself to be passive, for all the emanations and harmonious, luminous radiations that you have set in motion will protect you and prevent hostile forces from entering and ravaging you. You have to learn to be both man and woman. This is an extremely important exercise, my dear brothers and sisters, and you must never forget what I have told you today.

Now, I would like to add something to what I said about fullness and emptiness. As you know, every gesture has magical significance. Consequently, you must never go to someone's house in the morning and greet him with an empty container in your hand – a bucket or bottle, a cup or a shopping basket, for instance – because, unconsciously and without meaning to do so, you will be wishing him emptiness, poverty and failure for the rest of the day. You will say, 'That kind of thing is not important; nobody pays any attention to things like that,' but the fact that other people are unconscious is no reason for you to imitate them. They can do what they like, but we are here to learn the laws of life, and to train ourselves to be conscious, to be aware and in control of ourselves in whatever we are doing. I beg you to get this into your heads; I have been saying it repeatedly for years, but it is as though I had never said anything: when you go to say good morning to your friends, leave your empty containers at a distance and take them something full, or place some good thoughts and feelings in your heart and wish your friends a good day. If you know how to work with the positive forces of nature, others will love and appreciate and respect you.

In some countries there are women, witches, who know the magic influence of a full or empty container and who deliberately appear on the doorstep of the person whom they want to harm, with an empty container in their hands, just as he is coming out of his house. One can cause a serious and, sometimes, fatal accident in this way, so you must never, never do it, even unconsciously and, above all, not on purpose, for the penalty you will have to pay will be terrible.

And let me add just one more thing: the person you are going to visit has a right to be surrounded by empty containers in his own home but you, as you are approaching him, must not be empty; it is up to you to fill up his empty containers. He who goes towards another must be positively polarized; he must arrive with his hands full. Perhaps one of you might say, 'I'm not empty; on the contrary, I'm chock full of anger, remorse and animosity and I'm going to share all that with him.' Well, of course, there are different kinds of fullness... But the kind I'm talking about is a luminous, divine fullness. Obviously, it is also possible to be full of dung and go around smelling to high heaven for the rest of eternity.

The Bonfin, September 1963

Supplementary note:

The void seeks out fullness in order to be filled; fullness is attracted to the void in order to fill it with its abundance. But the void is so immense that one wonders whether it can ever be filled. However, as fullness is also immense, they seem to have been getting along together since the beginning of time and this is what makes the world go round.

And what about the human soul? The human soul is a virgin and must, therefore, be receptive, poor and humble in order to attract the Spirit of God and be fertilized by him. When fullness meets fullness they repulse each other; but humility, which is a form of poverty, is also a form of richness, because it makes it possible to approach God. You have to be humble towards God if you want him to fill you with his abundance; he cannot do that if you are already full and puffed up with pride. With regard to human beings, the situation is different; if you want to help other human beings – or simply avoid being overwhelmed by them – you have to be full. In other words, you have to be rich in front of men and poor in front of God.

The Bonfin, July 23 1963

Chapter Sixteen

THE TEACHING OF LOVE
IN THE MYSTERIES

Yes, my dear brothers and sisters, we must love. 'But we do,' you will say, 'That is just what everybody does; everybody loves somebody.' Yes, I know, but perhaps their understanding of love is not quite what it should be. In the great initiatic sanctuaries of the past, in the Mysteries, adepts were taught that love was the sole condition for true perfection, true liberation. And what do we see, nowadays? Just the opposite: because of the way human beings understand and manifest love today, they degrade and shackle themselves and, if they learn anything, it is hell that they learn, with all its torment, jealousy and revolt. They learn, yes, but only what is negative. We need to get back to the science that was taught in the initiatic sanctuaries. I remember that science, for I was there at the time; no one can deal with these questions, today, if he has not had past knowledge of them.

I know, also, that some of those who are now in the Brotherhood studied these things in the past, but did not complete their studies; they left their initiatic schools to take up another kind of life and this is the reason for their difficulties, today. In order to recover their knowledge, they must start to live, once more, according to the rules and laws that were taught, at that time, in the temples. They cannot bring this knowledge back to the surface of their minds if they do not live according to the rules of initiation.

In the sanctuaries, the disciples were taught about the loving relationship they should have with their Creator, with his creation and with all creatures. This teaching is contained, also, in the Cabbalah, which is the science that concerns the Creator, the world and man. It is always the same science that has been handed down through the ages ever since heaven entrusted it to men through the intermediary of the archangel Raziel. Human beings could never have had any conception of this splendour, this immensity, if the archangels had not made it known to them through the great initiates.

As I have said, therefore, love – and, first and foremost, love of the Creator – was taught in the sanctuaries. Without that love, man would be incapable of progress of any kind, for there would be no point of contact, no link with the world above. It would be as though you cut the cable that connected you to the central powerhouse: you would be unable to light your lamps or use your electrical appliances. This is why the very first thing the hierophants taught their disciples was never to cut the link that connected them to the central powerhouse, the Lord. Then they explained to them how to get their inner appliances and lamps ready, how to clean and purify them before switching them on.

The quintessence of this teaching about love has been summed up in the Gospels: *'You shall love the Lord your God with all your heart, with all your soul, with all your mind, and with all your strength. And you shall love your neighbour as yourself.'* Yes, but in between man and God is something else that we must love; between man and God there is the world, that is to say, all the different regions of the universe with all their inhabitants. Here, too, a complete science exists which explains how to communicate with the spirits of a particular region: what words to pronounce, what gestures to make, what perfumes to use, what symbols to place around one and what clothes to wear. There are not many Christian books that mention the hierarchy that exists between human beings and God. But, when Jesus said, *'No one comes to the Father except through me,'* he was expressing part of the science that was taught in the sanctuaries, for he was presenting himself as an intermediary between the Lord and human beings, as a medium, a transmitter.

There is a vast, living hierarchy between earth and heaven, and this hierarchy is represented in the Bible in the form of Jacob's ladder. When Jacob left Mesopotamia in obedience to an order from the Almighty, he went to sleep, one night, with his head on a stone. As he slept, he dreamed that he saw a ladder reaching from the earth to heaven, and angels ascending and descending on it. This ladder is the angelic Hierarchy mentioned in the Cabbalah: Christ, who links earth to heaven. To be sure, the word 'ladder' is very far from conveying any sense of the splendour of that hierarchy, but we have to find words that give some idea, however inadequate, of what we mean.

In the initiations, this ladder, this hierarchy, was represented by the hierophant. This is why the disciples who were studying true love took him as their starting point in their ascent to the Godhead, for it is impersonal love that contains the greatest blessings. Unfortunately, human beings, who know so little about all this, prefer to love not the Lord or their instructor but a man or woman, at the risk of ending with a disaster on their hands. This is what they have learned: they are ready to reject every other kind of love and centre all their love on some man or woman, saying, 'At least this gives me something to hold on to; at last I have something to enjoy.' But what a price they are going to have to pay and what bitter disappointments they are storing up for themselves. They will see all their hopes in ruins, simply because they put their faith in something that cannot be relied on. If you count on someone who is not in contact with heaven, who has no interest in trying to develop qualities and virtues, it is as though you put all your merchandise in a boat with a hole in the bottom; it is obviously going to sink, and all your treasures will sink with it. This happens all the time.

But if a disciple loves God first, with all his heart and soul, and if he sees his instructor, his Master, as God's representative, then he will be sustained and illuminated by these two disinterested affections and, when the time comes for him to love a man or a woman, the situation will be quite different: he will be able to do so without danger and without any tragic consequences. Yes, because those two higher forms of love are there to protect and counsel him by giving him intuition, clairvoyance and wisdom. In this way he will know fulfilment because his love will exist in all three worlds. But, in the absence of the first two kinds of love, human love inevitably ends in ashes, regrets and heartbreak.

Yes, human beings are so blind and thick-skulled that they are ready to quarrel and disagree with both God and their Master, whereas they are ready to put absolute trust in any imbecile. How can they be so stupid? The Lord, who possesses all powers, all knowledge, and their Master who is ceaselessly in touch with the Lord and has no thought but to help and enlighten them... it is they that human beings distrust and oppose. They are ready to trust a drunkard, a libertine, a crook, but they refuse to trust a Master. And yet, it is he who should be trusted, because he is the only one who will never wrong them in any way. Even if you love your Master and tell him, 'All I have is yours; take it,' he will say, 'No, no. Keep it. I don't need it.' If I tell you that you should love your Master, it is not for his sake but for yours, because it is you who will make great progress thanks to that love. It is for you, not for him; he has other things to think about. There, that is how you should understand the question. When I say that you should have a Master and that you should love him, you must understand this in the broadest sense. He can be here, in the physical world, or in the invisible world, but you need a Master to help and enlighten you, a Master who is very exalted and disinterested, a true servant of God.

You need to love and, since it is possible to love God and a Master without danger, why go and give everything to some charming little nonentity? Love whoever you want to, but in third place; if you do that, your love for God and your Master will guide you and keep you safe. As it is, you are not safe: you will be left to weep and moan and tear your hair, night and day, complaining, 'I never knew he – or she – would be like that.' No, of course you didn't; and you never will know, because you never ask the only ones who are capable of enlightening you. Are you surprised by what I say? Yes, well, I'm surprised too. I'm surprised every day, in fact, but for a quite different reason: I am constantly surprised to see how human beings think and behave.

The Bonfin, August 16 1970

Chapter Seventeen

LOVE IS EVERYWHERE

It is love that people are looking for, not a particular man or woman. The truth of this can be seen in the fact that a man will abandon his wife (or a woman her husband) because he has found love elsewhere, with another woman. It was not the woman he wanted, therefore, but love itself. And if he still does not find it with the second woman, he will go and look for it with a third and, perhaps, a fourth. So, it is the love that counts, not the individual man or woman, otherwise they would never leave each other. And suppose, now, that someone finds the love he is looking for on a higher plane, he will not need to go in search of it again since he already has it. It is because people have not found it that they go in search of it in a man or a woman.

Love, in reality, is everywhere; it is an element, an energy, which permeates the entire cosmos. But human beings are not yet ready to receive it into themselves through their skin, their ears or their brains; they are content to find some little pockets of it concealed in a few parts of a man's or a woman's body. This is where they look for love and this is why they content themselves with a few crumbs, without realizing that it exists in profusion throughout the universe.

Love is everywhere, my dear brothers and sisters, and this truth was revealed to me by a plant for, as I have already told you, I learn many things from stones, plants, insects and birds. One day in Nice I saw a plant hanging in the air; it did not have to put down roots into the soil because it was capable of drawing the nutrients it needed from the air. I looked at that plant for a long time and it said to me, 'Since I have succeeded in finding the vital element I need – love – in the air, why should I bury myself in the ground like all the other plants? I possess the secret of how to draw whatever I need from the air.' What an example for us! It opens up new horizons and shows that we, too, can find what we need elsewhere than in the physical dimension where we habitually look for it.

For the time being we are going to have to let people go on as before and look for love in the traditional places but gradually, in the future, they will be better prepared to find it in the atmosphere, where it is disseminated like dew. For human beings are like plants; some of them draw their vitality from mother Earth, others from the air, the sphere of thought, and yet others from the sun, from God himself, for God is love. Take dew, for instance: dew is water vapour that floats in the air and becomes visible only in the morning, when it condenses on plants. A lot of plants have no gardener to look after them, so nature devised this way of helping them by scattering these pretty little drops of moisture that keep all vegetation alive. Nature has the responsibility of watering the plants and, every morning, all over the world, she sprinkles them with dew. What is dew if not a form of love that has condensed? And what are the sun's rays if not a form of love that is projected? So, you see, everything in nature is love.

Now, let's take the example of respiration. With few exceptions, human beings are not yet capable of breathing through the pores of their skin; their respiration is not yet complete or ideal. But there are some yogis who have succeeded in doing this and who receive all the energies and vital nutrients they need through their skin. This is something you can practise, yourselves, at sunrise; you can concentrate on absorbing the sun's rays through your skin and storing them up in your solar plexus. In this way, after months and years of practice, you will feel that tiny mouths, tiny doors, are beginning to open; man has always possessed these doors but has never learned to make them function. In the future, once he has begun to breathe through his skin, he will even be able to eat and drink less, because he will have learned to absorb subtler elements.

Why do people always need a woman or a man in order to feel love? This is the root cause of all limitations, misfortunes, difficulties and dependence. Love is life; it is absolutely indispensable to us. The initiates themselves cannot live without it, but they look for it and gather it from all around them and then they distribute in all directions. They are constantly immersed in love: they breathe, eat and contemplate love, they think of love ceaselessly. This is why they don't need women: they already have love. Love is in them and all around them, gushing up and sparkling like a spring of water, filling them to overflowing; their whole being bathes in love. Why should they look for it elsewhere? Why should they destroy this sensation of fulfilment for the sake of something that will bring burning coals pouring down on them? I am not against love; on the contrary, what I am saying is that you must learn to find it everywhere. For my part, that is what I do: I find love everywhere. In fact I find it in you, too. You don't realize this, but you would be amazed to know how much love you pour out on me.

You want to find love, you say; very well, but you keep looking for it in the same places as everybody else, in those well-known, hereditary places that are reputed to be so fantastic... and it's not there. Oh, there is a little bit of love there, but only a few particles, certainly not enough to satisfy those who thirst for the whole ocean. This means that you are going to have to look for it in other places as well. It is like the dew: before it condenses and settles on the trees, grasses and flowers, it already exists in space. Everything that exists on the physical plane can be found, in a purer state, elsewhere. All the elements that are now material once existed in an etheric state; it was only gradually that they became condensed into gasses, then into water and, finally, into earth. Why not try to find them in this subtler state, therefore, instead of always looking for them too low down where they are already mixed with all kinds of impurities? It was in this way that the yogis of India discovered that, by respiration, they could take all the elements necessary to life from the prana. Even Western medical science has finally discovered that it is the subtlest elements, vitamins and hormones, which are the most important for our health.

You, too, must learn to look for love on the etheric plane, for that is where you will find it and, up there, it is not just a few drops of dew but an ocean from which you can drink as long and as deeply as you want, and no one will condemn you for doing so. If you trespass on your neighbour's lawn, because you haven't got a garden of your own and you have been told that it's good to walk barefoot in the dew, don't be surprised at what happens to you. You would do better to leave the little drops of dew alone and go straight to the ocean. There is nothing to pay when you go to the ocean; it is there, waiting for you, immense, infinite and inexhaustible. The only thing is that it is a little higher up. But when you reach it, it will flood into you and give you the plenitude you are seeking.

Obviously, there can be a lot of problems in all this. If someone asks me, 'Does this mean that I should never have intercourse with my wife again? That I must completely give up that form of exchange if I want to discover the subtler form of love that you are talking about?' I would have to tell him, 'I cannot answer your question just like that; it's very complicated. You and your wife must be together in this; she must agree with whatever you decide. You must solve this problem together, otherwise it will end in tragedy. And whose fault will that be? Mine, of course: I shall be accused of breaking up marriages and destroying the family.' The trouble is that people misinterpret what I say, so they don't know how to go about it. First of all, the husband and wife must agree; secondly, they should proceed gradually and not cease having relations suddenly. Very few people are capable of changing their way of life from one day to the next; most people would simply make themselves ill if they attempted it. You should do what a smoker does when he decides to give it up: if he stops smoking from one day to the next he will be so ill that, two days later, he will begin again. But if he does it gradually his organism will adapt and, one day, he will manage to stop altogether without any painful symptoms. The important thing is that, whatever we do, we have to find the right way to go about it.

So, don't start blaming me and saying, 'Ever since I've tried to follow the Teaching I've been utterly miserable.' And before? Were you really happy? No, I don't think so. You may have seemed happy, because, when a person makes no efforts of any kind, he seems to be in peace. But, meanwhile, impurities are building up in him and, in the long run, they result in suffering of one sort or another. Whereas, if you decide to purify yourself, of course you will begin by suffering, because of the revolution going on inside you but, in the long run, the improvement will be permanent. This is what you have to understand. In the first case, behind a veneer of happiness and peace, you are on the road to ruin. If you are not living correctly, you may say, 'I feel fine; there's nothing wrong with me,' but you will be wrong: you are like a house with a beautiful facade but whose beams are rotting away, eaten by worms. At the moment it is still standing, but it cannot last. Don't put your faith in appearances, therefore. You may have had to put up with a few minor inconveniences since you have been in the Brotherhood, but that is no reason to pull back now.

Sometimes, when people fast, they have the same reaction: as soon as they begin to feel a little discomfort, a headache or a faster pulse, for instance, they panic and refuse to fast any longer. They felt better as they were before. They don't know that fasting is a kind of diagnosis; it shows them the weak points of their organism, the spots where impurities have accumulated. You should not abandon the practice of fasting just because of a little discomfort. On the other hand, of course, if you have never fasted before, you should not fast for five or six days at once. Here, too, you have to give your organism time to adapt: begin by fasting for one day; later you can extend this to two and, gradually, to three days. You have to use your reason and know the right methods. If you rely on appearances or don't know how to go about something, you will, obviously draw false conclusions[1].

True joy is not to be found in physical intercourse. Take the example of two young people who are in love: what joy and inspiration fill their lives at the beginning, when they have still not exchanged so much as a kiss. They get up in the morning and go to bed at night thinking of each other, and the mere fact that the other exists, that they are going to see and talk to them, is enough to turn them both into poets. They write each other notes; they give each other a rose petal and it becomes a potent talisman. But, as soon as they begin to embrace, to sleep together, all these subtleties disappear. Their joy is not what it was, they don't think about each other in the same way, the time has come for quarrels, for paying off little scores. To begin with they were in Paradise; why didn't they let this Paradise last a little longer?

I know that you are going to object that you can't go on for ever with nothing but homoeopathic doses, smiles and sweet words; that you need something more substantial. Very well, but don't be surprised, later on, and don't put the blame on anybody else, when you find that you have to eat the soup you cooked for yourself. If a life of light and poetry is not what

---

[1] For a fuller discussion of fasting, see *The Mysteries of Yesod*, Complete Works, vol. 7.

you really want, if you need something more substantial, I have no objection, I am simply warning you. I am obliged to talk to you about that other degree of love which is so immensely superior that no words can do it justice. Everything else pales beside this sublime love which depends on no one and nothing else, in which you can live without interruption and which embraces all creatures. Yes, thanks to this love and in spite of all their faults and failings, all creatures become beautiful and agreeable and you love them.

Sèvres, January 11 1970

Chapter Eighteen

A BROADER CONCEPT OF MARRIAGE, I

I

Most human beings limit their love to such an extent that, apart from their husband or wife, they forget about everybody but themselves; nobody else exists for them. As a matter of fact, they themselves don't exist; goodness knows where they are – lost somewhere in space. Human beings are not yet accustomed to a broader, vaster understanding of love. The love they know is reduced in breadth and scope, mutilated and impoverished; it is no longer the divine love that pours forth to quench the thirst of all creatures. True love embraces all creatures without taking root beside any one in particular, without restricting itself. The only problem is: what reaction will people have if their partner begins to love everybody? They will say that the Teaching encourages all sorts of odd behaviour and, instead of liberating themselves, they will remain chained to their old conceptions. Well, if that's what they want, let them have it.

This Teaching is addressed to those who, recognizing that the old way of life can neither protect nor save them nor make them happy and free to come and go in heaven, are looking for a new life. It has been there for a long time, that new life, waiting for human beings to find it, but it could not be revealed to them before, because they were not ready to receive it. They would have done too much damage if they had received these revelations sooner, so it was better to leave them in their fetters. As long as human beings were still crude and primitive, their liberty had to be curtailed, so they were given partners to prevent them from causing turmoil wherever they went. This Teaching is not for everybody; it is only for brains and souls who will not use their freedom to do harm.

Now, don't turn what I am saying upside down: I never said that you should not marry and have children. I simply say that husbands and wives must be taught a broader concept of marriage and be less possessive and jealous. A husband should rejoice to see that his wife loves everybody; a wife should be happy to have a husband who is so great-hearted, and both of them would still be both wise and pure. In this way, marriage, with all its splendid rules and traditions, would be preserved and, at the same time, if the husband and wife broadened the scope of their consciousness, they would understand that, in the past, they had been too narrow in their outlook, that it was time to open up their hearts and love all creatures without contravening any of the rules of fidelity and wisdom.

This is the true solution. We are not opposed to marriage, nor are we in favour of free love as it has been practised in certain countries (where, incidentally, after some years of experimentation, they found that it was no better and, instead of finding a third solution, the right solution, they went back to the traditional way). Human beings are funny creatures: they always go from one extreme to the other without ever finding a third solution. But there is always a third solution for every problem and this is what I look for. There is a third solution for the problem of love, the problem of how to behave in regard to love, too, and as long as human beings do not know it, they will never be satisfied. Those who have decided to remain celibate often sense that they are missing something and regret not being married, while those who are married are no happier, and they regret not having remained single. In other words, no one has found the right solution, the third solution. But, once they find this third solution, everybody, whether married or single, will always be happy and fulfilled.

Marriage must not be abolished. It has existed for so many thousands of years that it has become an atavism with human beings and to do away with it would entail all kinds of complications. Suppose that everybody said, 'No: no more families; everyone must be free to do whatever they like with any man or any woman. Freedom for all!' After a while, people would see that this led to all kinds of serious anomalies in every aspect of life, physical, social, economic and psychic, and they would go back to family life. Then they would get bored with the family again and start to give free rein to licentiousness, debauchery and loose living until, exhausted and disgusted, once more, they went back to the family. And in this way the pendulum would swing back and forth from one extreme to the other until, at last, the third solution was found. Don't look for this third solution either in the family or in free love; it resides in our intelligence. It consists in understanding that there are other aspects of love, even more wonderful ways of manifesting it, other vaster and purer expressions, in which the husband and wife try to have a nobler, more exalted conception of each other and give each other real freedom.

Most people are incapable of achieving this conception of love; too many obsolete tendencies within them protest and rebel against it. But when two highly evolved human beings marry, they give each other this liberty in advance; they both rejoice in their freedom to love all human beings, knowing that there is no question of taking advantage of this to do anything stupid. The wife understands her husband and the husband understands his wife and, together, they move forward on the path to heaven, becoming more and more fulfilled and luminous, for they are living the true life that knows no limits. This is the best solution.

If you cannot find a husband or wife who is ready to give you that freedom, if you can only find someone who always wants to impose limits on your love, then you would do better to remain single because then, at least, you will be free to love whoever you want and nobody will have the right to reproach you for it. For if people are so narrow, egotistical and possessive, it is not worth tying oneself to them and being miserable for the rest of one's life.

The Bonfin, August 15 1962

Chapter Nineteen

SISTER SOULS

Every human being possesses a sister soul. When man leaped like a flame, a spark, from the bosom of his Creator, he was two in one and each of his two halves was the perfect complement of the other; each was the identical twin of the other. Later, these two halves became separated, each of them taking a different direction and evolving in its own way. During the course of their evolution they sometimes meet and, if they recognize each other, it is because each carries the image of the other in the depths of his being; each has put his seal on the other. Every human being, therefore, carries the portrait of his sister soul within him; it may be a very hazy image, but it is there, and this is why every man and woman comes to earth with a vague hope of finding a soul who will fulfil all his needs and with whom he may be united in total harmony.

You all know this; every one of you has always held on to the belief that, one day, you would meet that dear soul whose face you know so well. You continue to bear this image within you even though it is so deeply buried that you cannot see it clearly. Every now and then you will see someone in the street and exclaim, 'That's it. There she is!' as though the image within you and the face you were looking at had suddenly fused into one. In that instant, your whole life is changed and you do everything you can to find that person again. When you find her, or him, and speak to her, everything becomes marvellous, you feel life coursing through your being and you make progress in every area. And then, after a period of intimacy, you are disappointed, because you realize that this person is not really the one you were looking for, so you leave her and begin searching again. The same thing can happen a second time: once again you think you have found your sister soul in another being; once again you love her, and joy and inspiration flow within you. But the outcome is the same: once again you realize that this is not the being you have been looking for.

'Then it was all a mistake?,' you will ask, 'That person was not my sister soul at all?' Yes and no. It was your other half that came to visit you from the world beyond and who used this person as a vehicle for, very often, the two halves do not reincarnate at the same time. What really happens then, when someone gets this feeling that they have found their sister soul? From where she is in the world beyond, our sister soul thinks of us, wants the best for us and wishes us to be happy and, thanks to the mysterious bond between us, she senses our aspirations to a higher life, to beauty. So, in order to be with us for a little while, she enters another being. This is why, for example, a woman may suddenly find her beloved in a man; her sister soul has entered a temporary abode in this man and lets her feel her presence and her love, without the man even being aware that he is inhabited. However, as the woman (or the man: the same is true for both sexes) usually feels the need for physical relations with the man she has fallen in love with, her sister soul is driven away in sorrow. Obviously, the man makes the most of this error on the part of the woman who has taken him for her sister soul and, gradually, she begins to see that he is a liar and a thief and that her beloved has left her. Perhaps she will come back again in another man.

But the same experience is likely to repeat itself over and over again until people really understand the sacred aspect of love. When this happens, the two halves will really be able to come together: they will love each other, clothe each other in robes of light and dwell in perfect happiness, with no desire to look for less subtle contacts. They will know that to do that would be to sever the bonds that unite them to the primordial Light. But, before people reach this happy state, they are going to have countless disastrous experiences that leave them saying, 'I have eaten and drunk all I could; I'm sated and miserable; I've never found any joy or happiness in possessing someone.' It is criminal for someone to have tried all the women in the world and never to have found a lasting illumination. But human beings are content with such fleeting illuminations.

Sister souls are everything to each other; no other being in the world can fulfil them in the same way. This means, therefore, that all those you have ever encountered since the very first of your many incarnations, all your husbands and wives, all your lovers or mistresses, have left you because they were not for you. You may have been together for a while, but only for a while, like a pot with a lid that doesn't fit. Whereas two souls that God has created together fit each other, nothing can tear them apart and they have no fear of being separated. When one of the members of a married couple is afraid of their partner being lured away from them (and, as we all know, there is no reason why this should not happen), it is a sign that that partner is not really the beloved sister soul. A woman loves a man and he goes off with another woman; a man loves a woman and she leaves him for someone else... But sister souls can never do that; they recognize each other with absolute certainty and never abandon each other.

Human beings encounter their sister souls twelve times in the course of their earthly reincarnations. More often than not, however, this encounter leads to death because the conditions of their lives prevent the accomplishment of such a perfect, absolute love. Shakespeare's Romeo and Juliet is about this encounter between two sister souls.

One day in the future, sister souls will bring children into the world, but the manner in which they do this will be very different from that of men and women today. They will wrap each other in light and project their love towards each other and, from the atmosphere thus created, will be born currents of forces that will envelop them both. That which the man then gives to his wife will be absorbed by her in utter purity and, at this point, their work will have already attracted another being, their child, who will, naturally, be in perfect affinity with its mother and father. At the moment of the appearance of the spirit who is to be their child, a fluid will be projected into the solar plexus of the mother with which to envelop this spirit and, within a few moments, the child will appear before its parents, fully formed and looking just like them.

Obviously, as things are today, human beings are not capable of bringing children into the world in this way, although the phenomenon can already be seen in spiritualistic seances. When a medium is in a trance, a clairvoyant can see a fluid coming from her solar plexus and forming a luminous cloud and, shortly afterwards, a spirit becomes visible and can even be photographed. A spirit that incarnates in this way cannot remain visible for long, because the matter that clothes it is reabsorbed by the medium. In the future, however, when human beings give birth to children in this way, the matter will not simply be lent to the spirit as in a spiritualistic seance: it will be a permanent gift. Of course, for this to become possible, one day, human beings are going to have to work until they reach a state of absolute purity. The way in which children are created today is the way of animals. Why do people do it in the dark and in private? Because they have the feeling that it is unworthy of the Sons of God. God is not so cruel or avaricious as not to have given human beings another way of doing this but, in descending so deeply into matter, they have lost the secret of that other way.

Now, don't misunderstand me; it is not because you have just found out that your husband or wife is certainly not your sister soul that you must turn round and get rid of them. On the contrary, you must realize that you are partners, that you have some work to do together and that you must get along well with each other until the time comes for you to separate.

Sèvres, February 28 1942

Chapter Twenty

EVERYTHING DEPENDS ON
HOW WE SEE THINGS

All the dramas that human beings experience stem from the fact that they do not know how to look at things. You have a weakness for women – or for men – and, although you struggle and struggle against it, you never manage to overcome it because you don't know how to struggle. You can give yourself a nervous breakdown, in fact, by deluding yourself that you are strong enough to stand up to such formidable forces on your own; it is vain and presumptuous to do so, for what weapons are you going to fight them with? You think that you can stand up to these forces, because you don't know their power, but you will always be defeated by them, they will always give you a thorough thrashing.

In an initiatic school a disciple learns that, in order to overcome, he has to ally himself to a higher power that will fight his battles for him. Let's take an example. Suppose you want to avoid being seduced by a pretty girl who is there, in front of you, scantily dressed and very provocative. If you rely only on your own strength, the more you wrestle with the problem the stronger will be the temptation to ravish her. Whereas, if you know how to see the girl as an aspect, a reflection, of the divine Mother, not only will you never succumb to temptation but you will rise to a very high plane and spend days in a poetic state of wonder. Think that, with each girl and each woman you meet, it is the divine Mother who is doing you the honour of showing herself to you, that you are looking at one of her manifestations, that it is her face, her glance and her smile – and thank her for it. In this way, you will see every daughter of the divine Mother not as a temptation, but as a source of delight and fulfilment and indescribable enrichment. Wherever you go, you will feel that the earth is peopled with creatures who are there to gladden your heart and fill you to overflowing.

People fall victim to their own lusts and weaknesses until they are fit for nothing but the hospital, all because they don't look at things in the right way. They are forever struggling and wrestling with themselves, whereas they only need to know how to see things. This is the whole secret. And if you are a woman and are tortured by your conscience, because you are always attracted to men, you need never torment yourself again: look at them, simply, as manifestations of the heavenly Father. If you learn to see his splendour, his intelligence and his strength in them, they will no longer be a temptation; you will be out of danger, no longer on the edge of an abyss. A great deal of nonsense has been written about these questions, simply because people have never possessed the initiatic science that would have shown them how to see them correctly.

Of course, there will be times when you come across a rather sorry image of the heavenly Father: a drunkard, for instance. But that doesn't matter; tell yourself, 'That's rather a distorted, twisted reflection... I'd better leave him for later.' What can you expect? It's not the heavenly Father's fault; he certainly wanted to manifest himself in that man but the wretched creature dragged him into every bar he came to and the heavenly Father has had to abandon him; he wanted to take care of him, but... Or, again, you meet an old shrew who screams abuse at you, but even she is an aspect of the divine Mother. To be sure, she has let all those blessings slip from her; she should reflect the splendour of the divine Mother better but she has not managed to do so; circumstances have been against her and she deserves to be pitied. Perhaps, at bottom, she is a kind-hearted old thing and, if you ever needed help, she might well be more ready to give it than many a pretty young girl.

Work with this idea, therefore, that men and women are representatives of the heavenly Father and the divine Mother, and you will see what progress you make and what joy and riches this idea gives you. Even if he does not know it, every man, because of his structure and his emanations, has the power to link you to the heavenly Father. See men as an opening, a door, through which you can go in search of the heavenly Father because it is he, and he alone, who contains all things, who is Perfection itself. Every other being is no more than an aspect. In fact, even if you assembled all the men on earth, they could never accurately represent the heavenly Father; they could be no more than a pale, wholly inadequate reflection of all that he is. Envisage every man you see, therefore, as a bridge, an open door that allows you to approach the heavenly Father and, within five minutes, you will have almost forgotten about the person himself; your head will be filled with the heavenly Father. You don't need to talk to someone or get to know him: see him simply as an occasion for you to establish a link with your heavenly Father, be grateful to him for that, and then be on your way.

And, if you are a man and you meet an adorable young girl, look at her and try to admire the beauty of the divine Mother. Who do you think gave that girl her beauty, after all? She herself? If she had done so herself, she should be even more beautiful. As it is she cannot add a single hair to her head, nor add nor subtract a single millimetre from the length of her nose. Was it her knowledge of higher mathematics that enabled her to give such harmonious proportions to her body? She may never have done anything to deserve the marvels she manifests and, in that case, a higher intelligence must have given them to her so why not, rather, be enraptured by that intelligence? You see: if you reason correctly, you will always be obliged to seek out the author, the creator; you will want to say, 'Divine Mother, how can You make something so perfect? What intelligence You must have to be able to produce such pure, luminous, expressive forms. I admire You so much.' Stay with the divine Mother for a moment, speak to her and, in the meantime, the girl will have gone. But, don't regret her going. It is not she who matters: she has simply been an occasion for you to rise to the Being who gave her so many beautiful gifts. It is not the girl who deserves your love and consideration; still less is she worth your being troubled and unhappy and ruining your life because of her.

Try to understand, my dear brothers and sisters: all weaknesses, anomalies, seductions and transgressions are caused by not seeing things correctly. You see no further than the man or girl in the flesh, their physical body. Obviously, in these conditions, how can you expect not to succumb? You let yourself fall into the clutches of tremendous forces, and that's the end of you.

You have never thought of it that way, have you? And how did I discover these truths – and many more, besides? If you only knew how many more. But how can I communicate them to you? You're not ready. Even what I have been saying today will not really be understood or grasped and put into practice. You will be doing well if you have understood even five per cent of it. Even those who come here don't know the value of what they can learn in order to transform their lives. It all seems so remote, so impossible and unrealistic.

To be sure, it is difficult, I know that. But try to understand, all the same, because it will give you the key you need, otherwise you will flounder along, moaning, 'I can't resist, I can't do it.' And it will be true: you won't be able to resist, because you have never taken the trouble to understand what has been revealed to you. Learn to look, therefore, to see things correctly. I know what tragedies many families experience: if it is not the husband who cheats his wife, then it is the wife who is unfaithful to her husband. Their lives are a tissue of lies. But if they knew how to see things correctly they would both be strong and happy.

The Bonfin, July 1965

Chapter Twenty-One

A BROADER CONCEPT OF MARRIAGE, II and III

II

I have never reproached anyone for wanting to be rich. To my mind it is quite normal and I respect that desire: it is intelligent and only right to want to be rich. In fact, I want to be rich, too, so we understand each other: we are both seeking wealth. The only thing is that I wonder whether, when you have got what you want, you will be satisfied with it. As long as you have not found that other wealth, the wealth that Christ was talking about when he said, *'Lay up for yourselves treasures,'* what you have will not be worth much. This instinct to seek and amass treasure was put into man by God himself. The trouble is, though, that people look for it down below instead of looking for it above; that's the great difference.

As for you, if you look for wealth within you (for 'within' and 'above' are the same thing), it will satisfy you completely and you will feel rich, happy and free. I'm afraid I cannot say the same for others. So we have to say to human beings, 'You long for wealth and that is good, wonderful, but try to raise that longing to a slightly higher plane.' And I could say the same for man's sexual desire: who gave human beings this tendency to seek a man or woman? That, too, was the Lord's doing. And unfortunately they seek them only on the physical plane so that, even when they do find a partner, they are not happy.

All human beings want to find love; that is normal and legitimate. But they must ask themselves whether it is enough

to look for love only in one region, or if they should not also
look for it on a higher level. If you put the question this way
you will find the solution to many of your problems and avoid
a great deal of grief and tribulation. There is nothing wrong
in looking for love on the physical plane as long as you see it
as a starting point, a springboard that will help you to seek
the true love that exists on a higher plane. I know that what
you are looking for is your sister soul; everybody looks for
their sister soul except me. Why is this? Because I have already
found her. I know that that is going to make you wonder which
of the young girls here... But it's no good looking round you:
my sister soul is all the women in the world. To have only
one woman is asking for trouble but if you have every woman
in the world you'll be safe. So, all the women on earth are
my sister soul. This is how I look at it. On the higher plane, all
women represent just one Woman. On the higher plane, there
is only one Man and one Woman, Adam Kadmon and his
Beloved, whose reflection can be seen here, on earth, in a
multitude of men and women. There is only one Woman,
therefore, and it is she who is my sister soul. Each one of you
will ask, 'Am I included?' Yes, of course: everyone is included
in my sister soul.

Anyone who thinks that he has found his sister soul has,
in fact, found only a reflection of that sister soul who exists
above; it is not really her; it is only a reflection glimpsed in
another man or woman. Actually, the truth of this is shown by
the fact that each woman on earth reflects only one tiny part,
one feature, one aspect of the beauty of the cosmic Woman,
in her skin, her eyes or her hair, etc. All that beauty that has
been distributed to all the women of the world is the beauty
of the one, unique Woman, the cosmic Woman, the divine
Mother, who contains all splendour and all perfection. If you
are looking for perfect beauty, therefore, look upwards, to the
divine Mother, the Perfection of all splendour, all virtues. And
all the men on earth, each in his own way, some more and some

less, reflect a tiny part of the strength and beauty of the heavenly Father. If you love just one man or one woman, therefore, you can never be wholly satisfied, never truly fulfilled, because he or she does not possess every aspect of beauty.

Naturally, what I am saying must not cause you to neglect human beings and devote your love exclusively to the heavenly Father and the divine Mother. The father of a family, for instance, is a symbol of the heavenly Father, so you must love him and see him as a means of approaching your heavenly Father. And if you have an instructor, a Master, he too is a representative of the heavenly Father and the bond between you and your Master will make it easier for you to approach God himself. But don't delude yourselves: he can lead you to the heavenly Father, but he himself is not the heavenly Father. Everything, therefore, depends on how you see things. Beings such as Jesus and Buddha can help us to approach the heavenly Father more rapidly, because they represent him more perfectly than the father of a family, for instance, for how many men are capable of filling that role adequately? The father of a family may be a drunken, dull-witted illiterate but, from the purely symbolic point of view, he still represents the heavenly Father. And the mother, even if she is an ill-tempered shrew – who has never been tamed – it makes no difference: she represents, however inadequately, the divine Mother.

Don't think that, when the true philosophy prevails, that will be the end of love and marriage; on the contrary, it is then that human beings will love each other in the right way, because they will see things in their true light. Do you really think that it is intelligent for a girl to forget the rest of the world and cling to a little whippersnapper – even if he does have an adorable moustache – as though he could satisfy her every need? The need to love is a natural need but we have to know what to focus our love on, who to love and how. Get married, have children and be faithful to your husbands but don't delude yourselves: a husband and children cannot give you more than they have got.

For my part, I have studied only one path, I know only one thing: the power of love. We must learn how to love, for love is the only thing that can lead us all the way to the highest peak; nothing else can do it. A false understanding of love which leads to its energies being poorly controlled and regulated and aimed in the wrong direction, always results in hysteria, neurosis and depression. Love must always be brought onto a higher plane, raised to a higher realm until, at last, it reaches the realms of the heavenly Father and the divine Mother.

Sèvres, December 31 1963 (Morning)

III

I was talking to you, this morning, about the great universal Soul, the divine Mother, of which all women are a reflection. I did not say that men should love only the divine Mother, present in all the women in the world, and exclude all thought of marriage. Very few men are capable of this; most of them are capable of loving only one woman at a time, at least for the moment. Well, there is nothing wrong in loving one woman, but why not see her as representing all the women in the world? You will object that your wife would be far from delighted to hear you say, 'Darling, you represent all the women of the world to me.' True, but if women are also taught to see all the men in the world in their husband, this difficulty would be ironed out. I am well aware that the very imperfect culture we have today makes this extremely difficult, but given time and education it will come. One day, men and women will not be so jealous, narrow and personal. Besides, why are they jealous? Because they are ignorant. Let me prove this to you: when a married man is at peace it is because he is ignorant. If he knew all that went on in his wife's head and how many other beings go in and out and take something from her, he would not be so complacent. His wife is in communication, also, with entities of earth, water and air. When she looks at the sun, how many angels are with her, going up and down, kissing her, giving her presents? And her poor simpleton of a husband never says a word, because he doesn't see what is going on. It is only on the physical plane, if somebody actually touches her, that he reaches for his gun. And where she is concerned it is much the same, although to a lesser degree perhaps, for a man is less active on the psychic plane than a woman, so he communicates less frequently with the entities of the invisible world.

I am well aware that human beings will not find much room in their heads for this philosophy, because they have worked for thousands of years to establish a certain order of things; in fact, if you try to get them to step outside their traditions, you can even be in serious danger. But you must know this, my dear brothers and sisters: if you want to be free, happy and useful, if you want to live in the infinite, then you must try to find beauty, the beauty that exists in all women, in one Woman on high. See her and love her as an image of surpassing beauty in your mind, an image that contains and expresses everything that is beautiful, all colours, music and perfumes, all sweetness, life itself. To be sure, if disciples do this, it will not prevent them from loving other men and women but, as their hearts and souls are free to appreciate, love and admire the things of heaven, they will always be protected against giving in to temptation. And if, despite everything, they decide to get married without abandoning this heavenly philosophy, I am absolutely certain that they will be much freer and live in peace, light and joy.

If you are attached to one man, he will, of course, be very pleased and proud to see that you are his slave, that you can't get along without him, but there is no guarantee that you, yourself, will be particularly happy. And in the reverse situation, if it is the man who is so attached, so entangled and enslaved, the woman's vanity will, of course, take great satisfaction in the fact that the poor nincompoop can't get along without her, but is that a good situation for him? For thousands of years, men and women have chained their partners to them in order to satisfy their vanity. The fact that this might run counter to truth and, even, to common sense, does not matter as long as they themselves, their personality, is satisfied; never mind about truth or common sense. Men and women become gaolers for each other. But, when human beings are more enlightened about the question, this state of affairs will change. You will protest, 'It will mean the end of the family; it will lead to disorder and anarchy.' No, you need not fear that, because this kind of love is true love that will never stagnate; it always advances, always expands and flows and rises to the Lord. A man and wife will understand and agree with each other, they will work and scale the heights together. They will be partners, associates, with no jealousy between them and, at the same time, they will have a beneficial influence on the whole world.

Sèvres, December 31 1963 (Evening)

Chapter Twenty-Two

ANALYSIS AND SYNTHESIS

The Master reads the Meditation for the day:

'Analysis is a descent into matter and synthesis is an ascent towards the spirit. The higher one goes, the less detail one sees but, at the same time, one begins to get a view of the whole and to discern a greater variety of facts and objects. The higher one goes, the greater the need to synthesize. It is this synthesis that makes it possible to discover unity, the single principle that links all things together as one and, in this way, to advance towards true knowledge. To possess knowledge is to look at things from the highest possible point so as to see everything, and this knowledge brings with it power, health and joy. Power, health and joy can only be attained through the unification of all one's energies, by making all one's energies converge on one spot, on a point where divergence is no longer possible.'

This understanding of analysis and synthesis will, no doubt, surprise you, because no one has ever given this definition of them before. And yet, it is perfectly accurate. Analysis is a descent into matter: if you want to analyse things, you have to get closer to them and break them down into separate elements in order to study them more easily. Gradually, however, this separation of the elements ends in death. In fact, death is simply the ultimate, perfect analysis. Birth, on the contrary, is a synthesis: the elements come together and form a unity and a child is born.

The birth of a child is a symbol of the synthesis of all the different energies and particles.

Synthesis is life; analysis is death. This is why the modern tendency to analyse everything, which is so widespread, is dangerous. All specialists, for instance, are analysts. They concentrate on one subject, one organ, and neglect all the rest of the human being or of the universe. They are moving towards death, therefore. To be sure, specialization is necessary; we need specialists who know the details, but by dint of analysing everything one ends by losing sight of the whole.

Modern science works more and more with analysis and is constantly discovering smaller and smaller particles of matter; through analysis it decomposes, dislocates and disintegrates. And it tries to apply the same method to the study of human beings: split them open and cut them up into little bits. This tendency to split things up is so strongly emphasized and encouraged in every branch of science that it has even changed the moral and spiritual life of human beings: each individual tends to isolate himself, to set himself apart from others, and hostility, partisanship and war are the results. This is what comes of analysis. On the national level, patriotism, for instance, is often no more than a manifestation of this philosophy of universal isolation. Everybody is in favour of analysis: of dividing, separating, dislocating and tearing things apart. Even within the family unit, father, mother, parents and children are all so analytical that they have become completely intolerant; they spend their time splitting hairs. No one seems to understand that they should be paying much more attention to synthesis, because synthesis is love, mutual understanding and harmony.

Everybody rushes to analyse everything; everybody relies on analysis and their craze for analysis leads them to study microbes and disease. If human beings were healthy, if they relied more on synthesis, they would not need so much analysis. Why are people always analysing things, their blood, their urine and goodness knows what else? Because they have been analysed so much already that they need to live in a climate of analysis. Live in a climate of synthesis and you won't need analysis any more. You won't know what is in your urine, perhaps, but you won't need to, because you will be healthy. Everybody is in favour of analysis, of separation: even Brittany and Corsica are for analysis. Well, when everybody has become an analyst, France will be well and truly analysed... analysed to bits. As for me, I am on the side of synthesis; I am for all countries becoming one country. When this becomes a reality, life will flow freely, for synthesis is life, synthesis is eternity, immortality. But I know that very few will understand me; their mentality has been too distorted by the idea propagated throughout the world by newspapers, books, films and so on: the idea that we must continually uproot, exterminate and dissect things.

In fact, I will go even further and say that human beings, who choose only one woman or one man, are analysts and that this is why they have so many problems and so much misfortune and grief: because they have eliminated everybody else. They don't rejoice in anyone else, they can't even see anyone else, they don't want to know anyone else, all their attention is concentrated on one person. But in the Universal White Brotherhood we teach people to become synthesists, because we want to bring the whole world together, to love the whole world and not just one person, who will bring us an endless succession of problems. Oh, of course, I know that this makes you indignant. You think, 'How can he dare to talk like that about love and marriage and everything that is most sacred? He does nothing but disparage and belittle them.' Not at all, I am simply explaining how things really are from a philosophical point of view. The question of whether you prefer this or that is your business; I am certainly not going to meddle. All I do is explain things, in all innocence, and you cannot object to that.

Love is a synthesis: when you love someone you want to approach them, be with them, unite yourself to them. One learns by analysis, one feels and lives by synthesis. With analysis we cannot feel much and with synthesis we may not learn much but, at least we feel, we are stretched, we experience rapture and ecstasy. In fact, if human beings are less and less capable of experiencing divine, heavenly states, it is because they are too committed to analysis. When you first meet someone, don't you begin to analyse him? You look at his nose, his mouth, his gestures, his strengths and weaknesses, his profession and his income. Whereas, if you love someone, you don't want to know all that; you love him as he is, you have a feeling for the whole person, you vibrate in unison with him. This is synthesis. If, at some point, you are annoyed with him, you immediately begin to analyse and cut him up in little bits. Then, when you remember that you love him, you are ready to forgive him because, once again, you are looking at the whole person and forgetting the details. Synthesis does not dwell on minor details and, in this, it is just the opposite of analysis which not only dwells on them but, also, magnifies them so much that, for the sake of one flea, it burns the whole blanket. Because of one little failing, one is ready to massacre someone. The fact that that person is a son of God makes no difference; people have no eyes for that, they see only his defects.

Towards the end of the passage I read a moment ago, it says, 'It is synthesis that makes it possible to discover unity, the single principle that links all things together as one and, in this way, to advance towards true knowledge. To possess knowledge is to look at things from the highest possible point so as to see everything...' Yes, true knowledge is to be found in synthesis. The knowledge that can be obtained through analysis is not true knowledge, it is incomplete and superficial. You cannot know much about anything if you study its elements separately. To know something as it really is, you have to put all the elements together so that they produce something that they did not possess when they were separated; and that something is life. True knowledge is only to be found in life. Separate the elements and life is no longer there. The fact that a given element has specific properties and a specific smell or taste or weight is not essential knowledge, because there is no life in it. But, once you put all the elements together, something new happens and that something new is life. You can know all the properties of all the elements but if you have not found life it means that you have not found true knowledge. True knowledge, the knowledge that enables you to see the whole, is the knowledge of unity. Unity is the one most essential factor because it makes it possible for all your forces and all your energies to converge on one point. When this happens, these forces work together in peace and perfect harmony and you become really powerful, for unity belongs to the spirit.

If human beings do not hold this philosophy today, it is because they have chosen the path of matter. In itself, this is good, magnificent, and leads to many discoveries and great acquisitions. The only thing is that, if they stay on this path, they will find themselves so far from the unity of spirit, which, alone, is capable of maintaining harmony between individuals, they will become so hostile and egotistical, that they will end by destroying themselves. Whereas, if they choose the path of the spirit and turn their steps towards unity, love and synthesis, it will be possible for the Universal White Brotherhood to exist throughout the world, for all human beings will want to be united, to sing together, to rejoice and learn together. This is synthesis; it is not a question of being glued to each other like the elements of an object but of working together to establish the Kingdom of God, the Golden Age on earth.

By following the path of matter, human beings are allowing themselves to be destroyed. They think they are freeing themselves, whereas, in fact, they are burying themselves. They refuse to listen to the initiates, they know it all. Well the day will come when they will be completely crushed under this burden of matter that they are so attached to. If you work in the realm of matter while adopting the point of view of the spirit, you will have authority over it: it will obey you, because it will recognize your great strength. Otherwise, it will not obey you; it will say, 'Aha, I've succeeded in getting him into my clutches. He's ready to serve my every wish or whim. So much the better; now I can take advantage of him and make him my slave.' Matter, you see, is not afraid of man. If man spurns the spirit, he will just have to take what's coming to him, because no one has ever succeeded in freeing himself from matter except through the spirit; on the contrary, he becomes more and more tightly bound, chained, fettered; things inevitably end badly for him.

Believe me, here in the Universal White Brotherhood, you have a Teaching which can bring you eternal life. The only thing is that you must completely change the way you think and the way you live. For years, now, I have been showing you how to do so, and those who are here for the first time, must study and practise. It is no good thinking that you can understand and straighten out everything in one day. A student went to Germany, one day, to see a very famous professor of natural science, and said to him, 'Sir, I want to study natural science, but I want to complete my studies much faster than other students; is that possible?' 'Yes, it's possible,' replied the Professor, 'Look at nature: she only takes a few months to produce a pumpkin but she takes a hundred years to produce an oak tree. Which do you want to be: a pumpkin or an oak tree?' And I ask you the same question: do you want to be a pumpkin or an oak tree?

The Bonfin, August 25 1974

Chapter Twenty-Three

LOVE IS LIKE THE SUN:
IT ORGANIZES LIFE

I

Organization implies life; it is life that organizes things. Let water flow freely and it will arrange the sand and pebbles in its path. Let life flow freely and it will organize everything and, when life ceases to flow, everything disintegrates. In winter, when there is no sun, nothing grows and, then, with the light and warmth of spring, life begins to flow again, seeds stir and germinate and start sprouting. And what about man? As long as the spiritual sun does not shine, the divine life cannot flow in man, either, and all his seeds stagnate.

Everybody, even children, know that the sun causes seeds to germinate but they have not really understood what this means. If they had, they would look for the spiritual sun and seek to expose themselves more and more to its rays of wisdom and love so that it might cause the virtues, talents and qualities that God has sown in them to germinate. We need a spiritual sun, not only a physical sun, and it is thanks to that spiritual sun that the rivers will flow, the birds sing, the trees bear flowers and fruit.

There is a great deal that could be said about the word 'organization.' Human beings always understand it in the purely mechanical sense, but this is wholly inadequate. The great 'organizer' is love. When human beings love, they don't need any other organization, it happens spontaneously; each individual knows exactly what he has to do and everything runs smoothly. But take away love and you have to resort to threats and punishment, and even then nothing really works. If there is love in a family, things sort themselves out spontaneously, but if you take away the love and try to enforce order with a machine-gun, you won't succeed. When true love reigns throughout the world, there will be no more need to inflict rules and regulations on human beings, they will know what they have to do and do it, in perfect harmony with each other. Only love organizes things and causes them to grow and blossom. If there is love in a family or in society, you will never need to say, 'Do thus and so, and woe betide you if you don't.' Everybody will be taking pleasure in doing what they have to do; they won't need a law to oblige them. Laws are no longer necessary where there is love.

Law was instituted the day that love disappeared from amongst men. In fact, when men were still truly capable of loving and remaining faithful to each other, marriage did not exist as an institution either. It became an institution because human beings no longer knew how to love; they would marry and separate without even knowing why, so laws, sacraments and so on had to be invented in order to hold them together. When two people truly love each other, do they really need marriage licences, contracts, magistrates or clergy? And if they are determined to get a divorce, no amount of contracts, magistrates or clergy can do anything to prevent it. When true love is present, it doesn't need any props to make it last for eternity, not even the priest's blessing, because God has already given it his blessing. God is present in the love of those who love each other truly; in fact, it is their love that is the blessing.

I am not opposed to marriage and I am not opposed to a priest's blessing; I am simply explaining that they are human institutions which, in the absence of love, cannot really solve anything. This does not mean that you should not go to the

Registrar's office or to church to legalize your union. I am simply saying that those who love each other are already married by nature, even though they may not know it, whereas those who do not love each other, even if they have been duly married in church or in a Registry office, are not married in the eyes of nature.

Sèvres, May 8 1966

II

The understanding of human beings has sunk to such depths that they have mortified everything. For them, neither the earth nor the sun is alive, still less are they intelligent beings; man himself is the only intelligent being. But how could intelligence suddenly appear in the human brain if it did not already exist somewhere else? If man created his own intelligence, one is tempted to ask why he didn't do a better job of it: 'Why are you so dense and short-sighted? Since you are the author of your own intelligence, why didn't you give yourself a little more of it?' Logic obliges us to recognize that the intelligence that is partially manifested in the human brain, exists everywhere, and that human beings, through ignorance, are hindering their own evolution by mortifying everything.

The truth is that everything is intelligent, everything is divine, even rocks, even metals. Minerals represent the lowest rung on that immense ladder of life that reaches to the Lord himself, but they are alive. And the work of initiates is this: to get human beings to perceive this life throughout the universe and to be in communion with its purest and most intense aspects. This is why I lead you to the sun: if you know how to look at the sun, how to think of the sun and how to love the sun, it will help you to reach the higher levels of life; you will be creating a different current in your cells and your organism will begin to function differently, to emanate something subtle which, little by little, will attract the love of the whole world. For what human beings are really looking for is life. This is so cruelly true, in fact, that a woman can look at the face of the dead husband she adored and say, simply, 'Bury him.' This was the man who meant everything to her, whose looks, strength and intelligence she admired so much. But, now that he is dead, does she want to keep his body by her side? No; there is no more life in him, she has to give him up. We cannot cling to a body once the life has gone out of it; no one loves a corpse.

More and more, human beings are becoming corpses inwardly; they are stiff and cold: no warmth, no love, nothing magnificent emanates from them, and the poor wretches believe that this is how to succeed in life. No, no; they must begin by coming alive – and the only way to come alive is to emanate love. This is something that is very easy to practise: take a moment when nobody is about, for instance, raise your right hand and project all your love to the universe, to the stars, to the angels and archangels, saying, 'I love you, I love you, I love you; I want to be in harmony with you.' Gradually, as you get into the habit of emanating something vibrant and intense, you will become a living source, a fountain of love. Human beings think that it is safer to hide behind a cold, sinister mask that expresses neither love nor kindness; they don't see how detrimental this is to themselves. Just because some idiot has set the fashion of assuming a stony, frozen attitude, they think the clever thing to do is to imitate him, and now everybody imitates everybody else, as though they had found the crowning point, the peak of evolution. But this is idiotic; you must learn to emanate love so as to be alive, so that everything about you comes alive: your face, your eyes – everything. Sometimes, when I look at a person's eyes, I can find no response, nothing vibrates; their eyes are like stones. I cannot look at eyes like that, I have to turn my head away. Their eyes are dead. When will human beings begin to understand that it is life we love, not death?

You must get into the habit of vibrating, day and night, of constantly giving something of yourself to all the creatures of heaven and earth, of imitating the Lord and penetrating them with your love. For this is what the Lord does: he is only interested in infiltrating into his creatures so as to infuse his life and his qualities into them. Yes, this is how he works: by infusing his love into the whole of his infinite creation. It is thanks to this infusion of divine love that all the particles and currents harmonize with each other of their own accord. You can prove this for yourself: if someone has a headache, for instance, or a pain in his solar plexus, you can put your hand, very lovingly, on the part that hurts and, because of that love, the unruly particles that have been dashing about in all directions slip calmly back into place and the negative particles, that had infiltrated and caused the disturbance, are driven out. If your love is very strong and powerful, you can do this; otherwise, it is useless even to try.

If you want to be alive, love. 'Ah, now I understand,' you will say, 'I must go out and look for a man – or a woman.' No, no; that's not it at all; that would be inviting death. Every expenditure in this area is an invitation to death, spiritual death. Every time you squander this quintessence, which belongs to the brain, senselessly and uselessly, you weaken and coarsen yourself. And those who are simply inhibited are no better off, for they end by making themselves ill. The solution, therefore, is to send your love up to heaven; in this way it will not stagnate and accumulate until the dam bursts and everything is flooded. This is why we must love; night and day, we must love and send our love to every creature that needs it. When I come in to this hall and greet you, I send you all my love and, although you may not see it, it is I who feel happy and fulfilled in doing so. Why have you never understood the importance of greeting each other with love? When we greet each other, the angels and archangels who see us should be moved to say, 'Oh, how lovely! What beautiful light! Let's go down to those beings who greet each other with so much love.'

People meet and part from each other with no sign of love. Look at married couples: they kiss each other on the cheek, 'Goodbye darling; goodbye darling.' But the kiss is empty; it's a habit, a purely conventional gesture and that is very bad. Why kiss if that's all it is? When you kiss someone you must put something into your kiss that vivifies and resuscitates the other. Human beings have not yet learned what it means to embrace or how and when to embrace each other. A man will go and embrace his sweetheart when he is feeling dejected, because he is looking for consolation but, along with his kisses, he gives her all his misery and despair and she, poor girl, absorbs all that and then it is she who becomes ill. Men and women are constantly exchanging things and the Lord alone knows what it is they exchange... or rather, it is the Devil who knows. There is no law against embracing someone; on the contrary, but you must know when and how to embrace them so as to communicate eternal life to them.

I'm afraid, my dear brothers and sisters, that if I explained to you why I say that you don't even know how to embrace your beloved, you would be horrified with yourselves. In your own opinion, everything you do is exemplary, perfect. In the opinion of initiates, however, you are still very far from perfection.

The essential thing is life, love – for life and love are one and the same thing. This is why you must drag yourselves out of your present stagnant, prosaic, unexceptional way of life and aim for the highest ideal, that of emanating divine life, divine love. Don't say, 'I can't do it; I'm not sufficiently evolved; I might as well give up.' Even if your ideal is unattainable, impossible, don't abandon it; it is precisely because it is unattainable that it is so glorious. A goal that is readily attainable is not worth much. Everybody clings to things that can easily be reached, but I have always been deformed in this respect: I have always gone after something which I have known in advance can never be achieved, because it is too great, too exalted. Yes, but this is what stimulates me, this is what makes my life poetic and fills me with enthusiasm. If I fixed my sights on a more accessible target I would lose my enthusiasm. Psychology has never paid enough attention to this aspect of things. Perhaps you will say that this is not a question of psychology; on the contrary, that is just what it is: true psychology. Don't ask yourself if you are capable or incapable, therefore: just set to work to emanate divine life, divine love.

The Bonfin, July 14 1975

Chapter Twenty-Four

A MOTHER'S LOVE

Picture to yourselves a young girl who, before marrying and having children, gives first place in her heart to the love of God, purity and wisdom. She spends time, every day, in reflection, meditation and prayer, for she sincerely wants to lead an exemplary life. Then, one day, she marries and has a baby and, from that moment, it is her marriage, her family life and the life of her child that occupy first place in her heart and all the rest is forgotten. Now, I would like to analyse this attitude.

Of course, I know that everybody will say that this young woman is doing the right thing; it is only normal for a mother to sacrifice her spiritual life for the sake of her child. After all, she is a mother and it is her child; every father and mother will back her up in this. For my part, though, I refuse to go along with this point of view: this young mother has forgotten everything else; nothing is more important than her baby; she is ready to break all God's laws for the sake of her child. In fact, if he falls ill or dies she will even be very angry with the Lord and accuse him of being cruel and unjust. Everybody praises and admires such love – everybody but me, that is, for the fact that she loves only her own child and has no love to spare for other children or for God himself shows that it is really herself that she loves in her child; she is thinking more of herself than of him. Look at what she is really doing: she forgets about God and the light in order to devote herself wholly to her child and, in so doing, she is keeping him from all that is divine, from true life. Her child will never benefit from all that immensity, from the only thing in which he would find happiness and immortality, because her stupid love makes her snatch him away from it. Although she believes that she is looking after him, in fact, by keeping him away from light and harmony, she is leading him towards hell.

There is a traditional misunderstanding here, therefore, which has prevailed for thousands of years. A mother who truly loves her child must never turn him away from heaven, for it is only in heaven that human beings can find fulfilment. If she neglects God and thinks of nothing but her child, her thoughts will contain nothing divine and she will have only dead elements with which to nourish her child.

A mother must never attempt to care for her child without, first, turning to God for the life which she then transmits to him. In their stupidity, many mothers think that if they are not constantly paying attention to their child, he will die. On the contrary: he will resuscitate. Even if he were to die while her attention was turned to God, when she came back, she would bring him back to life. But, if she is always by his side and never turns to God, she could never bring him back to life if he died. You will say that it is very difficult to understand me. It is not so difficult: it is simply that if, in the midst of her occupations, a mother never turns to God – that is to say, to all that is alive and luminous – she will not be capable of radiating the luminous particles her child needs in order to become an exceptional being. Her love will be very commonplace and it will produce a very commonplace child. He may be alive and nicely turned out, but he will be just like every other child, because he will not have been brought up in the presence of God. A mother who has been instructed in initiatic science, on the other hand, will turn to God, saying, 'Lord, I come to You for the light, love, health and beauty I want for my child' and, when she goes back to her baby, she will impregnate him with elements that ordinary mothers have never heard of or felt. They say that they don't have time. They do have the time, but their selfish love forbids them to adopt such a philosophy. This is why the earth will be eternally populated with ordinary, unexceptional children: because their mothers were ignorant.

As long as fathers and mothers are so attached to their family that they dare not leave it, even for a few days, to go and learn something, they will never be capable of transforming it and making it really happy. You cannot transform the members of your family by sticking too close to them. It is not a question of leaving them physically, but of leaving them mentally, that is to say, of relinquishing your false notions of how to love and understand them. When someone gets married and has children, that's the end of them; they are subjugated, in the grip of an atavism. Women become 'mother hens'; the world is full of mother hens.

You will protest, 'But this is a crusade against our children.' Not a bit of it! I probably love your children even more than you do; in fact, it might be worth analysing the question. In any case, if there is anyone who loves your children, it is myself; I'm the only one. You don't really love them. I once knew a boy who asked his mother for money; he wanted it to pay for his latest escapades and he threatened to kill himself if she refused. His mother told him, 'Go ahead, my son. Go and kill yourself; the world doesn't need people like you. I wanted you to be a great and noble human being but you prefer to behave like a criminal. So, go and kill yourself; it's the best thing to do. I shall thank heaven when you are gone.' Well, thanks to that woman's courage, the boy took stock of himself for the first time in his life and ended by becoming a very remarkable man. Years later, he said to me, 'It was my mother who saved me.' If the mother had panicked and said, 'Oh, my darling boy, don't do that. Here, take the money,' she would only have encouraged him in his criminal ways. And then people say, 'But we love them.' They think that that excuses their stupidity and their lack of pedagogy and psychology. Instead of saying, 'Yes, I know that we've been very stupid and weak-minded,' they say, 'We love them.' Well, I for one don't believe them; behind those words I hear something else. 'What fools we are!' is what I hear.

A mother must not neglect heaven on the pretext of staying close to her child; on the contrary, she must take him with her to heaven, and she must tell him so. Even while he is still in the cradle and incapable of understanding, she must tell him, 'I'm taking you with me to heaven, to the world of light and harmony,' for the child's soul hears and understands. This is how mothers must begin to educate their children while they are still tiny, otherwise they will turn out to be perfectly ordinary human beings or, even, criminals. 'A criminal? No, no, he'll never be that; he's an angel.' Well, we'll see in a few years if he is an angel or not. If you are stupid, you'll see what kind of angel he is. But if you are intelligent, yes, he will be more than an angel; he will be a divinity. There; it is all perfectly clear and logical. What you may think about all this is another matter; what is really important is what I think. Learn to think as I do, for heaven's sake; be bold!

Abraham loved Isaac but he agreed to sacrifice him. God wanted to see whether Abraham loved him more than he loved his son. Fathers and mothers don't even realize that this question is still relevant and that it is addressed to them: who do you love most, your children or God? Well, as I say, God wanted to put Abraham to the test, so he asked him to immolate his son on the altar of sacrifice. You will say, 'But, couldn't God see that Abraham loved him; did he have to put him to the test to make sure?' Yes, of course, the Lord knew in advance what Abraham would do; he could see what was in his heart and mind. It was Abraham who didn't know which was strongest in him; it was he who needed to find out, and that is why God tested him: for his own sake. In the same way, all the trials that God sends us teach us something about ourselves. For it is we who don't know the extent of our endurance or our generosity, who don't know how strong, kind and intelligent we are or how weak and stupid. People have a lot of illusions about themselves, they say,' 'I'm a genius, I'm like this or like that... ,' but, at the first little trial, they surrender, and then they wonder how it could have happened. But Abraham proved that he loved God above all else; he knew that God had given him his son and that he had every right to take him away again.

Why don't mothers reason in the same way? They think they will save their child by neglecting the Lord; they believe that he will only be safe if they are always watching over him themselves. But how can they protect him if they themselves are not protected, having turned their back on the great Protector? What pride and vanity! Abraham, who was truly an initiate, did not rebel against God's will, he obeyed him and prepared to sacrifice his son. And, as God is not a bloodthirsty monster, at the last minute he told Abraham to sacrifice a ram in the place of Isaac. At that point, Abraham knew how far he was ready to go for love of God, he knew how much he was capable of sacrificing and that was all he needed to know. If a mother is not ready to do the same as Abraham, it shows, first of all, that she is not intelligent and, secondly, that she is too proud. In her ignorance, she imagines that she knows better than the Lord whether her child should live or die. With such a mediocre notion of love, even if her child lives, he will make her suffer a great deal, because, instead of leading him towards the light, she has done just the opposite: she has turned him from the light. As she sees it, it is her love that is primordial; it is the only thing that counts. But, later on, in one way or another, she will have to pay for this mistaken notion, because she is failing in her duty. Her duty is to be in heaven and to take her child with her.

You must never abandon heaven for anyone, not even for a child, not even for your husband or wife, for you can do them good only by remaining in heaven. If you turn away from the light for the sake of another human being, you will bring great misfortune on yourself; you will end by having neither heaven nor earth. In other words, you will lose both the Lord and those for whom you have made such a terrible sacrifice and find yourself alone. If you seek heaven, the earth will also be yours, for the earth is the faithful subject and servant of heaven and is always in attendance. But if you abandon heaven and cling to the earth, you will have neither heaven nor the earth; the earth will slip from you and you will be all alone.

If you always allow yourself to be ruled by sentimentality and blind attachment, you will suffer for it, sooner or later. If you want to avoid this suffering, you must give priority to intelligence, wisdom and God himself, then those you love will truly belong to you. All the children you love – yours or other people's – with a pure, divine love, belong to you; they don't belong to their mother if she loves them foolishly. You will think that this is impossible, that blood is thicker than water. Yes, the ties of blood are very strong but they are not the strongest, believe me; there are all kinds of ties. The truth is that only those whom you know how to love, whether children or men and women, belong to you. Outwardly, the ties of the flesh are the strongest but, in fact, members of the same physical family often have no affinity with each other, because they belong to different spiritual families. You can belong, physically, to a family of peasants, for instance, while belonging spiritually to a family of kings. Or the reverse: you can belong, physically, to a royal family and, spiritually, to a family of paupers and tramps.

Let's look at a man who truly loves his family and see what he does if they are in need. A man who truly loves his family will have the courage to leave them, for a time, and go and earn some money in another country, whereas someone who doesn't love them in the same way will not have the courage to leave them. At first sight, therefore, it seems that the first man abandons his family, but he does so in order to help them: he goes abroad and amasses a fortune and, when he comes home again, the whole family rejoices. But the man who did not have the courage to leave his family condemns both them and himself to lasting poverty. And, now, let's translate that: a true father, a true mother, will abandon their children and family and go abroad, that is to say, to the divine world, where they will amass a fortune and, when they bring their treasures back home, the whole family will be rich. Whereas he who has not understood this will stay with his family, but what will he have to give them? Nothing but a few odds and ends, a few stale crusts. The true father, the true mother, goes 'abroad.' For how long? That depends; it can be for half-an-hour or an hour, or it can be for a day or for three months, but however long it is, when they come back they have a fortune to share with their family.

You are bound to admit that I have some formidable arguments that can hold their own against all your logical objections. In fact, if there are some mothers amongst you who don't agree, let them come and talk to me about it. I will tell them, 'You say that you love your child, but analyse that love. If you really love him, you will go 'abroad' to that other country, if only for ten minutes or half-an-hour, then you will be able to give your child the abundance he needs.' Perhaps, in fact, the foreign country you must go to is here, at The Bonfin[1], and you must come here to earn a lot of money, that is to say, to gain a lot of knowledge and light that you can then pour out on your whole family.

Genuine love is a love that desires to lead others to the Lord. All other kinds of love are motivated by self-interest. A person

---

[1] 'The Bonfin' is the name of a property near Fréjus on the French Riviera. The members of the Universal White Brotherhood gather here in their hundreds every summer, to study the Teaching of the Universal White Brotherhood, dispensed in the daily lectures of the Master Omraam Mikhaël Aïvanhov, and to put it into practice in all their activities as they work, pray, sing and eat together.

will make someone's acquaintance, be very friendly with him and give him presents but, very often, his actions are motivated by the hope of obtaining his patronage or benefiting from his position in society. Human beings rarely know how to do something unselfish. Even when they give presents they always have their eye on their personal interest. Actually, this is inevitable; even the love of a great Master is motivated by interest. An initiate is also anxious to win favours, but the favours he is looking for are the love and protection of the Lord, and these, of course, are not material, earthly favours. The initiates seek the glory of God and this is the only legitimate favour to seek: to become like the Lord, to shine with his light, to create as he creates.

For my part, I cannot say that my love is absolutely disinterested; all I can say is that I have substituted one goal for another. It is to our advantage to love the Lord because, in doing so, we gain eternal life, we gain light and freedom. But this is not really self-interest, for eternal life, light and freedom are divine acquisitions. Thus, we have a form of self-interest and, at the same time, we struggle against a selfish interest; we try to overcome an inferior interest in order to gain a higher interest. If your only goal is to satisfy your lusts and instincts, your personality, then, of course, your self-interest is inferior. But if you want to satisfy other needs, a need for light, for eternal life, a need for the Deity, then you have a higher interest and this is the crux of the matter: your interest may be very inferior or it may be very exalted, but it will always exist. We say that we should be disinterested, but that is just for the sake of convenience. If we wanted to express it accurately, we should change the words we use and, instead of speaking of disinterestedness, speak of a 'higher interest.'

There, my dear brothers and sisters, there are still many questions that need to be elucidated but you need not worry; that will come. This is a school and there is a programme and certain problems to be solved each day. It is up to you to study well and you will find that all the other problems that worry you will soon be cleared up. Today, concentrate on this question of love: how to love your family and your children.

The Bonfin, August 10 1963

Chapter Twenty-Five

EMPTINESS AND FULLNESS:
THE MEANING OF RENUNCIATION

The Master reads the Meditation for the day:

'If a bottle is always full, how can you pour anything into it? You have to start by emptying it. This is also true of human beings: if a human being does not empty out his vices and pernicious habits, how can divine qualities and virtues ever pour into him? He's already full. This is what renunciation means: to empty oneself, to give up certain habits, to give up smoking, for instance, or lying or backbiting, so as to fill oneself with something else. As soon as one gives up a failing, a quality rushes in and takes its place. This is a law of physics. How can you fill someone who is already full of vices? There is nothing you can do about it. He can live close to the greatest of all Masters all his life long, but if he does not empty himself so that he can be refilled, he will never change.'

Anyone who has understood the meaning of sacrifice and renunciation knows that he consents to them for his own sake, so as to create a void within himself that can be filled with divine qualities. When someone does not understand this, he says, 'I'd be miserable if I gave up smoking or stopped going to bars and night-clubs.' No, it is just the opposite for, if he succeeds in giving up these tawdry little pleasures, they will be replaced by far greater pleasures of a higher order.

It's very simple: you cannot pour anything into a bottle that is already full. Obviously, if it is full of the Elixir of Everlasting Life, you must not empty it; but if it is full of dirt and mould, why treasure all that? Unfortunately, human beings are very good at filling themselves with impurities but they don't know how to empty themselves. From childhood they have been surrounded by people who were not fit to be models and who have handed on to them their own bad habits and their own distorted patterns of thought and behaviour; and now, if they want to get rid of all that, to be renewed and rejuvenated, to change their stereotypes, they are going to have to find other models, beings who are like suns. The only things people look for in life is a trade or profession, a family and a comfortable house; that's enough for them; they are quite content with this mediocre way of life. From time to time, they will read a few books and listen to some records, go for a walk or go to a few parties, and that's all. They never make any progress, therefore, they never add anything new, anything luminous or powerful to their lives and they have no inkling of how dangerous this sluggish life is or of all the physical and psychic illnesses that are prowling round them, just waiting for a chance to sneak in and to bite and gnaw at them. Cosmic intelligence did not use such marvellous skill in making man just so that he should chloroform himself and go to sleep: he was designed to advance constantly on the path of evolution. It is only in this way that he can trigger an intense, inner current of life that rejects all impurities. Otherwise, waste and dirt accumulate and he becomes a swamp.

I have often been asked about purity in love: when love is pure and when it is impure. It is very easy to answer this if you look at nature. In nature, everything that is dull, dirty and impure tends to sink to the bottom, whereas everything that is pure rises to the top. This is also true in human beings: all that is heavy and coarse collects down below and all that is light, pure and luminous rises to the head. This is why the eyes, ears, mouth, nose and brain are all located in our head, whereas other things are down below. Man is, as it were, divided into two parts, the higher and the lower, and these two parts correspond to his two natures, the lower nature, or personality, and the higher nature, or individuality. The love manifested by the personality cannot be pure; since the personality is connected to the subterranean world, its love is necessarily tainted by the selfish, heavy, drab elements of that world. The love of the personality is only concerned with taking and satisfying its own desires, so it cannot be very pure. To the blind, everything seems pure but not to initiates, for they can see the emanations, radiations and colours of every thought and feeling. A love that is very crude, primitive and sensual cannot be pure. Whereas the love of the individuality is pure, because it contains other elements, elements of generosity, intelligence, gentleness and disinterestedness.

Through their love, human beings give each other all kinds of filth which obstructs their vision and makes them incapable of enjoying heavenly sensations. Layers of selfish, sensual love build up into a barrier within them. If people decide to give a free rein to their lowest inclinations, they are free to do so, but they are making a big mistake. The initiates did not lay down rules and precepts in order to put obstacles in the way of love or to make people ill but to prevent them from sinking into the infernal regions in which they would lose everything. For, when a man lets himself be ruled by his personality, the scope of his activities and of his consciousness shrinks; he becomes dull-witted and blind and is incapable of receiving any of the blessings and wonders of the divine world.

Selfish love is necessarily impure. Love as it is practised by almost all human beings today, therefore, is impure: men and women spend their time exchanging filth, disease and vices. Everyone knows how to practise this ordinary kind of love, but it is going to take thousands of years to explain the other kind.

People simply cannot understand; they are incapable of forming a really clear idea of it and the more explanations they hear the more obscure it seems to be. This is because something is still missing inwardly; they are not ready for it.

Initiatic science tells us that privation is not really a loss; it is a substitution, a transposition, a transference into another world. It is a continuation of the same activity but with matter that is so pure and luminous that there is no longer any danger involved. You deprive yourself, for instance, of the pleasures of love on the physical plane in order to enjoy the far greater pleasures to be found on a higher plane. As a matter of fact, it is dangerous to deprive yourself of satisfaction on a lower plane unless you replace it by drawing from another source, by finding air and nourishment on a higher plane, otherwise all you do is inhibit yourself. To say that we must deprive ourselves, that we must renounce or sacrifice things, is simply a manner of speaking. In reality we should not deprive ourselves; we should simply transfer our activity onto a higher plane: instead of drinking water full of germs from a stagnant swamp, we should drink crystal-clear water at its source. To stop drinking spells death. If we are told not to drink, it only means that we must not drink sewage. We have to drink, but we must only drink celestial water.

As a matter of fact, an initiate deprives himself of nothing; he eats and drinks, he breathes, he loves; but he does all these things in regions and states of consciousness that are unknown to the man in the street. People are horrified by any mention of renunciation; they say, 'I'll die if I have to deprive myself.' And, indeed, they will die if they fail to understand that they must only deprive themselves for the sake of something better. You have to eat and drink; you have to breathe and love and create children; but you have to find a better way of doing these things and there is a complete science that could teach you this, but it is still unknown. But, as you see, the question is perfectly clear: nothing must be suppressed, only transposed and sublimated.

All our innate lower tendencies must be replaced by habits, tendencies and desires of a finer quality. Most people, when they want to get rid of their need to smoke, drink or sleep with women, try to suppress the desire without putting anything in its place but this is a very dangerous method; it unbalances them and plunges them into a void. You must compensate for what you are giving up; you must replace a lower desire by a higher one. This is why someone who wants to stop loving altogether is very wide off the mark: he must simply exchange the object of his love for another higher, more luminous object, otherwise he is condemning himself to death. Nature has planned everything perfectly: we all have to eat and drink and breathe and we must not do away with any of that; we must simply refine our needs or transpose them onto a higher plane.

Before deciding to renounce a strongly felt need, you must think about it carefully, for it is a very grave decision to make. You must find a way to replace this need. You must continue to satisfy it, therefore, by continuing to eat, drink, love and live but on a level that no longer exposes you to the same dangers. If you don't substitute something for your needs you will simply succumb once again.

Take the case of a man who constantly needs a woman: how can he overcome this desire? With the help of all the women in the world. Instead of restricting himself to one woman at a time, he must take an interest in all women, all at the same time, and this will be his salvation. Instead of following the road to ruin by wallowing in pleasure, night and day, with one woman, he must tell himself, 'I'm going to love every woman in the world.' In this way, as he cannot indulge his gross desires with all women at the same time, he will be saved. He can continue to love womankind by loving all women and, in doing so, he will be happy and at peace. And women can use the same method: instead of loving one man, they can learn to love all men and all men will fill them with joy, happiness and inspiration. As long as they fail to expand their consciousness in this way, they will always feel unhappy and dissatisfied and end by becoming spiteful and bitter. Remember this method. If you don't replace a desire, an attraction, a weakness, a passion or a vice by a different desire or a different attraction of a higher order, you will always be divided, in conflict with yourself – never forget this. In fact, if you lose the one you love, either because he leaves you or because he dies, you must replace him. But don't replace him with someone else who might also leave you; replace him with a great love for something celestial, something divine. In this way, you will no longer feel the void, for you will be filled with peace and serenity. People prefer to replace a husband, wife or lover with a different husband, wife or lover and that very rarely solves the problem.

However much I explain all this to you, it will never really be clear in your minds until you make it clear for yourselves by meditating and making the necessary inner adjustments. Things that are perfectly clear to me may not yet be clear to you, because you have a different structure, a different vision of reality. It is up to you, therefore, to do the work that needs to be done for these things to become clear to you. Once you achieve this, you will be in full possession of all that nature has given you and capable of using it with the same ease and accuracy as if you were working in a laboratory or an electricity plant: you will manipulate tremendous forces and currents without being electrocuted or pulverized by them. At this point, although nature gives you the right to do whatever you please with men or women, with anyone in the world, you will find that something strange has happened: you no longer have any desire to take advantage of that right. Your sense of beauty and your taste for perfection, for light and purity, will have developed to such a degree that you have absolutely no desire to descend into those dark, subterranean regions that border on hell; you prefer to remain in the higher regions, where you feel more at home.

Let me tell you a story. One day, a king was strolling in the countryside and saw a cow in a field. She was such a magnificent animal that he thought he would like to buy her. He sent a servant to make an offer but the owner of the cow was a sage, a wise old magus, and he did not want to sell her: she gave him milk, his only food, and he had no intention of parting with her. The servant brought this answer back to the king. As he could not buy the cow, the king decided to take her by force and sent several servants to seize her but, when they came to the old man's field, he stretched out his hand and paralyzed them. After a few minutes, he released them, saying, 'Tell your master that nothing he can do will make me give him my cow. He is rich and powerful and he must let me keep her, for she's the only thing I have.' When the king heard this, he was very angry and sent an army to bring back the cow, but the magus paralyzed the whole army and sent them home, as before. Then the king thought to himself, 'This magus must possess a secret science that gives him such power; I shall go and steal his secrets.' Disguising himself, he went to the magus and said, 'Venerable old man, I have come to learn from you, for your reputation for wisdom is very great throughout the kingdom. Please accept me as your disciple.' Of course, the old man recognized the king and could read his thoughts but he did not let the king know this and agreed to teach him. For years, the king practised his exercises of meditation and respiration, and prayed and fasted so much that, one day, thinking about the cow, he realized that he no longer wanted her. He, too, had become a magus and had absolutely no desire to possess the cow.

In the same way, someone who says to himself, 'I want every woman I can get my hands on...' decides to make a great effort to become handsome, seductive and irresistibly attractive. He begins to practise spiritual exercises, to pray and meditate and, in the end, his desire pales in comparison to all the discoveries he is making. He has begun to live in a world of

such beauty that he does not want to leave it. This is the goal
you must try to reach. There are some human beings in this
world – very few, of course – who have completely conquered
and risen above their sensuality, and these are the great initiates.
They have the right to do what they please, everything is allowed
but they have no desire to descend from the heights they have
reached.

And so, my dear brothers and sisters, you are going to reflect
on all this and understand that a divine philosophy exists that
is capable of giving you everything. Only you have to desire it,
accept it and commit yourself to it. Human beings think they
know all there is to know; they are not willing to learn. But,
gradually, I shall show you how little of what you know is really
worthwhile and where it is leading you, and you will be horrified
to see that you have been strutting about, as proud as peacocks
– but proud of what? Of your own ignorance. As the Bulgarians
say, 'Na gol toumbac srebarni pictofi,' which means, 'With silver
pistols on a naked belly.' In other words, he is destitute except
for his pistols and, with them, he thinks he can defy the whole
world.

The Bonfin, August 18 1975

Chapter Twenty-Six

THE BONDS THAT BIND US

The Master reads the Meditation for the day:

'Human beings have cut the bonds that bind them to each other and this rupture goes by the name of hatred and hostility, rancour, revenge and anarchy. Look at Israel and the Arab countries, at the United States and Vietnam. You will say, "But there is still a bond between them; they spend their time throwing bombs at each other". True, they still have ties with each other on the physical plane, since they are always slaughtering each other, but I am talking of the spiritual bond. It is this bond that has been cut and the cutting of it is called war.

Of course, there are still ties between adversaries at war. Look at two people who detest each other and come to blows: there is still a bond between them; they have never been closer, in fact, but it is in order to cut each other's throats. And others, who may be thousands of miles apart, can also be bound by very strong ties. But, when I speak of bonds or ties, I am talking about the kind of connection a mechanic or an electrician would understand. Suppose you have a machine that won't work because half an inch of wire is missing: I come along, connect up the missing wire, and there you are. The current is restored and your machine works. It all depends on that one little connection.'

I know that this subject is not new to you; you have already heard some lectures about this question of bonds. Everything in the universe consists of bonds; even our physical body is simply an agglomeration of bonds which, depending on their function, are called threads, fibres, filaments, tendons, veins or canals, etc. And it is this intricate web of threads that form tissues. But you know all that.

If you were clairvoyant, you would also see that men and women are entangled in bonds which tie them to quantities of other people. They think that they are apart from others, free and independent... if they only knew. Merely by thinking of someone you create a bond between you and him, because that is what thoughts are: bonds, threads. If you wish someone ill, your thought is like a lasso with which you capture him and drag him to you so that you can slaughter him. But if you love someone, your thought will be a duct that carries nourishment to him, a means of linking him to all that is best, so as to help and enlighten him. Thoughts and feelings, whether of love or hate, create bonds.

We hear a lot about the bonds of love, but there are also bonds of hatred. If you spend your time thinking about someone and trying to devise ways of injuring him, your hatred creates a strong link that binds you to him for goodness knows how long – perhaps even for several reincarnations. It is your desire to be rid of him that ties you to him. Hatred is a tie, love is a tie, and you will keep coming back, time and time again, to those you love or hate. The only way to be free of someone is to feel neither love nor hatred for him; to be indifferent. If you want to be rid of an enemy, therefore, try to be indifferent to him, otherwise, your hatred will create all kinds of problems for you. And the same is true of love: if your love is not pure, spiritual and disinterested, it will cause you endless problems.

But let's talk a little more about love. After all, this is the one subject that is always topical, always popular and important; there is hardly anyone, man or woman, young or old, who is not interested in love. When you think about hatred, it is all quite clear; there's not much to say about it except for the disastrous consequences it can lead to – and this is not always understood. But when it comes to love, nobody knows what to think. The whole question is so vast, so rich and complex; there are so many different aspects to it, that no one has ever managed to elucidate it satisfactorily. Just think of how many years I have been talking to you about love... So, again today, I want to talk to you about love, in the hope that at last you will have a clearer idea of what it is.

Everybody thinks that it is normal to love someone and to marry and have children. Nothing seems more natural. Nobody is astonished if you are in love, because they are all afflicted by the same disease. So much so, in fact, that they find it strange and absolutely abnormal if someone wants to introduce some changes in this area and get human beings to move to a higher level; people are astonished and hostile to the idea. But it is this that I want to talk about. As I have already explained in other talks, it was cosmic Intelligence that created the instinctive manifestations of love that are the same in man as in animals. But this state was not meant to be permanent; cosmic Intelligence has other plans for man. He is destined to reach a more highly evolved, more spiritual state. These two tendencies are represented in man by his lower nature, or personality, which is only interested in taking and satisfying its own needs, and by his higher nature, or individuality, which thinks of the welfare and happiness of others. Animals, even beasts of prey, show faint signs of this higher nature in the form of a maternal or paternal instinct which makes them hunt for food for their offspring and care for them, sometimes, to the point of sacrificing their own lives in order to protect them. Little signs of this kind prove that every creature possesses certain qualities planted in them by cosmic Intelligence, which are not yet fully developed for, in defending its young, an animal is, above all, defending its property. This is often true of human beings also; nevertheless, it is in human beings that the higher nature is most fully developed. Saints and martyrs and the great spiritual Masters have given extraordinary proof of their spirit of selflessness, sacrifice and renunciation.

If you read Volume 11[1], which deals with this question of personality and individuality, you will have a much clearer idea of the nature of what you manifest at every instant of the day in your thoughts and feelings, your plans for the future, your attitudes, etc. You will see that you are often inspired by your personality, that it is your personality that always leads you to dwell on other people's weak points, to doubt and distrust others. In fact, even when you are with an initiate, a Master, who points out your mistakes and failings, you refuse to accept his point of view. Instead of saying, 'Oh, Master, you must be right. I didn't think that things were as you say. But I trust you; you are so much more advanced than I am,' some people even reject what a Master tells them in order to help them, preferring to cling to their own limited point of view. How can you expect them to perfect themselves if they behave like that?

But the two natures, the individuality and the personality, become most apparent in relation to love. One young man loves a girl, but his love is really for himself; he is seeking to satisfy his own need and will think nothing of feeding on all her purity and beauty, all her fresh, young loveliness, and then discarding her like an empty lemon rind while he goes off to look for someone new. Whereas another will think of her welfare and seek to help and instruct her, to protect her and have a care for her future. This kind of love is more rare but it does exist and it is the love of the individuality. And this is the most important point. Now, listen to me carefully.

From now on, when you love someone, observe the needs that make themselves felt in you and you will begin to understand that what you had always considered to be absolutely normal, natural and innocent (because it is what everybody does) was, in fact, inspired by your personality. At that point, you must

---

[1] See *The Key to the Problems of Existence*, Complete Works, vol. 11.

decide to pay much less attention to your sensations, to the effervescence and all the volcanic eruptions that go on inside, and use some of those energies to evolve and understand and to grow in grace. In other words, you start to work with your individuality and your love becomes a vehicle that carries you to regions of splendour, to heaven itself. Whereas the other kind of love dulls and deadens you and makes you coarse and brutish; it will rob you of all your light and inspiration and make you an evil influence on others. So, there you have it: this is the truth and it is perfectly clear and simple. You can protest and disagree as much as you like, but that won't make it any less true.

To be sure, the manner in which the personality loves is normal and perfectly natural. I have never said that it was not natural. But the point is that what is natural for the personality is unnatural for the individuality, which is only waiting for the opportunity to manifest itself and blossom; as long as you continue to follow your primitive instincts, you are suffocating and repressing your individuality. I am not saying that this instinctive love has no reason for its existence and I don't deny that those who practise it are good at it, but I am in favour of progress, of taking things a step further: I am not saying that you should no longer love, but that you should raise your love a step higher. I often compare a human being to a skyscraper of a hundred or a hundred and fifty floors: the tenants on the first few floors get all the water they want, but those on the top floors die of thirst because the water never reaches them. You need pressure to send the water all the way to the top and the trouble is that, as soon as pressure begins to build up, people make haste to release it by consoling themselves with a man or a woman and there is nothing left for the top floor. You see how ignorant people are. This pressure is necessary in order to carry the water up to the brain and yet the first thing people do is try to get rid of it, on the pretext that they can't help it, that it is too painful. Whereas, on the contrary, they should be glad that it exists and try to hold on to it, because it is this that makes it possible to nourish the starving cells up in the brain. People become sluggish and dull-witted because the cells of their brain don't get enough water.

If some of you are not convinced, that is too bad for you, but there are others who are eager to move ahead and who need to be enlightened, so it is to them that I am speaking when I say that there are methods. What are they? Well, I was talking, only a moment ago, about bonds, threads, pipes, and I wonder if you have ever thought about the marvellous network of canals and ducts that cosmic Intelligence installed in man thousands of years ago? If this subtle etheric system is not functioning today, it is because human beings never use it to convey energy to the brain. In fact, does anyone even know that man possesses a system of ducts specially designed to carry sexual energies to the brain? Sexual energy is a prodigious force, but when it is used exclusively to nourish the physical body, the personality, it also nourishes hatred and war. It is capable of doing great things but, so far, it has only succeeded in encouraging human beings in an attitude of isolation and hostility. Primitive, instinctive love is closely allied to belligerence; he who is steeped in sensuality feels the need to conquer and dominate others, to destroy. A higher love, on the contrary, lends itself to spiritual conquests. Venus enhances Martian forces but, in both Venus and Mars, there are always two aspects, the higher and the lower. The higher love, the higher aspect of Venus, stimulates the higher aspect of Mars to set out in bold exploration of the divine world in order to give it material expression on earth.

And now, my dear brothers and sisters, what are you going to do with what I have just been telling you? Not much, I know. You have written it all down and will leave it lying about in your notebooks while you continue to feed your lower nature until it destroys everything. Oh, I know you will say, 'It's all so difficult, Master. We understand and agree, we feel that everything you say is absolutely true, but you don't realize how difficult it is for us to do what you say.' Yes, I know that it is difficult, but the fact that you know these truths will, one day, make it possible for you to put them into practice; if you don't know them you will never be able to put them into practice. So it is better that I should reveal them to you. For the time being you may be incapable of giving full expression to this splendour but you can keep trying until, one day, you manage to overcome the obstacles that stand in your way.

I know that one of these obstacles is fear, a fear that stems from ignorance. You think that you will be obliged to deprive yourself of every kind of joy and satisfaction. There is bound to be an aspect of privation, of course, but you will be depriving yourself of a weakness in order to acquire a strength; you will be depriving yourself of stupidity in order to acquire intelligence; you will be depriving yourself of something that entails problems and tragedies in exchange for something that brings you peace and happiness. What about me? Do you think that I deprive myself of anything? I am not so stupid. I deprive myself of nothing, all I do is exchange one thing for another. You will say, 'But you don't smoke, for instance.' If you only knew: I smoke other things, wonderful, heavenly things. As for the delicious wines I drink... No, the thing is that you have to deprive yourself of some tiny little pleasure in order to earn the right to taste a much greater pleasure.

Well, I'll stop there, but think about all this. And think about the question of bonds. Everything in the universe consists of bonds: the sun, stars and planets; trees and crystals; atoms and electrons, which are arranged along lines of force; faces; geometrical figures... Everything consists of bonds, threads, tissue. Look at your own physical body: it is simply a tissue, a fabric which you have woven yourself, and it can be beautiful or ugly, colourful or drab, symmetrical or asymmetrical. Everything is a mesh of threads woven together, and this is why it is so important to be careful about the attachments you form, the ties that bind you to people and things, for this is how you weave the garment you will have to wear in your next incarnation and to know how to do this is a science in itself. When you don't know how to weave or what threads to use, you are bound to make stupid mistakes. If you form a bond with a criminal, for instance, you will have to share his misfortunes, because you are associates, partners, collaborators. People never think about these things; they form bonds indiscriminately with anybody, even with the Devil himself. Think about this, therefore, and make sure that the bonds you form are only with highly evolved, radiant beings, with initiates, angels, archangels and divinities, otherwise you will not know a single bright day in your life, your whole life will be dark and terrifying.

Actually, as I have already said, this question of bonds goes much further than you imagine: every thought, every sentiment, every promise is a bond. Look around you: nobody tries to bind you with ropes, today, but they bind you with papers, contracts and signatures. If you commit yourself and sign a contract you are tied hand and foot and nothing can release you. But the bonds of the astral and mental planes are far more terrifying and people constantly bind themselves to others thinking that they are going to exploit them. Such bonds are invisible, to be sure, but they are the most tenacious, the most difficult to cut. Are you convinced, now? Meditate about this so as to be more aware of how terribly important it is... and be careful about the bonds you form, for your whole life is at stake.

The Bonfin, August 17 1975

Chapter Twenty-Seven

YOUTH AND THE PROBLEM OF LOVE

I

The Currents of a New Age

A new light is dawning in the world and men and women everywhere must be ready to understand it and apply it to their lives. The proof that it is coming is that everything is in a state of flux. Look around you: nothing like this has ever been seen before. Look at young people, for instance: they are no longer willing to follow the lead of adults and this, in itself, is proof that God is creating a new heaven and a new earth, for revolutions are always effected by human beings. Young people today are seeking happiness through sexual liberation and we must not condemn this; on the contrary, it is a sign that new conceptions are beginning to appear. At the moment, of course, it has still not been properly worked out; you must not imagine that every innovation will necessarily be wonderful or even acceptable: everything will have to be evaluated, revised and sanctioned by an authority of wisdom and light.

At the moment, therefore, we can only see the upheavals and revolutions in society, the outbursts of new forces; it is still unorganized; there is still a great deal of work to be done. This period is like the early periods when the earth was taking shape and volcanic eruptions broke through the half-formed crust. At that time, conditions made vegetable and animal life – particularly, human life – impossible. Plants, animals and human beings had to wait until all these untamed forces calmed down and hosts of intelligent beings had organized the earth and made it habitable. The inner condition of many people, nowadays, is a reflection of this primitive condition of the earth: they are in a constant turmoil of anger and revolt, of wild, uncontrolled sexual energy that erupts like a volcano and this shows the age of man: he is still living in the era in which the earth lacked the peaceful conditions necessary for the intervention of intelligent beings. As long as man allows brute forces to run wild within him, he is in too unsettled a state for the angels, archangels and initiates to do their work, so they give him time to calm down before trying to infuse light and wisdom into him. But when a man begins to be reasonable and in control of himself, he represents the earth as it is today and higher entities begin to take care of him: they plough and sow and tend the young plants, and a rich culture and civilization begin to take shape within him, that is to say, a numerous population of angels and glorious entities begins to inhabit him.

The turmoil in society today is a sign that the forces that are making themselves felt are still not orientated nor fully organized, but this will come. Entities capable of organizing all these conflicting currents will appear. Since the 'new heaven' already exists, the new light is beginning to break through the darkness. Don't be alarmed, therefore, when you hear about strange and terrible things happening in the world.

Young people, for instance, have never behaved like this before. In past eras they were more docile and obedient; I'm not saying that the situation was perfect, but it was different. Today, young people take pleasure in disobeying, they enjoy asserting themselves and showing their independence in every area and this will, at least, have the merit of forcing adults to re-evaluate themselves.

Young people today demand sexual freedom in the belief that it is this that will bring them fulfilment, joy and happiness. Unfortunately that is not so. Young people know nothing about man's structure, and it is this ignorance that will, in the end, utterly destroy their mental balance as well as their physical health and their intelligence. I have never said that you must repress all your desires. If you try to struggle against your sexual impulse it will simply destroy you; it is a force that has had thousands of years in which to develop and no man can withstand it. I am not preaching repression or inhibition; you only have to take one look at those who have repressed their sexual energy to see what it has done to them. But I am not preaching unbridled expression either, for this only entails other problems. In the more general area of education we see the same thing: if parents try to combat their children's faults and failings head-on, they only make things worse. They must not repress or oppose force with force, but guide and channel it and put it to work. But, as parents are ignorant, their children pay no attention to them and do as they please.

Besides, parents don't even bother to instruct their sons and daughters about sexual matters – this was particularly true in the past, when the custom was to keep children in ignorance of anything to do with sex. It is only very recently that people have begun to talk openly about sex education but this is not always an improvement, for now everyone wants to have their say in an area about which they are still very ignorant.

The other evening I watched a television programme in which doctors, parents and teachers were discussing the best way to explain to young children how a baby was born. They showed a film of a mother explaining things to her little boy of nine, and I was astounded to see how she did it. What a lack of psychology! She used all kinds of technical terms, talked about fertile periods, ovulation and so on, and the wretched child, who didn't understand a word, could only stare at her, wide-eyed. I was really sorry for him. Then, very crudely, she explained the father's role, talked about impregnation and gestation and finished with an explicit description of birth. The child, in his innocence, listened to what she said but it was obvious that he took nothing in.

That is no way to go about it. For my part, I would do it quite differently. I would begin by telling him about plants and flowers, explaining how a flower is fertilized by the pollen and how a fruit is formed. Then I would explain about insects and animals and show him how it happens in nature, in the fields and forests. In this way, the child would understand all the rest and it would be so much more poetic than describing how the man's organ becomes rigid in order to penetrate the woman's. That mother explained these things with the best will in the world, but it was a complete disaster. And there are many other areas in which human beings are clumsy and fail to get good results.

In every corner of the globe, starting with the United States and Scandinavia and including India and the Arab countries, we see that 'the pill' has made great progress. To begin with, it was seen as a way to ensure demographic balance in the world, but all kinds of other reasons that have nothing to do with demography have since made it popular, chief amongst them being the desire of both men and women to have their pleasure without the risk of consequences. Tell me frankly: does a fifteen-year old girl really need the pill? And yet they are allowed to have it at that age; in fact, in some schools, it is the teachers who distribute it to their pupils. Yes, the teachers.

I am not an advocate of asceticism, but I am not in favour of licentiousness either. By allowing young people to rush into exploring an area they know nothing about, you are opening the door to all kinds of physical and psychic disorders for them. They experiment with these things, but they don't know what the long-term consequences will be, that they will end by being physically ill and mentally unhinged. The truth is that neither those who encourage the use of the pill nor those who oppose it know anything about it. Those who encourage its use do so because they know that human beings are weak and they pander to that weakness, whereas those who oppose it are hypocrites, because they do so in the name of old traditions which they don't respect anyway.

Every sensation, every effervescence, every volcanic eruption entails the combustion of quantities of fuel. Human beings behave as though they had unlimited reserves of energy; they don't realize that every detail has been calculated in advance: when a human being comes into the world, he is given a certain supply of energy and if he behaves unreasonably and squanders it, the loss will be his; he won't be given any more. You will sometimes see someone who needs just one little drop more of life in order to finish his work, but he doesn't get it; this proves what I have been saying. Men draw on their supply of energy as though it were an inexhaustible ocean; they think they have a right to spend it without restraint. No, it has all been calculated. Today, thanks to the pill, people refuse to curb or moderate their behaviour; they don't realize that they are burning up all their reserves, all those combustible materials in the brain, and that they will become more and more debilitated and brutish. Now that they have the pill, people feel that they need no longer think before they act or exercise any kind of discipline or self-control... Just close your eyes and let yourself go.

If human beings are always so ready to squander their energies of love, it is because they are all in the habit of feeding only their personality. Nobody is interested in a collective, glorious, divine goal; they are only interested in their own profit and pleasure and think it normal to take it wherever they can. That is all very well but it means that men behave like animals. If you are interested in becoming something more, you must satisfy your individuality, your divine dimension, and not only your personality. In other words, you must have activities which are not for the sole purpose of satisfying your own craving for pleasure. For pleasure restricts man to such a narrow range of activities that he shrinks and wastes away until, one day, no one even notices his existence. If you want people to know that you exist, you have to work differently.

When I reveal these things to the young people who come here, when I talk to them about their future and about all the problems and complications in store for them if they continue in this way, many of them decide to change. You have no idea how happy that makes me. What a joy it is to see that all these young people were looking for what is right and good; it is just that they didn't know where to look. It is not really their fault, they have never been taught, but they are looking for something great and beautiful and noble. That is why I love working with the young.

And now, in closing, I will say this to all you young people: you all have your sweethearts, and that's good, but try not to 'devour' them completely, because it is very likely that you will end by tiring of so much effervescence. You will begin to be disillusioned and see only the negative aspects and your disappointment will rob you of all joy and inspiration. Why do you have to go to the lengths of tasting and experiencing what goes on underground in the sewers, in hell itself? Be content with beauty and that beauty will never end. The trouble is that, in their weakness, human beings destroy everything by wanting to know it all immediately; this is why they very soon find no more inspiration in each other and wish never to see each other again. They have seen too much, tasted and devoured too much and now they are glutted. It's all over; their great love is dead and buried. To begin with, their love gave them every blessing; they were in Paradise... and then they had to go and spoil it all for the sake of a few moments of pleasure. Why don't they try to restrain themselves for as long as possible so as to continue to benefit from that inspiration, continue to enjoy the Elixir of Everlasting Life? But no, they are in a hurry to 'go all the way'... and it all ends badly. Even when they get married and have children, they continue to live together from habit, to conform to convention or for the sake of appearances in front of their families and friends but, inwardly, they have been separated for years. It is the subtle, etheric sensations that feed the flame of love, it is they that adorn, strengthen and prolong life.

Sèvres, January 1 1967

II
Marriage

Nature has created human beings in such a way that they all need tenderness and affection, they all need some form of intercourse with others. This is a universal need and no one can doubt or deny it.

Take the case of a young girl who feels such a strong need for affection that, from one day to the next, without taking the time to reflect or really to know the character of the boy she is in love with, she decides to marry him. In order to satisfy that single need, she is obliged to accept everything about him, all his traits of character, his thoughts and his feelings – which may often turn out to be so crude that she cannot agree with them. To be sure, he gives her something, but to get that something she has to accept all the rest as well. And the situation is the same for all young men and women: for the sake of a few sensations, a few crumbs of joy and gladness, they are obliged to put up with all kinds of unpleasantness and they spend the rest of their lives complaining that they are unhappy and don't know what to do about it. Very often, in fact, in trying to escape from a situation that has become unbearable, they transgress all kinds of laws.

This is the sad reality: for the sake of a few little satisfactions, they all get entangled in inextricable complications. They feel a need and, in order to satisfy that need, they sacrifice all the rest. In their hunger for a few crumbs of pleasure, they are obliged to accept all the impurities and deformities of the person from whom they choose to receive those crumbs. Surely they could, at least, try to find someone who is pure, noble and full of light. My dear brothers and sisters, if you can't find anyone who answers to that description, be patient, don't get married for, if you do, you will pay too high a price for it. Unfortunately, very few human beings think of safeguarding their purity in order to do something really worthwhile; for the sake of a few pleasurable sensations, they open their doors to all kinds of impurities. Everything pales into insignificance in comparison with a little sexual titillation.

Before committing themselves to a love affair, young people should know the criteria that initiatic science can give them, so as to avoid falling into the arms of the first person who happens to come along. It is much better to be patient and wait until you find someone with whom you have a deep affinity, someone who will complete and fulfil you from every point of view – even from the magical point of view – then you can safely experience love with him or get married and have children. If you can't find someone capable of complementing you, don't attempt the experience with anyone else; it is simply not worth the price you would have to pay. Wait, keep looking and, when you find the right one, when your whole being vibrates in unison with heaven in a love such as only a poet could describe then, yes, do as your heart dictates. But to go and have ten, twenty, a hundred different experiences, to fritter yourself away, to defile and degrade yourself... really, it is a shame. It would be better, even, to refuse to try. If you want to find love, it must be true love, otherwise you're better off without it.

This is my advice, therefore, to young people: don't be in too much of a hurry; don't ruin your lives by rushing into a commitment with the first comer. Start by studying this question and trying to understand it clearly and, only then, go ahead and look for your beloved. But, above all, be sure to see if the one who attracts you is really capable of working with you, of treading the same path because, if he is not, you will spend your life together tearing each other to shreds. Make very sure that you are in harmony on the three levels, emotional, physical and intellectual, and that you are not simply letting yourself be blinded by the desire for pleasure. If you and your beloved have differing opinions about important things, don't tell yourself, 'Oh, that's not important. Eventually, we'll understand each other and everything will be all right,' because it won't. It will be just the opposite. After a time, when the novelty of certain pleasures has worn off and your feelings have lost their first fine edge, you will realize that your ideas, tastes and tendencies are too divergent, and arguments, fights and, eventually, separation will inevitably follow. Agreement on the level of ideas and tastes is extremely important. Physical attraction, even when it is accompanied by a little love, is not enough; lovers are very soon replete and disillusioned and if, in addition, there is a lack of intelligence and they are incapable of conversation that is always new and interesting, they end by being bored with each other.

There are people who are not physically in love but who adore each other because they always have a thousand things to tell each other, to explain, to discuss together, and it's a delight. Ideally there should be agreement on three levels: first, they should feel attracted to each other physically; secondly, there should be compatibility in the area of feelings and tastes for, if one prefers a lot of noise, for instance, and the other prefers silence, or if one likes to read and the other likes to dance, if one of them always wants to go out and the other always wants to stay at home, they will end by quarrelling. Finally, and this is the most important, there should be a strong community of ideas, of their goal in life, of their ideal. If harmony exists on all three levels, there is nothing more beautiful, more marvellous than the union of two beings; it is an inexhaustible source of joy, happiness and understanding.

Unfortunately, young men and women do not possess these criteria. They are too superficial and in too much of a hurry, and they rely on chance encounters to find a partner. Suppose someone shows you a sack full of snakes, lizards, doves, crocodiles and mice, and you say, 'I'll reach in and get hold of a dove.' If you put your hand into the sack, without looking, you are more likely to be bitten by a snake. You really have to be simple-minded to think that, blindly, by pure chance, you will pick on a dove or something equally harmless. People think that Providence is there for the sole purpose of helping the blind and protecting them from their own silly mistakes. On the contrary, as soon as Providence sees a blind person in the distance, she takes to her heels and leaves him to Fate and, as you know, Fate is very good at tormenting people. But if Providence sees two young people who use their eyes, she says to herself, 'Ah, I like that; I'll help them.' The extraordinary thing is that people who are blind and have already been bitten by a snake will often stretch out their hand to the same snake and be bitten again. I have known several very tenacious women who have done that: they said, 'I'm going to try again with the same one; perhaps he'll improve... ' But has anyone ever seen a poisonous snake or a crocodile mend its ways?

Physical attraction is important, to be sure, but it is not essential. How often one sees people who literally devour each other with love and then, not long after, detest each other... and yet nothing has changed physically. Take the case of a young man who gets married to a very lovely girl – everything about her is ravishingly beautiful and he is completely bewitched – but, when he finds out how superficial, unfaithful, capricious and stupid she is, his love dwindles rapidly. He is so repelled by that horrifying inner reality that even her beauty no longer has the power to move him. And the reverse can be true too: a young man can start going out with a girl who is not particularly pretty but, after a time, when he sees her wisdom, kindness, patience and spirit of self-sacrifice, he begins to love her more and more. To begin with, he found her rather unattractive but, now that he sees how beautiful she is inwardly, all the others pale by comparison, for she is loyal and faithful, sincere and even-tempered, always ready to console him, dress his wounds and give him good advice. The physical aspect is really not important to him any more; he adores her. When they go out together and people criticize or pity him for marrying such a plain woman, he thinks to himself, 'Poor fellows; little do they know what a pearl she is.' A lot of men have a very elegant wife whom they show off as though she were an ornament and every one congratulates them on their good fortune. When a man like this meets his friends, they can't tell that he has married a she-devil who torments him night and day, because he continues to take pride in showing her off and enjoys making other men envious. He suffers, but that doesn't matter: he continues to go to the opera and to parties in order to show off his wife. All he wanted was a piece of jewellery to brag about. Well, he has got his piece of jewellery and he is paying a very high price for it.

My advice to young men and women who want to get married is to avoid making any hasty decisions and to learn the laws of love, first. Once they have learned how to love each other and how to prepare to have children and bring them up, then they can decide to marry. But if they rush into it, later on, when the children are there and they are plagued by illness and other difficulties, the poor things are going to regret it and, in desperation, start consulting doctors and reading books in the hope of learning what to do. To begin with, they thought it was all great fun. They said, 'There's plenty of time to worry about that, later. It will be alright.' But it won't; not unless they study and prepare themselves in advance.

It sometimes happens that a member of the Brotherhood meets a very pretty girl in the world and marries her. Well, pretty she may be, but she does not want to follow the Teaching with him; she has no interest in the spiritual life and no desire to learn or to strive for perfection, with the result that the young brother finds himself in a quandary and, as often as not, he will abandon the Teaching for the sake of the silly little goose he has married. Well, that shows how stupid he has been and he is bound to suffer for it. The same thing can happen to a sister if she marries a man who is not willing to accept her ideas: for the sake of a young whipper-snapper she will be obliged to sacrifice all that is most wonderful in her heart and soul and end by being miserable. This is no way to solve your problems; don't be in such a hurry. You say, 'But we'll soon be old.' Well, it is better to marry when you're old but to marry the right person. Why rush into it? Do you want to suffer and get old even sooner? I have sometimes seen women who have been married for only three or four years and who were so aged by worry and privations that I did not recognize them. Whereas, when you find your Prince Charming, even if you're old, you will be young again, at once. Yes, even if you're ninety years old it makes no difference: you will be like a twenty-year old again.

The fact is that, whether you wait or not, whether you show discernment or not, if you are not ready, whatever you do will be a disaster. You must, at least, be prepared for marriage. Who will accept you if you are not ready? It's all very well to say that you want to marry a princess, the Queen of the heavens, what makes you think she would have you? If you are a weak and witless good-for-nothing, all you can hope for is to find a wife like yourself. Or, if you are a girl, you may be ravishingly beautiful but if you have nothing to say, if you have never read a book in your life and are abysmally ignorant, you will be incapable of understanding the man you love, still less of entertaining, encouraging and consoling him; you will have to rely exclusively on the charms of your body. Well, any man would tire of a woman like that very quickly; he would simply forget her because she has nothing to offer his soul or spirit. In fact, the more excellent the man she chooses the more miserable she will be, because she has not got the inner qualities that would satisfy him. If, for instance, he has artistic and spiritual interests which she is incapable of sharing, it would only be a cause for unhappiness, for she would see that he was so superior to her. If you have never done anything to prepare yourselves, you would do better not to fall in love with a prince or a princess.

The first thing, therefore, is to prepare yourselves, so as to be ready for whatever turns up, otherwise, I repeat, it will never work, even with the most wonderful person in the world: they will leave you for somebody better and more intelligent and you will be left to your tears. So, prepare yourselves and start to earn so much treasure, so many precious stones – that is to say, qualities and virtues – that you outshine everyone else. If you do this, then the one you love will be faithful to you. Why should he look for someone else? But nobody ever sees it that way: a girl sets her heart on someone, but how is she going to keep him? If she has so little to offer, she won't keep him for long. So, prepare yourselves. Prepare yourselves for years and years. You will say, 'But I'll be old and ugly.' That doesn't matter. You may be old and ugly outwardly, but so young and beautiful inwardly that your Prince Charming will never leave you. You must work and prepare yourselves without worrying about time or old age.

The question of love interests every human being; it will always fascinate them. More and more, in fact, they will think of nothing but love, live only in love, seek nothing but love and emanate nothing but love. Love will be the centre of everything; all things will converge towards love. Science, art and religion will share one and the same goal: to spread and infuse and propagate love. True happiness lies in the will to share one's love with everything that exists. At the moment, though, in view of the way human beings are constructed and of the education they have received, it is dangerous to give them one's love unless one also possesses great wisdom. I know too many poor girls who, inspired by their generous, loving heart, thought only of making a man happy and, then, found themselves sucked dry and discarded like an empty lemon peel. Before showing your love for someone, you must learn to love without being devoured. You must be able to say, 'The guests have had their fill and the cake is still whole.' In other words you are capable of nourishing all comers with your love without being any less magnetic, luminous or strong; indeed, you will be stronger and more magnetic and luminous. You will be able to 'nourish your guests' while remaining whole and intact. But, without this wisdom, you'll be lost: sucked dry and thrown away. Young people must listen to this advice for it is very important.

One day I told a young girl that she should love the man of her choice, but without letting him know and, naturally, she wanted to know why. So I explained, 'Because it is your love that makes you feel so full of happiness and vitality and gives meaning to your life and, as this young man is far from perfect, he is bound to spoil all that, even if he doesn't mean to, as soon as he knows you love him. Once you are both very strong and well prepared, there will be no danger in telling him you love him but, until then, go on loving him but hide it from him. If he were very advanced there would be no problem but his level of evolution is not sufficient to prevent him from trying to take advantage of you. He will say to himself, 'The door is open; what's to stop me going in?' and then there will be nothing left of your unspoiled youth. You will be so disillusioned that you will say, 'He didn't understand me; I detest him,' and that will be the end of your love. And it will be the end of you, too, for it is your love that gives you wings, and you must not sacrifice it for the sake of a boy who is incapable of understanding you. Since it is love that gives you wings, go on loving, but let it be a secret. Whether the boy deserves your love or not is not important: the important thing is that it gives you an impetus, a zest for life and the will to overcome all obstacles. So don't lose it, whatever you do. Always remember that it is not whom you love that matters, but your love itself, because it is this that nourishes you.'

Sèvres, April 13 1968

III

The Argument for Self-control

The Master reads the Meditation for the day:

'We look on every difficulty or inconvenience as an enemy. Well, let's take a closer look at that enemy. To primitive man, fire was an enemy. Fire, lightning, water, the wind, the earth, animals... they were all man's enemies and men struggled against them and died in the struggle. Then, in time, men began to tame these forces and discovered how useful they could be.

This attitude towards the elements can equally be applied to certain other manifestations of life, particularly on the psychic plane. Instead of running away from the little things that disturb you such as your sensuality, anger, vanity, jealousy and so on, you should explore these regions and get to know them so as to see what they really contain. The courage you show in doing this will lead you to understand that what you thought was an enemy is really a friend laden with gifts. A time is approaching when mankind will have a different attitude towards evil, when new educational methods will free them from the inner shackles that bind them.'

I have often talked about this before, about how man's attitude towards the forces of nature – water, air and electricity, for instance – has changed, and how he has learned to use them for extraordinary achievements. There's no doubt about it:

outwardly, man has won great victories over the elements. He has found all kinds of means and methods to make progress on the external level, because it is the external world that really interests him. This is not a bad thing; on the contrary, it is good. The only thing is that man pays no attention to his inner life and, on that level, the same dangers and catastrophes continue to hang over him.

I have often talked to young boys and girls who had questions in their minds about love, and they couldn't understand that physical intercourse with each other could be detrimental to them. On the contrary, to their way of thinking, it was a source of happiness and joy which enriched them and made them healthier. But that is not so, and I tried to explain it to them: 'Every physiological manifestation involves combustion. Even when you are only thinking or talking you are burning fuel and, when the emotions are involved, the consumption is considerably greater. When you have an overwhelming experience of joy or sorrow, the fuel that is burned leaves a residue of ashes and cinders and you have to sleep and give your body time to recuperate. Every manifestation, every emotion, every sensation involves an expenditure of fuel and energy. This being so, how can anyone imagine that in the effervescence of physical love, nothing is spent or lost?'

It is precisely in this area that the expenditure is greatest and that recuperation is most difficult, for the quintessences involved are of another kind and quality and, in the long run, a human being loses all his intelligence, beauty and subtlety.

This does not mean that you have to exclude all love and tenderness from life. Certainly not; the point is that you must live sensibly, intelligently and with a sense of the aesthetic. When one sees how people wallow in physical pleasure without any attempt to introduce a more spiritual element, one cannot help but be amazed and even shocked, because it is such a waste... such a terrible waste on every level. But it never occurs to human beings that perhaps they are wasting or losing something. They say, 'But these organs don't wear out.' True, it is not your sexual organs that wear out, but there is something in the brain that deteriorates and wears out. You must know this. As long as love stimulates and inspires you and gives you creative impetus, it is good; otherwise it is stupid. Most human beings make love in much the same way as they sit down to a meal: they feel obliged to eat something, mechanically, even if they have no particular feeling about it.

Let me tell you what I explained to a young girl who wanted me to tell her what was good and what was bad in respect to sexuality: was it preferable to live in chastity or to have sexual relations. This is what I told her: 'To begin with, I must tell you that, like everybody else, you are asking the wrong question. Everybody gives their opinion and declares that this is good and that is bad. But that is the wrong way of looking at it. Are those who choose to live in chastity and continence right to do so? It all depends on their goal: the results can be very bad but they can also be very good. Continence can make some people hysterical, neurotic and physically ill, and it can help others to become strong, well-balanced and healthy. And what about those who give a free rein to their instincts: are they right to do so? There is certainly something right in it. And does it do them good? To be sure, it can do them a great deal of good but it can also do them a great deal of harm. You cannot label everything either good or bad. Good and evil depend on another factor, on how you use your energies and the goal you are aiming for. Nothing is of itself good or bad, but everything can become good or bad.

'The question, therefore, is to decide, first and foremost, what your ideal in life is, what you want to become. If you want to become a soul, a spirit, an exceptional human being, if you want to discover the treasures of the spiritual world and be in communion with heaven then, of course, you will have to use restraint in certain pleasures or even give them up entirely so as to learn to sublimate your sexual energy. But if you do not have this high ideal, it would be idiotic to deprive yourself and try to live in chastity and virginity. In fact, you would almost certainly make yourself ill in the attempt, because your efforts would have no motivation to back them up.'

Needless to say, that young girl was astonished by my explanation because no one ever presents the question in this light. Things are either good or bad. But is it reasonable to want everybody to abide by the same rules, the same precepts, in this area? Try asking a hog to be chaste and virginal: it would gape at you, thinking, 'The man's crazy. What kind of a philosopher is he? What planet has he come from?' This is why I don't give the same advice to everybody.

For instance, someone will come and tell me that he thinks he should not marry and have children, because he is more interested in the spiritual life. But then, when I look at him and see how he is built, how he is constituted, I tell him, 'No, no. You would do much better to get married, otherwise the results will be disastrous: you would be very unhappy and become a nuisance to everybody else.' And then, to somebody who tells me that he wants to get married, I sometimes say, 'Get married if you like, but let me warn you that you are not built for marriage and you will be very unhappy.' A great many young men and women don't really know themselves and don't know what they should do. Each individual comes into the world with a mission, a particular programme to carry out; it is not he who chooses his tendencies and instincts. As I have always said, you can give a cat the best possible advice about becoming a vegetarian and giving up mice for dinner, etc., it will just look at you and say, 'Meow. How right you are!' But, even while you're still preaching to it, if it hears a faint scratching in the wainscoting, it will be off in a flash to catch the mouse. The mouse is far more to its taste than your sermon. How can you expect to explain to human beings – who are cats – that they must stop eating mice?

If there were some way of weighing what you gain from the sexual sensations you enjoy so much against what you lose by indulging in them, you would find that you lose almost everything and gain almost nothing, so it is not really worth sacrificing everything to pleasure. But, as people never remember that a sensation is short-lived and soon forgotten (yesterday's dinner is unimportant today), they continue to prepare a future of poverty for themselves. Whereas, if you make the effort to refuse, you may suffer for a moment but you will be preparing a magnificent future for yourself. In other words, you lose some passing sensations but you gain your whole future. People who never stop to think, say, 'I'm quite content; I'm happy this way,' and, of course, they are right: they are happy today but they have no future. This is the philosophy of the confirmed drunkard who finds his pleasure in alcohol: as long as he has something to drink he's happy. Yes, but if he goes on drinking, how are his employer and his family and friends going to react? He is preparing a future of degradation for himself. So, the sensation may be very pleasant but it doesn't last: his future is in the gutter.

You all know the account in the Bible of how Esau sold his birthright to his brother Jacob for a dish of lentils. For a sensation, a fleeting pleasure, he sacrificed his birthright as eldest son to Jacob. Not many people have thought much about this story or attempted to interpret it but most human beings are past-masters at depriving themselves of their most precious possessions in exchange for a moment of pleasure. Oh, yes; they are very good at this. But a disciple must be capable of renouncing certain pleasures for the sake of other acquisitions. To be sure, I am not saying that he has to give up everything, all at once. It is up to him to find out how to free himself, little by little, from all that hinders him from advancing on the path of evolution.

Do you imagine that those who became great spiritual Masters spent their lives in the pursuit of pleasure and sensual gratification? No, indeed! They knew privation, renunciation and disgrace. But their future is more glorious than that of the most glorious princes for this very reason: they trod the path of self-renunciation. Most human beings are terrified of renunciation; they are determined not to renounce anything, not to deprive themselves of anything; they are bent on gratifying all their needs and appetites. If they continue in this way, their future looks very bleak.

The Bonfin, July 31 1975

The Need for a Guide

Young people are always afraid that someone is going to take the things they love away from them, and this is why they avoid spiritual instructors or Masters: the fear that they will try to stop them from being happy. They vigorously defend their own tastes, opinions, hopes and desires and, in spite of their inexperience, embark on all kinds of ambitious schemes. But, as these schemes of theirs often turn sour, a great many youngsters end by being unhappy and disillusioned. Now, I would like to reassure them and dissipate this fear, for it is quite unjustified: there is no question of depriving them of any joy or pleasure; on the contrary, I want to show them how to enjoy life and have pleasure without harm to themselves, without damaging or destroying anything. It would, obviously, be very stupid to try to forbid these joys that are so natural. In the past many people, who were very poor psychologists and pedagogues, preached continence, privation and absolute chastity but, more often than not, the results were disastrous.

You must not think that, because you come to the Brotherhood, you're going to be told not to eat or sleep or get married and have children. Certainly not; we eat very well in the Brotherhood, we sleep very well and we get married and have children very well, also. It's wonderful, there's nothing missing here... except stupidity. And even that, if you really insist, you will find plenty of that; yes, even here. So this is what I have to say to young people: you know nothing about human nature yet, you have never had any real problems to contend with, so you think that everything is easy but, when you feel desires and instincts awakening within you, you will not know how to react or what to do about them and it is then that things will start to go wrong. There are certain things you have to know if you want to avoid making mistakes that will bring you unhappiness. 'Oh, we're young; we don't want to learn those things. It's all so boring.' That is what they say; I know that very well, but the trouble is that these things cannot be learnt at the last minute. If a girl is ignorant and has done nothing to prepare herself, she will be landed with a child. And the wretched girl, who is little more than a child herself, will be left to tear her hair because now there are two children. At this point she will look for advice, but it's too late; she should have been willing to learn before. But she wasn't interested before; she thought she didn't need to learn anything. Young people amuse themselves and laugh at adults and, even, leave home because they want to be independent and then, later, when things fail to turn out according to plan, they expect their parents to help them.

This is why I say that young people need proper guidance; they need to be enlightened and instructed. What can they lose by listening to me? I have never deprived anyone of his joys and pleasures or of his work; never. What I am saying is that whatever they do must be done better and, as they don't know how to make this improvement, they have to come and learn it here. Why are they so dead set against it; why are they so rebellious? Actually, I can tell you why: because they are all destined to suffer a great deal. This is what drives boys and girls to behave as they do: the need to suffer quite dreadfully. After all, what would they be deprived of if they came here? There is a certain lack of comfort and convenience, no doubt, and there are no swimming pools, gambling clubs or dance halls, but surely they can do without those for a week or two, or even a month? It wouldn't kill them. And think of how much they could learn. Otherwise, if they never learn anything and spend all their time amusing themselves, after a while, they will get less and less pleasure out of their amusements: nothing will be left but the serious things of life, the duties that life imposes on them and they will have no idea how to cope. Instead of learning and preparing themselves, they have been too busy having fun.

So, this is what I want to tell young people: 'No one will deprive you of anything; above all, no one will stop you loving and being loved, but you have to learn how to love. Of course, everyone knows the traditional way of loving, but there are other, higher degrees of love to be learned and you must learn them, for I foresee so much misery in store for those who refuse this light.' I am not clairvoyant but, when I know how someone reasons and how he behaves, I can see what lies in store for him; it is all too clear. Besides, let me tell you that, if young people are so determined not to listen to advice of any kind, it is because they are inhabited by entities who have an interest in keeping them as far away as possible from the light so that they can continue to feed on them. They think it is they who like this or dislike that but, in fact, it is these alien entities that manifest themselves through them.

Young people need not be afraid, therefore; they will not be deprived of anything. There are some delightful young girls here who are only fifteen, and they are just burning to know and experience certain things. I tell them, 'That's normal; nothing could be more normal. It's magnificent, marvellous. All that is sacred and divine. The only thing is that, to my mind, it is a little too soon. You should finish school and take the time to prepare yourself. Marriage is a very serious matter, you know. So don't worry: you won't be deprived of anything; you must just have a little patience.' In the long run, it is those who refuse to learn who deprive themselves of everything worthwhile, because they are incapable of exchanging their stupid ideas, their inferior desires and extravagant schemes for other, superior ideas, desires and schemes. It is they who will end by being unhappy. Each person has his own particular temperament which determines his likes and dislikes; that's natural. But if you don't allow your natural inclinations to be governed and guided by something higher, by intelligence, self-control, will-power, character and light, then I can tell you in advance that you are heading straight for the abyss. All these instincts and lusts are prehistoric tendencies; they have been with us for thousands of years and have never produced anything but carnage, massacres and catastrophes. Why abandon yourself to your primitive nature and not allow something higher to guide and direct you?

Let me illustrate this. You know how ships were constructed in the past: the stokers, whose job was to keep a head of steam on the boilers, were below decks. The ship advanced thanks to their labours but they couldn't see where it was going. There had to be a skipper up on the bridge to give orders and keep the ship on course but it was not he who kept it in motion. And this is an image of man: our emotions, feelings and instincts are the fuel that we feed into the boilers to keep our ship going but, if there is no one at the helm to keep it on course, it will be wrecked. A woman who was on a liner for an Arctic cruise, one day, asked the captain what would happen if they struck an iceberg. 'Madam,' said the captain, 'The iceberg would just keep going.' And the ship? No need to mention what would happen to the ship; it was only too obvious. And we can say the same for man: if his ship strikes an 'iceberg' – a symbolic iceberg – there will be nothing more to say. Man's captain is up here, in our head, and the stokers and engineers are in the rest of the body: the stomach, belly, sexual organs, etc.

This is why I say to young people: if you obey only the blind impulses of your desires, inclinations and spontaneous likes and dislikes, you are bound to strike an iceberg. Of course, I realize that it may be very pleasant, it may be sweet to the taste, but that will be no indication of the future that is in store for you.

Qualities of lucidity and discernment are indispensable but they are the fruit of thousands of years of experience; they are not given to the young. When you are young, therefore, you have to find someone to guide you, otherwise you will be shipwrecked. Whether you believe this or not, it has already happened... in millions of cases. That you should feel all these desires and impulses, therefore, is only to be expected; it goes without saying that every human being feels the urge of his instinctive forces, whether they come from the stomach, the intestines or the sexual organs, but that is no reason to let them lead you by the nose. If you continue to be ignorant, of course, you will continue to find enjoyment in a lot of things but that enjoyment will eventually be turned into suffering, disillusionment and regrets. Whereas the joys of an initiate are always pure gold. We must not deprive ourselves of joys and pleasures but we must see them for what they are and put better, purer, nobler and more beneficial joys and pleasures in their place.

I have never prevented anyone from being happy. There have been some puritanical, religious people who didn't understand human nature and who did a great deal of harm by trying to impose privations on people who could not bear them. It takes a great deal of psychological and pedagogical skill to direct other people. This is why, for thirty-eight years, I have been explaining points of view that could not possibly harm anyone who understands them correctly. In the Brotherhood you will never be deprived of anything; on the contrary, if you love someone, you will learn to keep him and to appreciate him even more. Otherwise, it will not be long before you lose him. We have to have a great deal of knowledge in order to protect and nurture our love and make it always purer, more spiritual and more divine, and I am here to give you that knowledge. I have spent my whole life experimenting these things for myself so as to be able to verify, substitute, transform and sublimate, and now, thanks to all these experiments, I can be very useful to you. But if you don't trust me and are afraid of being unhappy if you stay here, then you'd better go. I have no objection: it is you who will suffer. One day you will realize how stupid you were to behave so heedlessly and not even recognize where your true interest lay.

I can tell you one thing, my dear brothers and sisters, and that is that, wherever you look, you will never find a friend like me. Everyone else will abandon you or refuse to have anything to do with you just when you need them most, but I shall always be there to welcome you and to help and console you.

The Bonfin, September 3 1975

V

Send your Love to Heaven
Before Sending it to Human Beings

All adolescents have a great need to love and exchange with others. They feel this need as an obscure inner sentiment but are unable to define it or direct it towards anything specific. Doctors and psychologists have been studying the phenomenon for years but, even for them, it is not entirely clear. Only initiatic science can really bring any light to bear on the question.

Initiatic science teaches that a human being is composed of several bodies, physical, astral and mental, etc. In a child, it is the physical body that develops first: he sleeps and eats and moves about and touches things. Later, in the seventh year, it is the etheric body that manifests itself in the awakening of memory and a sensitivity to colours and perfumes as well as to human manifestations. This is why this period is so important for the later years, because all that a child sees and hears and experiences in his environment leaves its imprint on his etheric body and these imprints play an important role throughout his life. Although he may not understand what goes on around him and although his emotions are less highly developed than those of an adult, a child is very impressionable and everything is recorded in his subconscious. This is why those who take care of young children must see that they are not exposed to scenes of terror, perversity or violence, for they will bear the scars caused by such scenes for the rest of their lives, in spite of the best efforts of doctors, psychiatrists and so on.

From the fourteenth year, it is the turn of the astral body to awaken: the body of emotions, feelings and passions. And, as the astral body is potentially as strong in its negative as in its positive aspects, it can manifest itself just as easily in the need to rebel and destroy as in the need to love. To be sure, very young children can also have their likes and dislikes before they are fourteen, but they will not make themselves felt so strongly whereas, from their fourteenth year, they are subjugated by their feelings; in everything they do they are ruled and motivated by feelings. If a young girl or boy loves someone, all the arguments and explanations in the world will not alter their feelings; rather the contrary: instead of listening to reason they will hasten to give expression to that love. Or, if they do listen and submit, it will be from fear, obedience or respect for the adult, not because their feelings have changed, for it is their feelings that are in charge. From the twenty-first year it is the mental body that is awakened, the body of reason and reflection. Young men and women are better able to keep control of their feelings; they can diminish and restrain them or, on the contrary, amplify them and allow them to manifest themselves.

But, let's get back to that question of the awakening of the astral body at the age of fourteen. Before that age, a child tends to think only of himself: he eats and sleep, gets things dirty, grabs things for himself, etc. If cosmic Intelligence had not given man this need for a relationship of exchange with others, therefore, he would remain shut up in his own, selfish little world and the human race would soon be extinct. This is why, at the age of fourteen, adolescents begin to awaken to a sense of the collectivity, of the human community. They need to be in a group, to spend their time with other young people and get to know them. Other people's faces, words and attitudes move them. This is why they make dates and go dancing: because they are obliged to submit to this need for an exchange with others that has been implanted in them by cosmic Intelligence in order to ensure the propagation of the species.

Yes, but the great mistake of human beings is to consider only the physical, biological aspects of the question. The purpose of cosmic Intelligence was not limited to giving them this need to be together, this need to give each other pleasure and exchange caresses, kisses and presents and found a family. It intended to lead them towards a far greater, more spiritual, more glorious goal, that of creating the Universal White Brotherhood on earth. But the lower nature of human beings has had thousands of years in which to become extremely powerful and, as they have never been properly instructed or counselled, their love is still very personal and egotistical; they always tend to take things for themselves, to possess and dominate.

When adolescents are still very young, they are idealistic; they don't feel the need to shut themselves away in their own little world with someone of the opposite sex; on the contrary, they want to love everybody and work for the good of the whole world. But, before long, when they see how other people behave and because they have no one to guide them, their only idea is to start their own selfish, personal little family and, as all the members of this new family unit will be brought up in the same narrow, self-centred mentality, it will become an obstacle to the growth and development of the other Family, the universal Family. It's members will oppose the collectivity and universal brotherhood and, in this way, the little family will destroy the universal Family. In the future, however, thanks to this science, to the light of this Teaching which comes from far, far above us, the consciousness of human beings will expand to such an extent that they will work, in every way they can, to bring about the Kingdom of God and his Righteousness, the new Golden Age, the reign of the great Universal White Brotherhood, for this is the only way to achieve ease, freedom and happiness for the world.

So, from the age of fourteen, cosmic Intelligence gives adolescents this need to broaden their horizons, to get to know others and exchange with them. A young girl feels that she wants to love everybody, but others tell her, 'You're mad; it can't be done.' Of course, it seems completely stupid and impossible because she is still very weak and she doesn't realize that she will only be soiled and devoured, but all those people who give her advice are as ignorant as she is: they don't realize that, by pouring cold water on her generous impulse, instead of helping her to channel and control it, they are destroying it for ever. And a young boy who dreams of being a knight-errant and rescuing prisoners, of dedicating his whole life to doing good, undergoes such a brain-washing that he, too, soon conforms and becomes 'sensible' and never does any of the things he dreamed of.

If only there were other people, initiates, who could guide these young people's enthusiasm, it would be the greatest blessing. This is why, first and foremost, I advise young people who feel this divine desire to be sure to hide it, not to talk about it in front of idiots who, deluding themselves that it is their duty to give them what they consider to be good advice, will immediately destroy this splendid, shining impulse. Yes, you must simply keep quiet about it and, so as to give it expression and not let it die, you must try to find a quiet place where, from time to time, you can be alone to send all your love and light out into the world. Until such time as you are strong enough to manifest your love on the physical plane without danger, you must send it up to the world above. If you are in too much of a hurry to give outward, visible expression to it you will only be plundered by those who are neither considerate nor reasonable nor, very often, well intentioned. Many young boys have been 'initiated' by older women who have taken advantage of their innocence. There have even been cases of children's nurses who amused themselves by arousing the sexuality of their young charges... but we'd do better to leave all that to the psychologists who study such cases.

In order to avoid destroying this divine impulse, therefore, I advise all you young people to give it expression, first of all, in the invisible world. In this way you can be sure that luminous entities will take care of you. These spirits, who watch over us and see and record all that goes on, will help you to protect and nurture your divine impulse in purity and light, for it must not be allowed to wither away. Also, when the time comes, they will give you the conditions you need to see your way clearly and recognize those on whom you can pour out your love without danger and those you must not trust. This is something no educator knows anything about unless he learns it from initiatic science. It is an extremely delicate question, and it is of paramount importance for the young to be guided by instructors who can teach them to control and channel their impulses.

Sèvres, January 25 1976

Books by Omraam Mikhaël Aïvanhov
(translated from the French)

Complete Works

Volume   1 – The Second Birth
Volume   2 – Spiritual Alchemy
Volume   5 – Life Force
Volume   6 – Harmony
Volume   7 – The Mysteries of Yesod
Volume 10 – The Splendour of Tiphareth
                      The Yoga of the Sun
Volume 11 – The Key to the Problems of Existence
Volume 12 – Cosmic Moral Laws
Volume 13 – A New Earth
                      Methods, Exercises, Formulas, Prayers
Volume 14 – Love and Sexuality (Part I)
Volume 15 – Love and Sexuality (Part II)
Volume 17 – 'Know Thyself' Jnana Yoga (Part I)
Volume 18 – 'Know Thyself' Jnana Yoga (Part II)
Volume 25 – A New Dawn:
                      Society and Politics in the Light of Initiatic Science (Part I)
Volume 26 – A New Dawn:
                      Society and Politics in the Light of Initiatic Science (Part II)
Volume 29 – On the Art of Teaching (Part III)
Volume 30 – Life and Work in an Initiatic School
                      Training for the Divine
Volume 32 – The Fruits of the Tree of Life
                      The Cabbalistic Tradition

Brochures

301 – The New Year
302 – Meditation
303 – Respiration
304 – Death and the Life Beyond

By the same author:
(Translated from the French)

Izvor Collection

201 – Toward a Solar Civilization
202 – Man, Master of his Destiny
203 – Education Begins Before Birth
204 – The Yoga of Nutrition
205 – Sexual Force or the Winged Dragon
206 – A Philosophy of Universality
207 – What is a Spiritual Master?
208 – Under the Dove, the Reign of Peace
209 – Christmas and Easter in the Initiatic Tradition
210 – The Tree of the Knowledge of Good and Evil
211 – Freedom, the Spirit Triumphant
212 – Light is a Living Spirit
213 – Man's Two Natures: Human and Divine
214 – Hope for the World: Spiritual Galvanoplasty
215 – The True Meaning of Christ's Teaching
216 – The Living Book of Nature
217 – New Light on the Gospels
218 – The Symbolic Language of Geometrical Figures
219 – Man's Subtle Bodies and Centres
220 – The Zodiac, Key to Man and to the Universe
221 – True Alchemy or the Quest for Perfection
222 – Man's Psychic Life: Elements and Structures
223 – Creation: Artistic and Spiritual
224 – The Powers of Thought
225 – Harmony and Health
226 – The Book of Divine Magic
227 – Golden Rules for Everyday Life
228 – Looking into the Invisible
229 – The Path of Silence
230 – The Book of Revelations: a Commentary
231 – The Seeds of Happiness
232 – The Mysteries of Fire and Water
233 – Youth: Creators of the Future
234 – Truth, Fruit of Wisdom and Love
235 – 'In Spirit and in Truth'
236 – Angels and other Mysteries of The Tree of Life
237 – Cosmic Balance, The Secret of Polarity
238 – The Faith That Moves Mountains
239 – Love Greater Than Faith

By the same author
(Live Lectures)

Life Recordings on Tape

KC2510AN – The Laws of Reincarnation
(Two audio cassettes)

Compact disc

CD5009AN – The Seed
CD5016AN – The Role of the Mother during Gestation (*2 CD*)

Videos (french/english)

V 4605 FR – *The Activity of the Soul and Spirit:*
How They Can Manifest Through Us.
How Can We Modify our Destiny?
L'activité de l'âme et de l'esprit et notre travail
pour qu'ils se manifestent à travers nous.
Comment peut-on changer sa destinée?

V 4606 FR – *How Can We Purify our Physical Body*
Despite the Pollution
of the Atmosphere and Food?
Comment peut-on purifier le corps physique
malgré la pollution de l'air et de la nourriture?

World Wide - Editor-Distributor
Editions PROSVETA S.A. - B.P. 12 - F- 83601 Fréjus Cedex
(France)
Tel. (00 33) 04 94 19 33 33 - Fax (00 33) 04 94 19 33 34
Web: www.prosveta.com

Distributors

AUSTRALASIA
SURYOMA LTD - P.O. Box 2218 – Bowral – N.S.W. 2576 Australia
e-mail: info@suryoma.com – Tel. (61) 2 4872 3999 – fax (61) 2 4872 4022

AUSTRIA
HARMONIEQUELL VERSAND – A- 5302 Henndorf am Wallersee, Hof 37
Tel. / fax (43) 6214 7413 – e-mail: info@prosveta.at

BELGIUM & LUXEMBOURG
PROSVETA BENELUX – Liersesteenweg 154 B-2547 Lint
Tel (32) 3/455 41 75 – Fax (32) 3/454 24 25 – e-mail: prosveta@skynet.be
N.V. MAKLU Somersstraat 13-15 – B-2000 Antwerpen
Tel. (32) 3/231 29 00 – Fax (32) 3/233 26 59
VANDER S.A. – Av. des Volontaires 321 – B-1150 Bruxelles
Tél. (32)(0)2 732 35 32 – Fax. (32) (0)2 732 42 74 – e-mail: g.i.a@wol.be

BULGARIA
SVETOGLED – Bd Saborny 16 A, appt 11 – 9000 Varna
e-mail: svetgled@revolta.com – Tel/Fax: (359) 52 23 98 02

CANADA – UNITED STATES
PROSVETA Inc. – 3950, Albert Mines – North Hatley (Qc), J0B 2C0
Tel. (819) 564-8212 – Fax. (819) 564-1823
in Canada, call toll free: 1-800-854-8212
e-mail: prosveta@prosveta-canada.com / www.prosveta-canada.com

COLUMBIA
PROSVETA – Calle 149 N° 24 B - 20 – Bogotá
Tel. (57) 1 614 88 28 – Fax (57) 1 633 58 03 – Mobile (57) 310 2 35 74 55
e-mail: kalagiya@tutopia.com

CYPRUS
THE SOLAR CIVILISATION BOOKSHOP – BOOKBINDING
73 D Kallipoleos Avenue - Lycavitos – P. O. Box 24947, 1355 – Nicosia
e-mail: cypapach@cytanet.com.cy – Tel / Fax 00357-22-377503

CZECH REPUBLIC
PROSVETA – Ant. Sovy 18, –České Budejovice 370 05
Tel / Fax: (420) 38-53 10 227 – e-mail: prosveta@iol.cz

GERMANY
PROSVETA Deutschland – Heerstrasse 55 – 78628 Rottweil
Tel. (49) 741-46551 – Fax. (49) 741-46552 – e-mail: prosveta.de@t-online.de

GREAT BRITAIN – IRELAND
PROSVETA – The Doves Nest, Duddleswell Uckfield, – East Sussex TN 22 3JJ
Tel. (44) (01825) 712988 - Fax (44) (01825) 713386
e-mail: prosveta@pavilion.co.uk

GREECE
RAOMRON – D. RAGOUSSIS
3, rue A. Papamdreou – C.P. 16675 – Glifada - Athenes
Tel / Fax: (010) 9681127 – e-mail: raomron@hol.gr

HAITI
PROSVETA – DÉPÔT – B.P. 115, Jacmel, Haiti (W.I.)
Tel./ Fax (509) 288-3319 - e-mail: haiti@prosveta.com
HOLLAND
STICHTING PROSVETA NEDERLAND
Zeestraat 50 – 2042 LC Zandvoort
Tel. (31) 33 25 345 75 – Fax. (31) 33 25 803 20
e-mail: prosveta@worldonline.nl
ISRAEL
Zohar, P. B. 1046, Netanya 42110
e-mail: zohar7@012.net.il
ITALY
PROSVETA Coop. a r.l.
Casella Postale 55 – 06068 Tavernelle (PG)
Tel. (39) 075-835 84 98 – Fax (39) 075-835 97 12
e-mail: prosveta@tin.it
LIBAN
PROSVETA LIBAN – P.O. Box 90-995
Jdeidet-el-Metn, Beirut – Tel. (03) 448560
e-mail: prosveta_lb@terra.net.lb
NORWAY
PROSVETA NORDEN – Postboks 5101 – 1503 Moss
Tel. (47) 69 26 51 40 – Fax (47) 69 25 06 76
e-mail: prosnor@online.no
PORTUGAL & BRAZIL
EDIÇÕES PROSVETA
Rua Passos Manuel, n° 20 – 3e E, P 1150 – 260 Lisboa
Tel. (351) (21) 354 07 64 – Fax (351) (21) 798 60 31
e-mail : prosvetapt@hotmail.com
PUBLICAÇÕES EUROPA-AMERICA Ltd
Est Lisboa-Sintra KM 14 – 2726 Mem Martins Codex
ROMANIA
ANTAR – Str. N. Constantinescu 10 - Bloc 16A - sc A - Apt. 9,
Sector 1 – 71253 Bucarest
Tel. 004021-231 28 78 - Tel./ Fax 004021-231 37 19 - e-mail : antared@pcnet.ro
RUSSIA
EDITIONS PROSVETA
143 964 Moskovskaya oblast, g. Reutov – 4, post/box 4
Tel./ Fax. (095) 525 18 17 – Tel. (095) 795 70 74
e-mail: prosveta@online.ru
SPAIN
ASOCIACIÓN PROSVETA ESPAÑOLA – C/ Ausias March n° 23 Ático
SP-08010 Barcelona – Tel (34) (93) 412 31 85 - Fax (34) (93) 318 89 01
aprosveta@prosveta.es
SWITZERLAND
PROSVETA Société Coopérative – CH - 1808 Les Monts-de-Corsier
Tel. (41) 21 921 92 18 – Fax. (41) 21 922 92 04
e-mail: prosveta@swissonline.ch
VENEZUELA
PROSVETA VENEZUELA C. A. – Calle Madrid
Edificio La Trinidad – Las Mercedes – Caracas D.F.
Tel. (58) 414 22 36 748 – e-mail : betty_mramirez@hotmail.com

The aim of the Universal White Brotherhood association
is the study and practice of the Teaching
of Master Omraam Mikhaël Aïvanhov,
published and distributed
by Prosveta.
All enquiries about the association should be addressed to:
Universal White Brotherhood
The Doves Nest, Duddleswell, Uckfield
East Sussex TN22 3JJ, GREAT BRITAIN
Tel: (44) (0)1825 712150 – Fax: (44) (0)1825 713386
E-mail: uwb@pavilion.co.uk

Achevé d'imprimer en juin 2004
par Barnéoud Imprimeur
53960 Bonchamp-lès-Laval - France

Dépôt légal : Juin 2004
1er dépôt légal dans la même collection en France : 1987